EATING ITALY

EATING ITALY

JEFF MICHAUD

WITH DAVID JOACHIM

PHOTOGRAPHY BY
KELLY CAMPBELL

RUNNING PRESS
PHILADELPHIA · LONDON

GAIA, THIS IS YOUR BOOK. IT TELLS THE STORY OF HOW YOUR MOTHER AND I MET AND FELL IN LOVE. I HOPE YOU GET AS MUCH JOY OUT OF IT AS WE PUT INTO IT. TI VOGLIO TANTO BENE PICCOLA! (MY LITTLE GIRL, I LOVE YOU VERY MUCH!)

GAIA

CONTENTS

FOREWORD

In the spring of 2005, my business partner, Jeff Benjamin, and I were at Ca'Marcanda, the Gaja-owned vineyard in Tuscany. In between cellar tours and tasting, I was on the phone with Jeff Michaud. At that time, he was the chef at The Bedford Village Inn in New Hampshire. Jeff Michaud and I had been talking about opening a restaurant together in Philadelphia since he returned to the States from his three-year journey in Italy. We had three previous phone calls about it, but they all ended with me saying, "I don't think it's going to happen." We just couldn't strike a deal with the developer. (Coincidentally, *Ca'Marcanda* means "the house of endless negotiations.")

This last phone call, however, ended differently. "It's a done deal!" I exclaimed. "Get yer ass back to Philly!"

I could hear Jeff's eagerness through the phone. Although, when I think about it, I don't know who was more excited: him or me.

Some people just inspire you to do better. Perhaps it's the work ethic they possess. Or maybe it's the endless questions they ask until every possible scenario has been exhausted and they finally understand exactly what is going on. People like that make you strive for perfection, never accepting mediocrity. Why do something that's just good enough when you can make it great with only a little more effort? I always look for that kind of determination in cooks, and it's what initially drew me to Jeff Michaud.

We first met in 1998 at the Food & Wine Classic culinary festival in Aspen, Colorado. This was just a few weeks before I signed the lease for Vetri, my first restaurant. At the time, Jeff was working at Aspen's Caribou Club under chef Miles Angelo, a good friend with whom I had worked in the early '90s.

"He's you," Miles said to me, "only 10 years ago."

At the time, I really didn't think much of the comment, but it stayed with me.

Miles called me a few years later, saying "Remember that kid, Jeff? Well, I can't teach him anything else, and he needs to get out of here. He needs to learn something new—you have to take him."

I was in the process of looking for a cook, so I had Jeff come out and work at Vetri for a couple days. I didn't realize it then, but it was as if my own son had come to work at the restaurant. He set the tone in the first month.

"Do you know how to make bread?" he asked eagerly.

"Yes," I replied.

"Then why don't you make it?"

"There's just not enough time or room in the restaurant, Jeff."

"Why? I don't understand. I think we can do it. Will you please show me?" he implored.

Have you ever seen a child badger a parent to the point of exhaustion? Jeff pushed me until I relented. I agreed to make bread. We made a beautiful rustic loaf with a natural starter that we let ferment and grow for two weeks, feeding it three to four times a day. It was like our little pet. The bread turned out perfect. Soon after serving that first loaf, we stopped ordering bread. We have made our own bread at Vetri ever since.

And so it began. My life for the next two and a half years was packed with exploratory trips to markets and farms and early-morning lessons on curing sausage and making pasta. At a certain point, I even let him work the pasta station. There's a first for everything! You name it—if Jeff wanted to learn it, he asked and asked and asked until he got his way. It reached the point where he only had to ask once, and I would give him a fatherly, "Whatever you want," knowing full well the torture I would go through if I said no. The funny thing is, without realizing it, I got as much out of his education as he did. Jeff's passion is infectious, and those torturous yeses eventually turned to anticipation. I looked forward to the next challenge we could tackle together. Sometimes we all need a push in the right direction, and Jeff was pushing with all of his might. Vetri was livelier and more exciting than ever. To this day, those ambitious ideals have not changed. The restaurant has been a platform of learning for everyone who has worked there, and in large part, we have Jeff Michaud to thank.

In 2001, I took Jeff on his first visit to Italy. He was 23, and we went to Vin Italy, the wine fair in Verona. That trip changed his life. The entire time his eyes were as big as beach balls looking at everything around him. . . the food, art, culture, and yes, the women. That trip began the great love affair with Italian food and culture that he continues to this day. Jeff always knew that cooking was what he wanted to do, but now he knew for certain that Italy was the place in which he wanted to do it. Shortly after we returned, Jeff made plans to move to Italy.

Through the years we kept in touch from afar. I visited him during my research trips, and it was clear that he had gone "native" and was fully immersed, soaking up everything he could. I wasn't the least bit surprised. "You get out of life what you put into it." It's such a simple adage, but it's the very *modo*—the manner—in which Jeff lives his life.

In early 2007, we opened Osteria in Philadelphia with Jeff at the helm. Another person, given the same opportunities that Jeff had would not have achieved the same level of success. But Jeff excelled in Italy and at Osteria because he puts absolutely everything he has into absolutely everything he does. It's all in, all of the time.

That's why I'm so excited about *Eating Italy*. This book is a true, complete journal of Jeff's travels, experiences and adventures in Italy. Reading it makes you feel as if you are right there with him. . . discovering, tasting, and cooking. A dish always tastes better when you hear the story behind it. From Venice to Florence and Piedmont to Lombardia, Jeff leaves no stone unturned when sharing the moments that led to all of these beautiful recipes.

Eating Italy also illustrates how the ambition that first drew me to Jeff continues to grow and evolve. Jeff doesn't simply cook Italian food. He lives it. If this book is anything, it's evidence of that. But it's much more. It's the impassioned work of a chef who has lived more than most and who still has a great deal to share with us. I, for one, am thrilled to be along for the ride.

—MARC VETRI

AT FIRST I KNEW NOTHING ABOUT ITALIAN FOOD

Restless. Ambitious. Headstrong. That was me as a teenager. I wasn't planning on sticking around Nashua, New Hampshire, for too long. At age thirteen, I got my first job at Kinsley House of Pizza, a Greek pizza place around the corner from my house. They started me out folding pizza boxes, and before long I was slicing tomatoes. Then I asked if I could make the dough. By the time I was a high school sophomore, I was cooking all the pizzas.

My high school had a two-year culinary program, and I jumped on it for junior and senior year. Cooking seemed like good honest work, and I had a knack for it. I saw it as my ticket out of town to discover new places, new people, and new ideas. At sixteen, I started working at the Hilltop Steak House and Butcher Shop, a chain restaurant in the Northeast. A year later, they made me kitchen manager of the place. We did a thousand covers a day, and with that kind of volume, I really learned how to work a kitchen.

Going to culinary school seemed like the next logical thing to do. I enrolled in the Culinary Institute of America and graduated in 1998. For my externship, I went as far away as possible: Aspen, Colorado at the Caribou Club. Within a year, the chef, Miles Angelo, offered me a job as sous chef. I learned everything I could in his kitchen, paid attention, and said, "Yes, Chef," more times than I can remember. A few years later, I became executive sous chef and stayed on for four years.

As a young professional, I'd made good progress in my career. But, as usual, it wasn't enough for me. I was still restless. We cooked mostly American, Southwestern, and Asian food at Caribou. I wanted to learn more. I heard that Marc Vetri was looking for a sous chef, so I flew to Philadelphia to apprentice with him. At that point, Italian food wasn't really part of my repertoire. Sure, I made pizzas at Kinsley House as a teenager, but that was barely Italian food. The differences between the two restaurants were like night and day. Vetri's kitchen was half the size of Kinsley's, but the food we turned out in that tiny space was on another level entirely. We made pasta, bread, and sausage in-house, and cut fish and meat to order. Everything was prepared from scratch. By hand. With pristine ingredients. That spring, I took on the sous chef job at Vetri and put my nose to the grindstone. I made it a point to come in early every day to learn the fundamentals of Italian cooking. Once a week, I took wine classes with Marc's partner and wine expert, Jeff Benjamin.

After a few months, what continued to amaze me about Italian cuisine was its stubborn simplicity. We used a minimum of ingredients. The flavors were uncomplicated. The plating was spare. If you didn't execute everything to perfection, you could easily screw it up. Compared to all my other training, learning to cook Italian food was like trying to find a needle in a haystack, searching for a tiny sliver of culinary perfection buried deep in a mountain of madness. It was just the kind of focus I needed in my career.

Marc and Jeff noticed how I took to the cuisine, and how inspired I got. That spring, they brought me to Vin Italy, an international wine expo held annually in Verona. Every Italian wine you could imagine was there, and you could sample them all. The food was like nothing I'd ever tasted—heaps of locally made salumi and cheese—all of it artisanal, beautiful, and incredibly delicious. Each day of eating, drinking, sampling, and talking got me more and more excited.

When we arrived back home, I knew what I had to do. I had to pack up my life, once again, and move to Italy. A window had opened up inside me. During that trip, I felt a real connection to Italian food and wine but even more so to Italian people and culture. I can't fully explain it. . . the Italian lifestyle was just so different from what I was used to

in America. It was a breath of fresh air, and I wanted more.

I've never been afraid to stick my nose into things. Sometimes you just have to put yourself out there and take risks. I had no idea if living in Italy would lead to anything good, but I knew I had to go. I took on a second job, and scrimped and saved for months. I scrounged up enough money to last me one year.

This book tells the story of what happened next. I'd planned to stay a year and ended up staying for three. I hoped to find a paying job and ended up finding my wife. I fell head-over-heels in love not only with a woman but also with her family, her cuisine, and her culture. Each chapter takes you into the Italian towns and villages that shaped me the most, like Alme, where I trained with Italy's youngest Michelin-starred chef; Cinque Terre, where Claudia and I spent our first romantic getaway; Leffe, where I snagged my first executive chef position; and Trescore Balneario, where Claudia and I got married just before we opened Osteria in Philadelphia. The recipes I learned and the dishes I created along the way are all here. And there's plenty of detail about restaurants, wineries, bars, markets, and inns all over Italy, so you can experience the places where I cut my teeth and discovered the world's most welcoming cuisine.

After those first few years in Italy, I came back a different person. I was a better chef for sure, but more important, I had a sense of purpose. My ambition wasn't blind anymore. I found love in my work and in my life. I realized that good cooking is about putting your heart and soul on a plate. It doesn't matter whether you cook at home or in a restaurant kitchen. Cooking has to be something that you enjoy and feel in your body. If it's not, you taste it right away in the food.

That's the Italian way of cooking that I try to convey in these pages. I hope the stories and recipes here help you find that kind of joy in your own cooking—no matter what style of cuisine you prefer.

PALADINA

THE BUTCHER'S APPRENTICE

I ARRIVED AT THE MANGILI BUTCHER SHOP AT FOUR IN THE MORNING IN EARLY 2003. I'D VISITED ITALY A FEW TIMES BEFORE, BUT THIS TIME I SAVED UP ENOUGH MONEY TO STAY AND WORK FOR A YEAR. SOME FRIENDS SET ME UP TO WORK UNPAID AT A SMALL, FAMILY-OWNED BUTCHER SHOP IN PALADINA, A TINY TOWN JUST NORTHWEST OF BERGAMO.

When I got there, a line of calves stood near the back door, and the holding area stank of cow shit. I had some butchering experience but couldn't speak Italian. The Mangili family didn't care. There was work to do. An old man with salt-and-pepper hair said something to me in Italian, handed me a small knife, and led me to the kill floor. His knife was a giant medieval-looking ax with a long wooden handle and curved blades on each side. The kill floor was made of terra-cotta tile that sloped to the center to drain the blood. A veal calf had just been shot and was hanging upside down on a hook. The old man lifted his axe and cut the head clear off the animal. One perfect swipe! He hung up the head and we started skinning the calf together.

For hours, I stood with the axe man at a big white table in the back room as he showed me how to butcher various cuts of veal, such as shank, breast, and shoulder. Before I knew it, the axe man was motioning for me to stop. It was lunchtime. They closed the butcher shop and we all went upstairs to eat. Everyone started talking, and I learned that the axe man was Maurizio, a brother-in-law in the Mangili family. The two main owners were Oliviero and Francesco Mangili. One of their daughters, Alexandria, worked the front counter with the customers. Even though I was a complete stranger—and an American—no one was nervous about having me in the house. They completely opened their doors to me. I had a dictionary in my back pocket and pieced together some of what they were telling me. Oliviero

and Francesco's grandfather started the butcher shop two generations ago. There were a couple of other butchers in Paladina, but the Mangilis were the only ones that raised their own cattle on their own farm. The veal calves came in on Wednesdays. The steers on Thursdays. Pigs were Mondays. Goats and lambs, Tuesdays.

It struck me how relaxed the whole family was around the table. They nibbled on salumi and cheese, talking and laughing. Francesco made jokes and winked at everyone. Maurizio had a glass of wine with an ice cube in it. Oliviero took a quick nap.

This was new to me. I wasn't used to stopping in the middle of the afternoon to enjoy a peaceful lunch—or, for that matter, starting the day with a leisurely cappuccino and croissant. The Italian lifestyle had a comfortable rhythm. It was slower than the amped-up American rat race.

As lunch went on, my mind wandered back to the previous day and the long plane trip from Philadelphia to France to Bergamo. I remembered seeing the mountains, rivers, and valleys from 20,000 feet (6 km) up. The snow-capped Alps tower above the North and the Apennine Mountains jut up from the green plains in the south. These two mountain ranges create a paradise of fertile valleys and rivers that you can grow just about anything in. Lombardy is so desirable that every neighboring country, including France, Austria, and Germany, has held control of it at some point in history. The local economy accounts for a big chunk

of Italy's gross domestic product. It's full of hard-working people. And cows. Most of Italy's cattle are raised on the lower plains of Lombardy. Pigs thrive more in the north around Bergamo. So it's no surprise that beef, cheese, and sausage are some of Lombardy's most important foods.

Oliviero snapped me out of my reverie when he tapped me on the knee. We cleaned up lunch, went downstairs, and opened up the butcher shop again, working until about five o'clock. We butchered all the veal for the week, then hosed down the entire shop and closed for the day. When we were done, it was so clean you could eat off the floor.

Our days went on like this for five months. Maurizio taught me everything he knew about farming and butchering animals. I visited the family farm where the animals were raised. I learned how to kill them as quickly and

humanely as possible. I gutted and skinned them; broke down half-ton steers into sides of beef; and let the meat rest for two weeks to develop flavor before cutting it into steaks. Sometimes little old ladies would come in and order half a steer, specifying how much of it they wanted ground for *polpettini* (little meatballs) and what parts they wanted cut for freezing and sharing with their families. Maurizio showed me how to hang big pieces of beef off the edge of the table to let gravity help with the heavy butchering.

The Mangilis took me in like family. Maurizio had me over for dinner. Francesco and Oliviero brought me to local fairs, where they showed off their prized cows—just like at county fairs in the United States. But instead of the overalls American farmers wear, Italian farmers wear Gucci jeans and Louis Vuitton shoes—even while stomping around in cow shit!

Seeing this entire process, day in and day out for the better part of a year, gave me a new respect for Italian food. I realized how important farming is to the economy and the cuisine of northern Italy. When I cooked, I was no longer just grilling a rib-eye steak. I was grilling a rib-eye steak from the local Fassone breed of cattle that was raised and butchered by someone I knew and respected. When I snacked on cheese, it was no longer just fuel to get me through the day. I was enjoying creamy formagella made from goat's milk by an award-winning local cheese maker named Battista. Everything I ate became more important. More meaningful. It made me feel more grounded. Seeing the love and care that went into preparing the food made every bite taste better somehow. And it made me curious to learn even more.

Beef Tartare with Fried Egg Yolk and Parmigiano

•

Carne Salata with Red Onion, Celery,
and Olive Oil

•

Whole Braised Beef Shank
with Buckwheat Polenta

•

Bucatini with Pig Testina

•

Veal Tongue Salad with Escarole
and Salsa Rossa

•

Veal Shoulder Roasted in Hay
with Grilled Peach Salad

•

Pork Neck Cannelloni
with Heirloom Tomatoes and Basil

•

Whole Roasted Pig's Head

•

Whole Roasted Pork Shoulder
with Pickled Vegetables

•

Pappardelle with Veal Ragù and Peppers

•

Grilled Lamb Rack with Favetta
and Roasted Pearl Onions

BEEF TARTARE with FRIED EGG YOLK and PARMIGIANO

MAKES 4 SERVINGS

½ small red onion, cut through the root end

About 1 cup (235 ml) whole milk

About ¾ cup (175 ml) olive oil, divided

3 tablespoons (45 ml) red wine vinegar

8 ounces (225 g) beef tenderloin, trimmed of fat

Salt and freshly ground black pepper

Canola oil, for frying

2 Belgian endives, cut in a thin julienne

½ cup (30 g) chopped fresh flat-leaf parsley

1 cup (100 g) plain, dry breadcrumbs, sifted

4 large egg yolks

Parmigiano cheese for shaving

The tartare at Mangili butcher shop was like none I'd ever had. As a chef, I was used to chopping raw beef by hand for tartare. Almost every restaurant I worked in served it that way—in tiny cubes. But at Mangili, they ground the raw beef twice in a meat grinder. The grinder cut down all the connective tissue in the meat and made it super-creamy. Traditionally, tartare is served with arugula, lemon, and Parmesan. Once in a while, you see egg yolk. I thought it would be cool to roll an egg yolk in breadcrumbs, deep-fry it, and serve it over the tartare. When you cut into the crispy yolk, it runs all over the meat and makes it taste even creamier.

Chill four serving plates. Thinly slice the onion on a mandoline (or use a very sharp knife). Separate the onion into slivers in a large bowl. Add enough milk to cover the onion and let stand at room temperature for 30 minutes to extract the raw onion taste. Drain the onion slivers, rinse them and the bowl, and return them to the bowl. Add ½ cup (120 ml) of the olive oil and the vinegar, stirring to mix. Marinate the onion for 2 hours at room temperature.

Put the beef and all the parts of a meat grinder in the freezer for 20 minutes. Grind the cold beef twice on the small (¼-inch/10-cm) die of the meat grinder. Season the beef to taste with salt, pepper, and olive oil.

Heat the oil in a deep fryer or deep saucepan to 350°F (175°C). You can check the heat by sprinkling in small pinches of breadcrumbs to see whether the oil sizzles instantly and fries them up golden brown.

For each serving, mold the beef mixture in a 6-inch (15-cm) ring mold (or a large cookie cutter) on a cold plate. Lift off the ring to unmold.

Toss the endives with the marinated onion and top each serving of beef with the mixture. Sprinkle the parsley on top.

Put the breadcrumbs in a shallow bowl and carefully add the egg yolks, one at a time, to coat thoroughly without breaking the yolks. Use a slotted spoon to carefully lift the yolks from the crumbs. Gently shake off the excess crumbs and turn each yolk into the fryer, frying for exactly 12 seconds. Remove each yolk with a heatproof slotted spoon and place gently on top of the endive salad.

Drizzle the remaining olive oil around the plate, along with a few grindings of cracked black pepper. Using a vegetable peeler, shave 3 slivers of Parmigiano over each serving.

CARNE SALATA with RED ONION, CELERY, and OLIVE OIL

MAKES 8 SERVINGS

3 pounds (1.25 kg) beef eye of round, trimmed of fat

3½ tablespoons (35 g) rock salt

1½ teaspoons (6 g) granulated sugar

½ teaspoon (6 g) curing salt #2 (see page 277)

½ teaspoon (1 g) freshly ground black pepper, plus more to taste

⅛ teaspoon (0.25 g) ground mace

⅛ teaspoon (0.25 g) ground coriander

⅛ teaspoon (0.25 g) freshly grated nutmeg

⅛ teaspoon (0.25 g) ground cloves

1½ teaspoons (1.75 g) chopped fresh rosemary

1 small red onion, thinly sliced (about 1 cup/160 g)

1 cup (235 ml) whole milk

2 ribs celery, julienned (1 cup/100 g)

2 tablespoons (30 ml) red wine vinegar

½ cup (120 ml) olive oil

2 tablespoons (7.5 g) chopped fresh flat-leaf parsley

Salt

You always see *carne salata* in Italian butcher shops. It's usually made with horse meat that's salted, cured, and then boiled. Horse meat just became legal in the United States and is still very hard to get, so I make mine with beef eye of round. It comes out fantastic. My wife's family slices their *carne salata* meat paper-thin and serves it with raw onion. They soak the onion first in milk so it loses its bite. (You can also soak the onion in vinegar.) After that, a little celery, parsley, and olive oil is all you need to round out the salad.

Place the meat in a plastic tub or wide nonreactive bowl. Mix together the rock salt, sugar, curing salt, ½ teaspoon (1 g) of the pepper, and the mace, coriander, nutmeg, cloves, and rosemary. Rub the spice mixture all over the meat, cover, and let cure in the refrigerator for 4 days, rotating the meat every day and dousing it with the liquid that settles in the bottom of the tub or bowl.

On the fourth day, transfer the beef to a very large Dutch oven. Add half of the leftover curing liquid and enough water to cover the meat by ½ inch (1.25 cm). Cover and bring to a simmer over medium heat, then adjust the heat so that the mixture simmers very gently. Simmer until the meat is cooked through, about 155°F (315°C) internal temperature, 1 to 2 hours. Remove the pan from the heat and let the meat cool in the liquid in the pan. If you're not serving right away, cover and refrigerate for up to 3 days before slicing and serving.

Meanwhile, soak the onion in the milk for 30 minutes. Rinse the onion and pat dry. Mix together the onion, celery, vinegar, oil, and parsley. Season to taste with salt and pepper.

Slice the beef very thinly and toss with the salad to coat. Use tongs to arrange the slices on a platter and top with the salad.

WHOLE BRAISED BEEF SHANK
with BUCKWHEAT POLENTA

This is a butcher's dish if I ever saw one. A whole beef shank is a big piece of meat with a giant bone running through it. It's fit for a caveman. If you shop at a farmers' market or know your butcher pretty well, it should be easy enough to get a whole beef shank. You can also just use crosscut shanks. Either way, you'll be braising the shank in the traditional northern Italian style. The people who live in and around Bergamo are known as *polentone* (poh-len-TOE-nay), or polenta eaters. They love to braise big, tough cuts of meat on the bone and then serve them in gravy on a mound of warm, creamy polenta. Here, I mix the polenta with some buckwheat flour for a darker, earthier flavor to match the rich taste of the marinated and braised shank.

Fit the shank in a very large nonreactive Dutch oven or large stockpot. Add the wine, 1½ cups (175 g) of the carrots, 1½ cups (150 g) of the celery, 1½ cups (250 g) of the onion, and the sachet. Cover and refrigerate for 24 hours.

Remove the shank from the marinade, strain the liquid, and reserve the liquid and sachet. Discard the vegetables.

Preheat the oven to 325°F (160°C). Pat the shank dry and season with salt and pepper. Dredge the shank in the flour, shaking off excess flour. Heat the oil in the Dutch oven or an ovenproof braising pan over medium-high heat. Add the shank and sear until browned all over, about 20 minutes total. Transfer the meat to a plate. Add the remaining ¼ cup (40 g) of carrots, ¼ cup (25 g) of celery, and ¼ cup (25 g) of onion to the pan. Cook over medium heat until the vegetables are lightly browned, about 5 minutes. Add 1 quart (1 L) of the reserved marinade and the reserved sachet to the pan. Pour in just enough veal stock to cover the meat by three-quarters. Cover the pan and braise in the oven until tender, 2 to 3 hours.

Remove the meat from the pan and cut the meat from the bone. Cut the meat into bite-size pieces, discarding excess fat and gristle. Alternatively, you can serve the meat on the bone, family style. Either way, strain the vegetables from the braising liquid and pass them through a food mill. You could use a food processor instead of a food mill, but the resulting texture isn't quite as coarse and good tasting. Return the milled vegetables to the pan, along with a few cups of the braising liquid to thin them out. Boil the mixture over high heat until reduced in volume by about half and thick like gravy, about 15 minutes. Lower the heat to keep the gravy warm, and then skim off any excess fat and season to taste with salt and pepper.

To serve, ladle some buckwheat polenta onto each plate. Place the warm beef on top and drizzle with the reduced sauce. Garnish with the chopped herbs.

MAKES 4 TO 6 SERVINGS

4 pounds (1.75 kg) beef shank

3 quarts (2.75 L) red wine (about 4 bottles)

3 medium-size carrots, chopped (1¾ cups/215 g), divided

3 medium-size ribs celery, chopped (1¾ cups/175 g), divided

1 large yellow onion, chopped (1¾ cups/275 g), divided

1 sachet of 1 sprig rosemary, 3 sprigs thyme, 1 bay leaf, 5 black peppercorns, 1 cinnamon stick, and 2 whole cloves (see page 277)

Salt and freshly ground black pepper

About ½ cup (60 g) *tipo* 00 flour (see page 277) or all-purpose flour, for dredging

2 tablespoons (30 ml) olive oil

2 cups (475 ml) Veal Stock (page 279)

6 cups (1.5 L) Buckwheat Polenta (page 281)

1 tablespoon (3.5 g) chopped mixed fresh herbs (parsley, rosemary, and thyme) for garnish

BUCATINI with PIG TESTINA

MAKES 4 SERVINGS

1 small pig's head (4 to 5 pounds/1.75 to 2.25 kg)

3 quarts (3 L) 3-2-1 Brine (page 280)

3 sprigs thyme

1 tablespoon (6 g) ground cloves

1 tablespoon (6 g) freshly grated nutmeg

1½ teaspoons (3 g) ground allspice

½ teaspoon (1 g) freshly ground black pepper

1 teaspoon (6 g) curing salt #1 (see page 277)

1 large yellow onion, chopped (1½ cups/240 g)

3 medium-size ribs celery, chopped (1½ cups/150 g)

2 large carrots, chopped (1½ cups/ 185 g)

1 pound (450 g) fresh Bucatini (page 283), or 1 (12-ounce/340 g) box bucatini

2 tablespoons (30 ml) olive oil

2 tablespoons (30 ml) freshly squeezed lemon juice

¼ cup (15 g) chopped fresh flat-leaf parsley

3½ ounces (100 g) Parmesan cheese, grated (1 cup)

Salt and freshly ground black pepper

Pig is the meat of choice in northern Italy, and most butcher shops carry *testina*. It's a terrine made from pig's head and shaped in rounds, squares, or rectangles. One day, I had the idea to try it with pasta. I made the terrine, chopped it up, and sautéed it with some olive oil and bucatini, a kind of thick, hollow spaghetti. Some of the liquid from the testina nestled inside the hollows and blended perfectly with the pasta. Bucatini has more bite than spaghetti, so it still made a nice contrast to the soft, creamy pig's head. And with all those warming spices—the nutmeg, cloves, allspice, and black pepper—the dish had great aroma. There's no butter here, but it's pretty rich from the testina.

Rinse the pig's head and set aside. Make the brine; add the thyme, cloves, nutmeg, allspice, black pepper, and curing salt and puree everything together. Pour the brine into a stockpot or large tub, submerge the pig's head in the brine, cover, and refrigerate for 4 days.

Put the pig's head and 1½ quarts (1.5 L) of the brine in a very large Dutch oven. Add 1½ quarts (1.5 L) of water and the onion, celery, and carrots, cover, and bring to a boil over high heat. Lower the heat so that the mixture simmers gently and simmer, covered, until the skin cracks and the meat is fall-apart tender, 3 to 4 hours. Let cool in the liquid.

Carefully transfer the pig's head to a large cutting board. Strain the braising liquid and discard the solids. Return the braising liquid to the pan and boil over high heat, uncovered, until reduced in volume by about half, 40 to 50 minutes.

Cut the skin, meat, and fat from the head and chop into pieces the size of a half-dollar. Remove the skin from the tongue and discard it, and then coarsely chop the tongue; set it aside. Line an 8 x 4-inch (20 x 10-cm) loaf pan with plastic wrap, leaving a generous overhang to cover the top of the pan. Combine the skin, meat, and fat (including the tongue) in the pan and add enough of the reduced liquid to saturate but not quite cover the meat. Cover with the overhanging plastic and put a heavy weight on top (canned tomatoes or beans work well). Refrigerate overnight with the weight.

Bring a large pot of salted water to a boil. Add the pasta, and cook just until tender, 2 to 3 minutes if fresh or 8 to 10 minutes if dried.

Meanwhile, heat the oil in a large sauté pan over medium heat. Finely chop about 12 ounces (about 2 cups/340 g) of the *testina*, add to the pan, and sauté for 2 to 3 minutes. Stir in the lemon juice, 1 cup (235 ml) of the pasta water, and the parsley.

Drain the pasta and add to the sauce, along with the Parmesan and salt and pepper to taste. Cook until the sauce is creamy and coats the pasta, 2 to 3 minutes. Serve hot.

VEAL TONGUE SALAD with
ESCAROLE AND SALSA ROSSA

Before you turn away, hear me out. I've heard so many people say they are disgusted by veal tongue, but when they taste it, they end up loving it. Forget your preconceived notions about eating tongue. It's just another piece of meat. And it's damn good! Think about it. The most flavorful cuts of meat come from the areas of the animal that get the biggest workout, such as the shoulder (chuck) and—you guessed it—the tongue. It's packed with flavor. That's why you see veal tongue in every butcher shop in Italy. I've breaded it, fried it, slow-cooked it, and grilled it. It's good every which way. But my favorite technique is to brine it, slow-simmer it until it's tender, then slice it super-thin. With a salad of roasted tomatoes and peppers (*salsa rossa*), it's really worth a taste.

For the veal tongue: Rinse the tongue and set aside. Add the thyme and cloves to the brine, and puree everything together. Pour the brine into a medium saucepan, submerge the tongue in the brine, cover, and refrigerate for 4 days.

Pour off three-quarters of the brine and add enough water to cover the tongue by 1 inch (2.5 cm). Cover and bring to a simmer over medium heat, then adjust the heat so that the liquid simmers gently. Simmer until the tongue is almost fall-apart tender, about 190°F (88°C) internal temperature, 1 to 1½ hours. Remove the pan from the heat and let the tongue cool down in the liquid.

When the tongue has cooled, remove and discard the skin. Refrigerate the tongue for up to 2 days or use immediately.

For the salsa rossa: Preheat the oven to 500°F (260°C).

Slice the tomatoes in half lengthwise and scoop out all the seeds. Toss with the garlic, 1 teaspoon (6 g) of salt, ground black pepper to taste, sugar, thyme, and olive oil. Lay the tomatoes cut-side up on a rimmed baking sheet and put the sheet in the oven. Turn off the oven and let the tomatoes dry in the oven overnight, 8 to 10 hours. The next day, chop the tomatoes, reserving the oil in the pan separately. (In a pinch, you could substitute soft, oil-packed sun-dried tomatoes for the oven-dried tomatoes here.) Toss the tomatoes in a medium bowl, along with the roasted peppers, anchovies, parsley, vinegar, and 1 tablespoon (15 ml) of oil from the roasting pan. Season with salt and pepper.

To serve: slice the veal tongue very thinly, about ⅛ inch (3 mm) thick, and toss gently with 2 tablespoons (30 ml) of the reserved olive oil from the pan in a bowl. Toss the escarole with 1 tablespoon (15 ml) of the reserved olive oil. Place the tongue slices in piles on plates or a large platter. Place the escarole in piles near the tongue and top the escarole with the *salsa rossa*. Garnish with cracked black pepper, Maldon sea salt, and mixed herbs.

MAKES 6 SERVINGS

Veal Tongue:

1 veal tongue, about 1½ pounds (675 g)

2 sprigs fresh thyme

2 whole cloves

1½ quarts (1.5 L) 3-2-1 Brine (page 280)

Salsa Rossa:

10 plum tomatoes

4 garlic cloves, minced

1 teaspoon (6 g) salt, plus more to taste

Freshly ground black pepper

½ teaspoon (2 g) granulated sugar

Leaves from 2 fresh thyme sprigs

1 cup (235 ml) olive oil

1 cup (90 g) Roasted Red Peppers (page 278), chopped

4 anchovy fillets, chopped

2 teaspoons (2 g) chopped fresh flat-leaf parsley

½ teaspoon (2 ml) sherry vinegar

To Serve:

1 ounce (28 g) escarole, torn into bite-size pieces

Cracked black pepper for garnish

Maldon sea salt for garnish

Minced mixed fresh herbs (parsley, rosemary, and thyme) for garnish

VEAL SHOULDER ROASTED IN HAY
with GRILLED PEACH SALAD

In Piedmont, Walter Eynard of Ristorante Flipot is famous for roasting big cuts of meat in hay—especially lamb. The hay imparts an earthy grassiness to the meat. When I got back to the States, I thought I'd give it a whirl. My farmer, Glenn Brendle from Green Meadow Farm, was making a delivery to Osteria one week in the fall, so I asked him to bring me some hay. We butchered a lot of veal at Mangili, so I figured I'd use veal instead of lamb. It came out awesome. All it needed was some sweetness and bitterness to round it out. So I grilled a few peaches and tossed them with cut-up radicchio and pistachios for a quick salad. The amounts here are great for a crowd but if you want to serve fewer people, get a four-pound (1.75 kg) roast and cut the recipe in half.

MAKES 8 TO 10 SERVINGS

1 bone-in veal shoulder roast, about 8 pounds (3.5 kg)

1½ gallons (5.75 L) 3-2-1 Brine (page 280)

Clean hay, a few big handfuls, enough to completely cover the veal, plus more for serving

4 peaches

½ cup (120 ml) blended oil (page 276), divided

2 tablespoons (30 ml) balsamic vinegar

1 small head of radicchio

1½ tablespoons (14 g) chopped raw unsalted pistachios, preferably Sicilian

Salt and freshly ground black pepper

In a stockpot or large, clean tub or plastic bag, submerge the veal in the brine. Cover (or seal) and refrigerate for 4 days.

When you're ready to start cooking, soak the hay in water for 1 hour.

Preheat the oven to 450°F (120°C). Remove the veal from the brine, give it a rinse, then place it in a Dutch oven and pack the wet hay around it. Roast uncovered until the hay smells dry and the meat begins to brown, about 1 hour.

Lower the oven temperature to 300°F (150°C). Add enough water to come one-quarter of the way up the meat, then cover the pan and braise in the oven until the meat is tender (about 190°F/88°C internal temperature), 4 to 5 hours. Let cool slightly, then remove the meat from the pan and discard the hay. You can cover and refrigerate the meat for up to 4 days at this point.

About an hour before you're ready to serve, preheat a grill to medium-high heat. Cut the peaches in half lengthwise and discard the pits. Coat the peaches with 1 tablespoon (15 ml) of the blended oil. Coat the grill grate with oil and grill the peaches just until grill-marked but not mushy, 2 minutes per side. Cut each peach half into quarters lengthwise.

Pour the vinegar into a medium bowl and whisk in 6 tablespoons (90 ml) of the blended oil. Core the radicchio and cut it into 1½-inch (3.75-cm) squares. Add to the bowl, along with the grilled peaches and pistachios. Season to taste with salt and pepper and toss gently.

To finish, preheat the oven to 425°F (218°C) and roast the whole shoulder on a large baking sheet until crispy on the surface, 20 to 25 minutes.

Place the remaining hay on a large serving platter and set the roast on it. Loosely assemble the salad around the roast. Serve hot, discarding any large fat deposits as you carve the roast.

PORK NECK CANNELLONI with HEIRLOOM TOMATOES and BASIL

Here's a way to use a part of the pig that's usually forgotten. You do see the neck used to make cured *capocollo*, but not much else. I decided to braise it down, grind it, and stuff it into cannelloni with cheese and eggs. It was one of the best pasta fillings I ever had. Ask your butcher or farmers' market vendor for pork neck. They'll be happy to sell it to you cheap because no one asks for it. If you can't get pork neck, use boneless pork shoulder or shank instead. Either way, there's so much flavor here, all you need are some quick-sautéed heirloom tomatoes to pull the whole thing together. It's a great late summer dish when you're up to your ears in overripe tomatoes. This recipe makes a large casserole, so you have plenty of leftovers (which taste even better the next day). If you want less, cut the recipe in half.

MAKES 8 TO 10 SERVINGS

Pasta and Filling:

2 tablespoons (30 ml) extra-virgin olive oil

2½ pounds (1.125 kg) boneless pork neck or pork shoulder, cubed

1 medium-size yellow onion, chopped (1 cup/160 g)

2 medium-size carrots, chopped (1 cup/125 g)

2 medium-size ribs celery, chopped (1 cup/100 g)

4 ounces (115 g) chopped prosciutto (scraps are fine if you have them)

½ cup (120 ml) white wine

20 ounces (570 g) fresh whole-milk ricotta cheese (2½ cups)

5 large eggs

Salt and freshly ground black pepper

8 ounces (227 g) Egg Pasta Dough (page 282), rolled into 2 sheets, each about 1/16 inch (1.5 mm) thick

1 quart (1 L) Béchamel Sauce (page 281), divided

3½ ounces (100 g) Parmesan cheese, grated (1 cup)

Heirloom Tomato Sauce:

8 garlic cloves, minced

1½ cups (375 ml) extra-virgin olive oil

4 pounds (1.75 kg) heirloom tomatoes

24 fresh basil leaves

Salt and freshly ground black pepper

For the pasta and filling: Heat the oil in a Dutch oven over high heat. Add the pork in batches to prevent overcrowding, and cook until browned all over, 8 to 10 minutes. Transfer the meat to a bowl, and add the onion, carrots, and celery to the pan. Cook until the vegetables are soft but not browned, 5 to 6 minutes. Add the prosciutto, and cook for 2 minutes. Return the meat to the pan, add the white wine, and simmer until the liquid reduces in volume by about half, 10 minutes or so. Lower the heat to medium-low, cover, and simmer until the meat is extremely soft, 3 to 4 hours, adding a little water, if necessary, to prevent sticking. The meat should fall apart in shreds when poked with tongs. Remove the pan from the heat and let the mixture cool down in the pan. Refrigerate the whole pan until the mixture is cold, at least 1 hour or up to 1 day.

Put all the parts of a meat grinder in the freezer for 15 minutes to chill them. Grind the cold meat mixture on the small ($\frac{1}{4}$-inch/6-mm) die of the grinder. Weigh out 2 pounds (1 kg) of the mixture and reserve the rest for another use. (You may have about 4 ounces/115 g extra—add it to tomato sauce or use it to top bruschetta.) Put the 2 pounds (1 kg) of ground pork in a bowl and stir in the ricotta cheese, eggs, and a generous amount of salt and pepper. Spoon the mixture into resealable plastic bags and refrigerate for at least 1 hour or up to 3 days.

Lay the pasta sheets on a lightly floured work surface and cut into 4-inch (10-cm) squares. You should get about twenty squares from each sheet, forty total.

Bring a large pot of salted water to a boil and fill a large bowl with ice water. Drop the pasta squares into the hot water a few at a time, quickly return the water to a boil, and cook for 15 to 20 seconds just to blanch them, stirring gently to prevent sticking. Immediately transfer the pasta to ice water to stop the cooking. Lay the pasta squares on kitchen towels and pat dry; they will be delicate and some may stick, but you should have plenty.

Preheat the oven to 500°F (260°C). Turn on convection, if possible.

Pipe a 1-inch (2.5-cm)-thick line of the cold filling along one edge of each pasta square. Starting at the filled side, use the edge of the kitchen towels to lift and roll the pasta to the edge of the unfilled side to enclose the filling.

Spread a thin layer of béchamel over the bottom of a 4-quart (3.75-L) baking dish (or use individual dishes, if you like). Place the cannelloni on top, seam-side down, and top with the remaining béchamel. Sprinkle with the Parmesan cheese, and then bake until the cheese melts and browns on top, 8 to 10 minutes.

For the heirloom tomato sauce: Heat the garlic and oil over medium-low heat in a sauté pan for 3 to 4 minutes. Thinly slice the tomatoes and add to the pan. Raise the heat to medium, and cook until the tomatoes fall apart and the sauce thickens, about 20 minutes, stirring now and then. Chop the basil and stir into the sauce, along with salt and pepper to taste.

To finish, spoon the sauce on top of the cannelloni.

WHOLE ROASTED PIG'S HEAD

Jonathon Sawyer was the inspiration for this recipe. He's the chef at the Greenhouse Tavern in Cleveland and is completely dedicated to zero-waste cooking. I invited Jonathon to do a dinner with me at Osteria in Philadelphia. Jonathon saw me cutting off a pig's head and throwing it out (we roast a small pig almost every day at the restaurant). "What the hell are you doing?" he screamed. "You're throwing away good food there!" He kept the head and roasted it whole with a Coca-Cola glaze. Since that day, I started roasting all our pig's heads. But now I use beer cooked down with some orange juice and chili flakes to make an *agro dolce* (sweet-and-sour) glaze. It's become a cult classic. At Osteria, we only have so many heads a week, so people call in advance to order it. When it comes to the table, the whole roasted pig's head looks kind of macabre. But it tastes 100 percent awesome.

MAKES 2 TO 4 SERVINGS

Pig's Head:

1 small pig's head (4 to 5 pounds/1.75 to 2.25 kg)

3 quarts (2.75 L) 3-2-1 Brine (page 280)

1 tablespoon (6 g) ground fennel seeds

1 medium-size yellow onion, chopped (1½ cups/240 g)

2 large carrots, chopped (1½ cups/185 g)

3 medium-size ribs celery, chopped (1½ cups/150 g)

1 sachet of 1 sprig rosemary, 3 sprigs thyme, 1 bay leaf, 5 black peppercorns, and 1 garlic clove (see page 277)

1 quart (1 L) Chicken Stock (page 279)

Beer Agro Dolce:

12 ounces (375 ml) beer (I like pale ale, but almost any beer will do; in the fall I use a chestnut beer from Baladin called Noël)

½ cup (100 g) granulated sugar

¼ cup (60 ml) sherry vinegar

Juice of 1 orange

Big pinch of chile flakes

½ teaspoon (1 g) black peppercorns

Bruschetta:

5 thick slices rustic bread

Olive oil, for brushing

Salt and freshly ground black pepper

Raspberry, apple, or another seasonal jam of your choice

For the pig's head: Rinse the head and set aside. Make the brine and stir in the ground fennel seeds. Submerge the head in the brine, and refrigerate for 4 days.

Put the head in a large Dutch oven or other pot that will hold it comfortably. Add the onion, carrots, celery, and sachet to the pot. Pour in the stock and just enough water to come about halfway up the head. Cover and bring to a boil over high heat.

Preheat the oven to 325°F (160°C). When the liquid comes to a boil, transfer the pot to the oven, and cook, covered, until the head is tender, 4 to 5 hours. The skin on top of the head should start to split and the cheeks should feel soft to the touch. When the head is done, carefully remove it from the pot (heatproof silicone gloves work well), put it on a rimmed baking sheet, cover, and refrigerate. When the head is cool, use a knife to remove the skin from the cheeks and snout, peeling away the skin but leaving the meat and fat. Score the fat around the cheeks. Leave the skin on the top of the head so the ears remain attached. Remove the tongue, and remove and discard the skin from the tongue.

For the beer agro dolce: Combine the beer, sugar, vinegar, orange juice, chili flakes, and peppercorns in a pot and bring to a boil over high heat. Boil until the liquid reduces in volume to about ⅔ cup (150 ml) and becomes a thin syrup, 10 to 15 minutes. Strain and set aside.

For the bruschetta: Heat a grill or broiler to medium-high heat. Brush both sides of the bread with oil and season with salt and pepper. Grill or broil the bread until toasted, 1 to 2 minutes per side.

Preheat the oven to 450°F (230°C). Put the pig's head and the tongue in a roasting pan or on a rimmed baking sheet and pour the agro dolce evenly over the head and tongue, brushing it to cover completely. Transfer to the oven and roast for 5 minutes. Pull out the pan and turn the head onto one cheek, spooning the sauce from the pan evenly over the head and tongue. Roast for another 5 minutes. Remove again from the oven and turn the head on the other cheek, spooning the sauce all over the head and tongue. If the sauce gets too thick, add a little water to the pan to thin it enough to be pourable. Roast for another 5 minutes. The total roasting time will be 15 to 20 minutes. Put the head right side up on a large plate or platter, with the tongue alongside it. Spoon the remaining sauce over the head.

Serve with the bruschetta and jam. Invite guests to pick meat from the head (the cheeks are especially rich and delicious). The tongue can be sliced into serving pieces.

WHOLE ROASTED PORK SHOULDER with PICKLED VEGETABLES

In American markets, you see two kinds of pork shoulder—Boston butt (the upper part of the shoulder) and picnic ham (the lower part near the foreleg). At the Mangili butcher shop in Italy, I sold the whole shoulder, including both sections. Together, they weigh about fourteen pounds (6.25 kg). It's a good-size hunk of meat. If you can't get a whole shoulder, look for pork butt or picnic ham with the skin on. If you can only get skinless pork butt, you can still make this dish. You won't get any cracklings, but it'll be delicious anyway. Set out the whole roasted shoulder and let your guests pick at the meat and vegetables. Perfect for a party. The pickled vegetables add some acid to cut through the fat of the pork and the sweetness of the *vincotto* glaze. *Vincotto* is "cooked wine" that's reduced until it's thick, sweet, and syrupy, sort of like balsamic syrup. You can find it at good Italian specialty shops.

MAKES 10 TO 12 SERVINGS

1 bone-in skin-on pork butt or picnic ham (about 8 pounds/3.5 kg)

1 cup (135 g) kosher salt

1 cup (200 g) granulated sugar

¾ teaspoon (1.5 g) ground fennel seeds

¾ teaspoon (1 g) freshly ground black pepper

½ cup (120 ml) vincotto (see recipe headnote)

1 packed cup (225 g) light brown sugar

5 cups (200g) torn romaine lettuce

5 cups (500 g) mixed pickled vegetables for garnish

Rinse the pork, and then pat it dry. Combine the salt, sugar, fennel, and black pepper, and rub the mixture all over the pork in a tub or large resealable plastic bag. Cover or seal, and refrigerate overnight.

Preheat the oven to 275°F (135°C). Transfer the pork to a large Dutch oven and add 2 cups (475 ml) of water. Cover and braise in the oven until the meat is tender, about 190°F (88°C) internal temperature, 4 to 5 hours, checking periodically and adding water, as necessary, to keep the liquid level about three-quarters of the way up the meat.

Carefully transfer the shoulder from the pan to a rimmed baking sheet and cover with foil. Save the cooking liquid in the pan. The liquid should measure about 1 quart (1 L). Add the vincotto and brown sugar to the liquid, and bring to a boil over high heat. Boil until the liquid reduces in volume by about half and becomes a thin syrup, 20 to 25 minutes.

Preheat the oven to 375°F (190°C). Brush the vincotto syrup all over the pork shoulder. Heat the pork in the oven until warmed through, 20 to 30 minutes. Raise the heat to 500°F (260°C). Cook until the pork is hot and the skin is crisp, 10 to 15 minutes, stopping every 5 minutes to brush the glaze from the bottom of the pan over the pork. You may need to add about 1 cup (235 ml) of water to the pan to keep the syrup from burning as it cooks.

Line a platter with the lettuce and carefully transfer the pork to the platter. Garnish with the pickled vegetables and serve the meat whole drizzled with any remaining glaze. Allow guests to crack the skin and pick off pieces of the meat, dragging them in the glaze and alternating with bites of pickled vegetables.

PAPPARDELLE with VEAL RAGÙ and PEPPERS

When I got back to Philadelphia after working in Italy for three years, I was buzzing with inspiration. I'd just opened Osteria, and toward the end of that summer in 2007, the menu ideas were coming fast. I was doing some really innovative cooking. But sometimes, I would walk into the garden outside the restaurant and crave the classic combinations, such as sausage and peppers. Our pepper plants were going crazy that summer. We had cherry peppers, cayennes, red and green bell peppers, Marcona peppers, and horns of the bull. I grabbed a mix of sweet and hot peppers off the plants, sautéed them, and mixed them with a ragù made from veal rib. Use whatever mix of sweet and hot peppers you have on hand. The heat level should end up being mildly spicy—just a little kick. And if you buy veal rib, the butcher might have it rolled and tied already. For this recipe, just untie it and open it flat before seasoning it.

Rub the veal with the kosher salt and cracked black pepper. Cover and refrigerate for 2 hours to lightly cure the veal. Then rinse it off and pat dry.

Cut the veal into two or three manageable-size pieces and dredge them in flour. Heat 2 tablespoons (30 ml) of the oil in a Dutch oven over high heat. When hot, add the veal and sear until golden brown on all sides, 4 to 5 minutes per side (sear in batches, if necessary, to prevent overcrowding the pan). Transfer the veal to a plate.

Add the onions, carrots, and celery to the pan and lower the heat to medium. Add the sachet, and cook until the vegetables are golden brown, 10 to 12 minutes, stirring now and then. You want a little caramelization on the vegetables, but not too dark. Add the wine, raise the heat to high, and boil until the liquid reduces in volume by about half, 15 minutes or so.

Preheat the oven to 300°F (150°C).

Add 1½ quarts (1.5 L) of the veal stock to the pan. When it comes up to a simmer, add the seared veal, which should only be covered by liquid about halfway. Adjust the amount of veal stock as necessary.

Cover the pan and braise in the oven until the veal is tender but not easily falling apart, 2 to 3 hours. Chop the veal into bite-size pieces and then return it to the sauce. Discard the sachet.

Meanwhile, roll the pasta dough out into 2 sheets, each about 1/16 inch (1.5 mm) thick. Lay the pasta sheets on a lightly floured work surface and trim the edges square. Cut crosswise into strips a little less than 1 inch (2.5 cm) wide, preferably with a fluted cutter.

Heat the remaining 2 tablespoons (30 ml) of oil in a large, deep sauté pan over medium heat. Add the peppers, and cook until just tender, about 5 minutes. Add the veal ragù, and cook until slightly thickened, 5 minutes or so.

Bring a large pot of salted water to a boil. Add the pasta, and cook until tender yet still firm, about a minute. Drain and add the pasta to the sauté pan, along with the butter and Parmesan. Cook, stirring gently, until the sauce is creamy, 2 to 3 minutes. Taste, then season with salt and pepper and serve hot.

MAKES 6 SERVINGS

2½ pounds (1.125 kg) boneless veal rib

2½ tablespoons (21 g) kosher salt

½ teaspoon (1 g) cracked black pepper

All-purpose flour, for dredging

¼ cup (60 ml) olive oil, divided

2 medium-size yellow onions, finely chopped (2½ cups/400 g)

3 large carrots, finely chopped (2¼ cups/275 g)

1 whole head celery, finely chopped (2¼ cups/225 g)

1 sachet of 1 sprig rosemary, 3 sprigs thyme, 1 bay leaf, 5 black peppercorns, 5 parsley stems and 2 garlic cloves (see page 277)

1 quart (1 L) dry white wine

2 to 2½ quarts (2 to 2.5 L) Veal Stock (page 279)

8 ounces (227 g) Egg Pasta Dough (page 282) rolled into 2 sheets about 1/16 inch (1.5mm) thick

2 long hot or cherry peppers, seeded and cut into narrow strips

2 red or green bell peppers, seeded and cut into narrow strips

4 tablespoons (56 g) unsalted butter

1 ounce (28 g) Parmesan cheese, grated (1/3 cup)

Salt and freshly ground black pepper

GRILLED LAMB RACK with FAVETTA and ROASTED PEARL ONIONS

A couple of years after I returned to the United States, my wife, Claudia, asked me to bring home some fava beans for dinner. It was springtime and she made a rustic fava bean puree with grilled lamb rack. It was exactly like the one her Uncle Bruno made for us years before when we started dating in Italy. I like to cut the lamb rack from the whole saddle, French it, and then tie it myself. But most U.S. butchers sell Frenched lamb racks already tied. When you cross-cut the rack into portions, each piece should have a nice long rib bone that you can use as a handle to hold the meat while dragging it into the fava puree. That's how Uncle Bruno eats it.

For the *favetta*: Bring a large pot of water to a boil and fill a large bowl with ice water. Add the whole fava pods to the boiling water and blanch for 1 minute. Transfer to the ice water to stop the cooking. When cool, pluck the favas from the pods, then pinch open the pale green skin and pop out the bright green fava beans. You should have about 4 cups (750 g).

Place the fava beans in a food processor, turn it on, and slowly add just enough olive oil until the beans catch and the mixture forms a rustic, slightly chunky puree. Season to taste with salt and pepper.

For the roasted pearl onions: Preheat the oven to 500°F (260°C). Toss the onions with 2 tablespoons (30 ml) of the olive oil and season with salt and pepper. Spread the onions in a single layer on a rimmed baking sheet and roast until tender and golden in color, 10 to 12 minutes, shaking the pan once or twice. Let cool slightly, then slice any large onions in half lengthwise. The onions can be roasted up to 2 days ahead.

Put the vinegar in a blender and slowly add the remaining 3 cups (750 ml) of oil until blended and emulsified, 1 to 2 minutes. Season generously with salt and pepper. Pour the vinaigrette into a medium saucepan and add the onions.

For the lamb racks: Heat a grill (preferably with oak wood) to medium heat with both high- and low-heat areas.

Season the lamb racks with salt and pepper. Scrape the grill grate clean, coat it with oil, and grill the racks over a high-heat area of the grill until nicely grill-marked, 5 to 7 minutes per side. Move the meat to a low-heat area of the grill, cover, and cook to medium rare (135°F/57°C internal temperature), about 10 minutes more.

Warm the onions and vinaigrette over medium heat.

Use two large dinnerware tablespoons to scoop up and shape the *favetta* into football shapes (quenelles). Place a quenelle on each plate just a little left of center. Remove the butcher's twine from the lamb racks and cut into portions between each bone. Place two portions on each plate. Mix the mint into the onions and spoon the onions on top of the lamb, reserving some of the liquid to drizzle around the plates.

MAKES 8 SERVINGS

Favetta:

4 pounds (1.75 kg) young fava beans in the pods

½ cup (120 ml) olive oil

Salt and freshly ground black pepper

Roasted Pearl Onions:

12 ounces (56 g) red pearl onions, peeled

3 cups (750 ml) plus 2 tablespoons (30 ml) olive oil, divided

Salt and freshly ground black pepper

1 cup (235 ml) red wine vinegar

30 mint leaves, cut into chiffonade

Lamb Racks:

2 Frenched lamb racks, about 4 pounds (1.75 kg) total, trimmed and tied

Salt and freshly ground black pepper

Olive oil, as needed

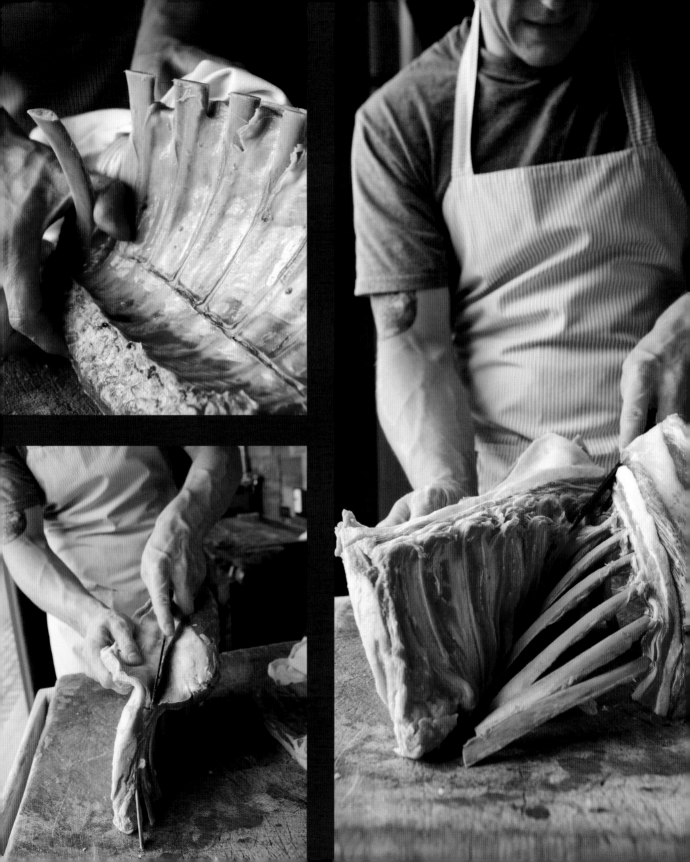

ALME

A MAESTRO IN THE KITCHEN, AMORE IN THE DINING ROOM

WHEN I PICTURE ITALY IN MY MIND, I SEE ALME.

The town is only the size of a football field. It has a church, a movie theater, one good bar, and an awesome *gelateria* (ice-cream shop) called Paradiso. But that's about it. Frosio Ristorante is what makes the place famous. The restaurant sits inside an eighteenth-century villa that has an ancient look with a modern touch. It's like a yellow-painted ice cube dropped in the middle of a classic Italian village.

When I started working there as a stage (an unpaid kitchen apprentice), I'd been in Italy for nine months or so. I had finished up at Mangili butcher shop and then cooked at Loro, which recently earned its first Michelin star. The chef at Loro was Antonio Rochetti, who has since become a good friend of mine. Antonio taught me so much. It was only the two of us in the kitchen, and we did everything from butchering animals to making bread, pasta, and desserts. I couldn't imagine a better introduction to cooking in Italy. But after a few months, it was time to move on. I really wanted to cook at Frosio. The food there totally blew me away. Antonio had worked there years ago, and he and the chef were friends, so Antonio set me up to work with him.

Paolo Frosio, a thoughtful, sensitive chef, was one of the first to put the province of Bergamo on the culinary map. After culinary school, Paolo trained in France and Los Angeles, and then came back home brimming with experience. He opened his restaurant in 1990 at the age of twenty-three and he earned a Michelin star just over a year later, making him Italy's youngest-ever Michelin-starred chef. With his training and background, he created magnificent plates of food, staying true to what the locals grew up eating but going way beyond what a typical *osteria* or trattoria could do.

The Frosio family has been in the food business for more than one hundred years, so it was easy for Paolo to blend the local and global at his restaurant. His aunt raises full-breasted duck and guinea hens on her farm, and his sister provides him with Taleggio cheese that she ages in caves until it gets firm and pungent. He would make a creamy *fonduta* (fondue) with the Taleggio and spoon it over two poached eggs from his aunt's birds, all on toasted brioche. Then he shaved fresh black truffles over the top. Simple, but mind-blowing. The truffles were usually dug out of the ground the day before in Val Brembana, not too far away.

Just about everything we cooked at Frosio was tied to the food and culture of Bergamo. Our meat came from one of the area's best butchers, Franco Cazzamali, who is considered a master of beef the way a sushi chef is a master of fish. Cazzamali uses Fassone, the local white cattle that everyone calls *la granda* (most-prized beef). It has a dark red color, lots of marbling, and big flavor that really shines when shaved for carpaccio.

The cheeses that didn't come from Paolo's sister came once a week from Vecchio Larry (Old Larry), a big, burly guy who owned a rustic restaurant outside Milan. As a side business, he sold local cheeses, such as stracchino, strachitunt, robiola, and formagella. Vecchio Larry was a huge Celtics fan and loved Larry Bird. When he found out there was an American in the Frosio kitchen, we started talking sports. Every week, he'd come into the kitchen, joking, laughing, and talking trash.

Vecchio Larry is a character, or a *personaggio*, as they say in Italy. Camillo, Paolo's older brother, is another *personaggio*. Camillo runs the front of the house and wine service at Frosio Ristorante. He's thin, walks slightly hunched over, and loves to drink sparkling wine and crack jokes about Americans. He's a big football fan. The Super Bowl came around while I was working there, and Camillo organized a Super Bowl party for the staff. That February, he bought

hamburgers and Budweisers, and we stayed up until three in the morning to watch the game.

The biggest thing I learned from Paolo Frosio is that nothing goes to waste. He used the stems and leaves from every plant and the skin and bones from every animal that came into that kitchen. He was a master at opening up the walk-in, pulling out a bunch of scraps, and making a meal that would blow you away. We'd come to the end of the workweek, and the last party of six would come into the restaurant and ask for a tasting menu. "Shit!" Paolo would say to the cooks. "We don't have anything left!" Then he'd open up the walk-in, grab a piece of mullet, some pork trimmings, some vegetables, and make an incredible five-course tasting menu. I learned how to do that from him. When you get in a whole pig, you use the whole thing, nose to tail.

When you get fennel, you use the fronds; you chop the stems. You make pesto from celery leaves. That's how you save money: you use everything.

By late winter of that year, I started feeling more comfortable in Italy. I'd picked up a few more words since working at Mangili. Just enough to get by. When April rolled around, the weather started getting warmer, and we opened the kitchen windows to let in some air. I had been working the apps and pastry stations but also did entrées with Paolo. One night, Matteo, one of the cooks who used to work there, came in for a birthday dinner with an old friend of his. They both got the *degustazione di carne,* the meat-tasting menu. For an appetizer, I shaved raw Fassone beef and plated it with blanched, pencil-thin asparagus and shaved Parmigiano-Reggiano. I also made Paolo's poached eggs with Taleggio *fonduta* and black truffle on brioche. I served them crispy sweetbreads with Parmigiano *fonduta* and grilled Treviso radicchio, then pork shank osso buco with saffron rice *crema.* And for dessert, molten chocolate flan. I also served them chestnut cannoli, *torrone semifreddo,* and one of my specialties, *piccola pasticceria* (petit fours).

Around midnight, we finished up in the kitchen. I went into the dining room to say hi to Matteo, and he introduced me to the birthday girl, Claudia. I said literally three words to her: "*Ciao. Sono* Jeff." (Hi. I'm Jeff.) I was still learning the language, and my already-small vocabulary deserted me. Matteo and I talked for a few minutes before they got up to leave. I couldn't help noticing Claudia's tight jeans as they walked out the door.

The next morning, I called Matteo because we had dinner plans. It was restaurant week and Bergamo's top restaurants were running dinner specials: thirty-three euros for anyone age thirty-three or under. We set a time and place to meet, and then I asked Matteo, "Do you think Claudia would like to come with us?"

Crispy Sweetbreads with Parmigiano Fonduta
and Grilled Treviso

•

Canederli with Cabbage and Speck

•

Doppio Ravioli with Duck and Chestnut

•

Fettuccine with Braised Rabbit and Porcini

•

Grilled Halibut with Mussels and Chanterelles

•

Pork Shank Osso Buco with Saffron Rice Crema

•

Chocolate Flan

•

Chestnut Rice Pudding with Persimmon

•

Rhubarb Tartellette with Italian Meringue

CRISPY SWEETBREADS with PARMIGIANO FONDUTA and GRILLED TREVISO

MAKES 4 SERVINGS

1 pound (450 g) sweetbreads, preferably veal thymus

1 head Treviso radicchio

¾ cup (175 ml) olive oil, divided, plus some for drizzling

Salt and freshly ground black pepper

¾ cup (95 grams) *tipo* 00 flour (see page 277) or all-purpose flour

4 ounces (1 stick/115 g) unsalted butter

6 sage leaves

1 cup (235 ml) heavy cream

1 teaspoon (2 g) cracked black pepper

1 ounce (28 g) Parmesan cheese, grated (¼ cup)

2½ tablespoons (37 ml) sherry vinegar

1 tablespoon (3.75 g) chopped mixed fresh herbs (parsley, rosemary, and thyme)

Extra-virgin olive oil for garnish

Back in 1996, when I was training at the Culinary Institute of America, we always poached sweetbreads before sautéing or pan-frying them. When I got to Italy, I saw Paolo Frosio doing the same thing. But I always thought that pre-cooking gave sweetbreads a chalky texture. I had learned from Marc Vetri that you can just soak them in ice water before cooking them. That's how I like to do them. With a quick pre-soak, the sweetbreads stay nice and meaty and fry up crispier.

Rinse the sweetbreads in cold water, then soak in a bowl of ice water for 10 minutes. Pat dry, then remove the outer membrane from the sweetbreads. Cut the sweetbreads into 1-ounce (28-g) portions, about the size of two fingers, and refrigerate for up to 8 hours. It's important to keep the sweetbreads cold right up until you cook them.

Heat a grill to medium heat. Quarter the head of Treviso lengthwise, drizzle the pieces with a little olive oil, and season with salt and pepper. Brush the grill grate with oil and grill the Treviso until charred on all sides, 2 to 3 minutes per side. Set aside.

Season the sweetbreads all over with salt and pepper, then dredge in the flour, gently shaking off excess flour.

Heat the butter and ¼ cup (60 ml) of the olive oil in a large skillet over medium heat. When the butter starts to foam, add the sage leaves. Use a spoon to baste the sage with the butter mixture until the sage is crispy, 3 to 4 minutes. Remove from the pan and drain on paper towels; season lightly with salt and pepper. Add the sweetbread pieces to the pan, and cook until darkly browned and crisp all over, about 15 minutes, turning once or twice. Transfer to paper towels to drain.

Combine the heavy cream and cracked pepper in a small saucepan over medium heat. Cook until steam begins to rise from the cream but it doesn't simmer, 3 to 4 minutes. Whisk in the Parmesan until melted. Strain the mixture through a medium-mesh strainer into a small metal bowl, discarding the solids. You will be left with a creamy Parmesan sauce (*fonduta*). Set the bowl into another bowl of hot water to keep warm until ready to serve (if you put it over direct heat the Parmesan will coagulate on the bottom).

Put the vinegar in a bowl or small food processor and slowly whisk or blend in the remaining ½ cup (120 ml) of olive oil until thickened, 1 to 3 minutes. Season with salt and pepper to taste. Cut off and discard the Treviso cores, then cut the grilled Treviso into ¼-inch (5-mm) chunks and toss in a bowl with the vinaigrette and herbs. Keep warm or rewarm gently just before serving.

Spoon about ¼ cup (60 ml) of fonduta onto each plate, and place the sweetbreads on top. Garnish with the grilled Treviso, fried sage, and a drizzle of extra-virgin olive oil.

CANEDERLI with CABBAGE and SPECK

Most American restaurants have a quick staff meal in the middle of the day before dinner service. When I worked in Italy, staff meal was like no other I'd ever had. We actually sat down for thirty to forty minutes and enjoyed a three-course meal. At Frosio, one of the cooks, Francesco Cereda, made these bread gnocchi for staff meal one day and they blew my mind. He soaked some leftover bread in milk, mixed in sautéed onions and eggs, and boiled the dumplings like pasta. The canederli were unbelievably light and fluffy, and he served them with only brown butter, Parmesan, and fresh sage. It was simple and beautiful. Canederli come from Trentino, so I like to serve them with cabbage and Speck, two ingredients that are a huge part of Trentino cooking. That chewy, salty spark ties the whole dish together. If you can't find Speck, use coppa or prosciutto.

Whisk together the milk, 5 tablespoons (70 g) of the melted butter, and the eggs, parsley, salt, nutmeg, and ½ teaspoon (1 g) of black pepper in a large bowl. Stir in the cubed bread, then the 6½ tablespoons (50 g) of flour. Let stand for 30 minutes.

Bring a large pot of salted water to a boil. Put the remaining 1 cup (125 g) of flour in a bowl, then scoop the bread mixture into small balls about the size of golf balls and drop them in the flour, rolling them gently until dusted with flour. Shake off the excess flour. The canederli will be loose and soft. Drop the dusted canederli in the boiling water, in batches, if necessary, to prevent overcrowding, and cook until they float, 4 to 5 minutes. Remove from the boiling water with a slotted spoon and transfer to a bowl or plate.

Meanwhile, heat the remaining 4 tablespoons (55 g) of butter over medium heat until deep amber in color, about 5 minutes, swirling the pan for even browning. Set aside.

Heat the oil in a large sauté pan over medium heat and add the cabbage, cooking it just until tender, about 5 minutes. Taste and season with salt and pepper.

Divide the cabbage among plates, top with the canederli (four to five per serving), and sprinkle with the Parmesan. Drizzle with the browned butter and scatter the strips of Speck over the top.

MAKES 4 TO 6 SERVINGS
(18 TO 20 DUMPLINGS)

¾ cup plus 2 tablespoons (100 ml) whole milk, at room temperature

9 tablespoons (125 g) unsalted butter, melted, divided

2 large eggs

1 tablespoon (3.75 g) chopped fresh flat-leaf parsley

1 tablespoon (18 g) salt, plus more to taste

½ teaspoon (1 g) grated nutmeg

½ teaspoon (1 g) freshly ground black pepper, plus more to taste

8 ounces (227 g) white bread, crust removed, cubed (from 8 to 10 slices)

6½ tablespoons (50 g) sifted *tipo* 00 flour (see page 277) or all-purpose flour, plus about 1 cup (125 g) for dusting

2 teaspoons (10 ml) grapeseed or olive oil

8 ounces (227 g) savoy cabbage, julienned (2 cups)

1 ounce (28 g) Parmesan cheese, grated (¼ cup)

2 ounces (56 g) cured Speck, coppa, or proscuitto, thinly sliced into strips (½ cup)

DOPPIO RAVIOLI with DUCK and CHESTNUT

Toward the end of summer 2008, I was developing the fall menu for Osteria in Philadelphia. I thought back to the *doppio* (double) ravioli that Paolo Frosio made when I was there, which contained two different fillings. Genius! I wanted some chestnuts on our fall menu, so I decided to try duck and chestnuts. With some chestnut flour in the pasta itself, the combination was perfect. Thanks for the inspiration, Paolo!

MAKES 6 TO 8 SERVINGS

Duck Filling:

2 pounds (1 kg) bone-in duck legs

Salt and freshly ground black pepper

2 tablespoons (30 ml) blended oil (page 276)

½ small yellow onion, chopped (⅓ cup/52 g)

1 medium-size carrot, chopped (⅓ cup/40 g)

1 medium-size rib celery, chopped (⅓ cup/33 g)

4 cups (1 L) red wine

1 sachet of 2 sprigs parsley, 2 sprigs rosemary, and 2 sprigs thyme (see page 277)

1 large egg

1 ounce (28 g) Parmesan cheese, grated (¼ cup)

Chestnut Filling:

1 tablespoon (15 ml) olive oil

1 tablespoon (14 g) unsalted butter

½ small yellow onion, chopped (⅓ cup/52 g)

1 small garlic clove, minced

8 ounces (227 g) peeled chestnuts (1⅓ cups), thawed if frozen

4 ounces (113 g) fresh whole-milk ricotta cheese (½ cup)

½ ounce (14 g) Parmesan cheese, grated (2 tablespoons)

1 large egg

Ravioli:

8 ounces (227 g) Chestnut Pasta Dough (page 282), rolled into 2 sheets, each about 1/32 inch (0.8 mm) thick

8 ounces (2 sticks/225 g) unsalted butter

6 ounces (170 g) peeled chestnuts (1 cup), sliced

8 sprigs thyme

1¾ ounces (50 g) Parmesan cheese, grated (½ cup) for garnish

(continued on next page)

For the duck filling: Remove any excess fat deposits from the duck legs. Rinse them well, then pat dry and season the duck all over with salt and pepper. Heat the oil in a Dutch oven or large, deep saucepan over high heat. When the pan is smoking hot, add the duck and sear on both sides until well browned, 10 to 12 minutes total. Transfer to a plate or platter. Pour off all but a few tablespoons of fat from the pan, and then add the onion, carrot, and celery; cook over medium heat until soft but not browned, 3 to 4 minutes. Return the duck to the pan, pour in the wine, and add the sachet. Bring to a simmer, then adjust the heat so that the liquid simmers gently. Cover and simmer gently until the duck is very tender, just about to the point of easily falling apart, 2 to 3 hours. Remove from the heat, and remove and discard the sachet. Transfer the duck to a plate or platter. Strain the broth, reserving the broth and vegetables separately. Pick the meat and skin from the bones, discarding all the bones. Grind the meat, skin, and reserved vegetables on the small die of a meat grinder. Fold in the egg and cheese, and season with salt and pepper. Spoon the filling into a resealable plastic bag and refrigerate for up to 2 days. Refrigerate the braising liquid as well.

For the chestnut filling: Heat the oil and butter in a sauté pan over medium-low heat. When the butter melts, add the onion and garlic, and cook until soft but not browned, 8 to 10 minutes. Add the chestnuts and season with salt and pepper. Add enough water to cover the ingredients, increase the heat to medium, cover, and cook until the chestnuts are tender enough for a fork to slide in easily (sort of like that of boiled potatoes), 15 to 20 minutes. Drain and reserve the cooking liquid. Transfer the solids to a blender and puree with just enough of the cooking liquid to make a thick, smooth puree that's roughly the texture of ricotta cheese, scraping down the sides of the blender as necessary. Fold in the ricotta, Parmesan, and egg. Spoon the filling into a resealable plastic bag and refrigerate for up to 2 days.

To make the ravioli: Lay a pasta sheet on a lightly floured work surface and dust with flour. Trim the ends to make them square, then fold the dough in half lengthwise and make a small notch at the center to mark it. Open the sheet so it lies flat again and spritz with water. Cut a corner from each bag of filling and pipe the fillings in ½-inch-wide columns along the length of the pasta, leaving ½-inch margin around each column of fillings and stopping at the middle of the sheet. (See photo at right, but note that the pasta sheet has been rolled in a commercial pasta machine and is about twice as wide as what you get from a typical consumer pasta machine.) Neaten up the columns of filling with your fingertips. Lift up the empty side of the pasta sheet and fold it over to cover the filling. Gently press the pasta around each strip of filling to seal (it helps to use a long wooden dowel or chopstick). Use a fluted pasta cutting wheel or a sharp knife to cut the ravioli into rectangles. When cut, each ravioli should have two fillings in it. Repeat with the remaining pasta dough and filling. You will have about sixty ravioli.

Bring a large pot of salted water to a boil. Add ten to twelve ravioli at a time, and cook just until tender, 4 to 5 minutes.

Meanwhile, melt the butter in a large, deep sauté pan. Add the chestnuts, thyme, and 1 cup (235 ml) of pasta water. Skim and discard the fat from the reserved duck braising liquid and add 1 cup (235 ml) of the braising liquid to the pan. Remove the cooked ravioli from the pasta water with a slotted spoon and add them to the pan, simmering until the sauce coats the pasta, 3 to 4 minutes. Season with salt and pepper. Divide among plates and sprinkle with Parmesan.

FETTUCCINE with BRAISED RABBIT and PORCINI

You see thick, hearty *ragù* (stew) on every menu in northern Italy. But I wanted to try and make a ragù that was delicate instead of heavy. Rabbit and porcini came to mind right away. In Italy, eating rabbit is about as common as eating chicken is in the United States. It made perfect sense. The rabbit is lean, and the porcini are earthy. Plus, Italian rabbits are big and richer-tasting than the ones you see in the States, so they stay rich and moist even when braised down into a ragù. Don't worry if you can't find Italian rabbits for this dish. Farmed American rabbits work fine. The dish just comes out tasting a little leaner.

MAKES 6 TO 8 SERVINGS

1 pound (450 g) Egg Pasta Dough (page 282), rolled into 4 sheets, each about ¹⁄₁₆ inch (1.5 mm) thick

4 ounces (113 g) dried porcini mushrooms (about 1½ cups)

2 rabbits (about 3 pounds/1.3 kg each)

Salt and freshly ground black pepper

¼ cup (60 ml) olive oil, divided

1 small yellow onion, finely chopped (²⁄₃ cup/105 g)

½ cup (120 ml) white wine

2 cups (480 g) canned plum tomatoes, preferably San Marzano, cored and crushed by hand

4 tablespoons (56 g) unsalted butter

2¾ ounces (78 g) Parmesan cheese, grated (¾ cup), divided

Lay a pasta sheet on your work surface and cut the pasta crosswise into 12-inch (30.5 cm) lengths, making sure each one is well floured. Run each piece of pasta through a fettuccine cutter and fold it gently onto a floured tray. Repeat with the remaining pasta dough. Dust with flour, cover, and freeze for up to 3 days.

Soak the porcini in hot water until soft, about 15 minutes. Pluck out the mushrooms and finely chop. Strain the soaking liquid through a fine-mesh strainer and reserve.

Rinse the rabbits and remove the innards and excess fat deposits. Remove the hind legs and forelegs by driving your knife straight through the hip and shoulder joints. Cut each leg in half through the center joints. Snip through the breast bones with kitchen shears, then cut the rabbits crosswise into five or six pieces each. Season the rabbit pieces all over with salt and pepper. Heat 2 tablespoons (30 ml) of the oil in a Dutch oven over medium-high heat. Add the rabbit pieces in batches to prevent overcrowding, and sear until golden brown on both sides, about 5 minutes per side. Transfer to a platter.

Preheat the oven to 350°F (175°C).

Add the onion to the pan, and cook over medium heat until soft but not browned, 4 to 5 minutes. Add the wine, stirring to scrape the pan bottom. Simmer until the liquid reduces in volume by about half, 5 minutes. Put the tomatoes in a food processor and pulse until finely chopped, and almost pureed. Add the tomatoes to the pan, along with the chopped mushrooms and the rabbit pieces. Add just enough of the reserved porcini liquid to barely cover the rabbit pieces. Cover and braise in the oven until the rabbit is so tender it falls apart, about 2 hours. Remove the rabbit, let cool slightly, and then pick the meat from the bones, feeling for small bones with your fingers. Shred the meat and discard the skin and bones. Put the braising liquid through a food mill or puree it briefly in a food processor. If the pureed braising liquid is thin, boil it until slightly thickened. Return the shredded meat to the pureed braising liquid.

Bring a large pot of salted water to a boil. Drop in the pasta in batches to prevent overcrowding, and stir after a couple of seconds to prevent sticking. Cook until tender, 30 seconds to 1 minute, depending on whether it is refrigerated or frozen. Drain the pasta and reserve the pasta water.

Add the remaining 2 tablespoons (30 ml) of olive oil and 2 cups (475 ml) of the pasta water to the ragù. Bring to a boil over high heat, and then lower the heat to medium and simmer gently for a minute or two. Add the cooked pasta, stirring constantly to prevent sticking. When the sauce is slightly reduced and coats the pasta, add the butter and ½ cup (50 g) of Parmesan. Season with salt and pepper to taste and stir until the butter melts completely, 1 to 2 minutes. Transfer to plates and garnish with the remaining Parmesan.

GRILLED HALIBUT with MUSSELS and CHANTERELLES

Frosio had a way of making sauce that I'll never forget. He would put some stock in a pan with a tiny amount of butter and olive oil, simmer it down, and then shake the hell out of it until it got thick and creamy. When I got back to Philadelphia, I thought that kind of sauce would be perfect if we made it from the juices of steamed mussels. It was early summer, chanterelles and halibut were both in season, and the ingredients practically combined themselves.

Heat the grapeseed oil in a 2-quart (2-L) pot over medium heat. Add the onion, and cook until soft but not browned, about 4 minutes. Add the garlic, and cook for 1 minute. Add the mussels, along with the wine. Cook until the wine reduces in volume slightly, and then add enough water to come about halfway up the mussels. Cover, bring to a simmer, and steam over medium heat until all the mussels open, 10 to 12 minutes. Discard any mussels that have not opened. Remove the mussels from their shells with a melon baller or small spoon, keeping the mussel meat as whole as possible. Strain the stock at least twice through cheesecloth or a clean coffee filter to remove any grit.

Heat 4 tablespoons (60 ml) of the olive oil in a large sauté pan over medium-high heat. Add the mushrooms and sauté until soft, about 5 minutes. Season with salt and pepper. Add the lemon juice and ½ cup (120 ml) of the mussel stock, scraping the pan bottom and simmering until the liquid reduces in volume and starts to thicken when stirred, 5 to 8 minutes. When the sauce has a creamy consistency, add the scallions, parsley, and reserved mussel meat, and cook for 1 minute. Taste and adjust the seasonings. Remove from the heat and keep warm.

Heat a grill to medium-high heat. Season both sides of the fish with salt and pepper and coat with oil. Scrape the grill grate clean and coat it with oil. Grill the fish until deeply grill-marked on one side, about 4 minutes. Rotate 90 degrees for crosshatch grill marks and continue grilling until the flesh turns white about halfway up the sides, 3 to 4 minutes more. Flip and cook until the fish is just a little moist and translucent in the center, about 125°F (52°C) internal temperature, 5 minutes or so.

Spoon the mushrooms and mussels on opposite sides of each plate and place the grilled fish in the middle. Add the remaining 2 tablespoons (30 ml) of olive oil to the mushroom pan and gently shake and swirl the pan until the sauce becomes creamy and thick, about 30 seconds. Drizzle the sauce over the fish and around the plate.

MAKES 4 SERVINGS

2 tablespoons (30 ml) grapeseed oil, plus some for oiling the fish

1 small yellow onion, thinly sliced into half-moons (½ cup/80 g)

1 garlic clove, smashed

2 pounds (1 kg) mussels, cleaned and scrubbed

½ cup (120 ml) dry white wine

6 tablespoons (90 ml) olive oil, divided

6 ounces (170 g) chanterelle mushrooms, thinly sliced lengthwise (about 2 cups)

Salt and freshly ground black pepper

1 teaspoon (5 ml) freshly squeezed lemon juice

4 scallions, thinly sliced (green parts only)

¼ cup (15 g) chopped fresh flat-leaf parsley

4 (6-ounce/170-g) skinless halibut pieces

PORK SHANK OSSO BUCO with
SAFFRON RICE CREMA

When they hear "osso buco," most people think of veal. But *osso buco* just means "bone with a hole," which is what you see in a crosscut piece of leg. I thought, why not make osso buco with pork shanks instead of veal? They're even richer and more deeply flavored than veal. Otherwise, the flavors here are classic Milanese: braised shanks, saffron risotto, and lemon-garlic-parsley gremolata for punch. The pork makes all the difference. This recipe will feed two hungry people, but if you have a braising pan big enough to hold eight shanks in a single layer (or if you have two pans), double the amounts to serve four people.

MAKES 2 SERVINGS

Pork shanks:

4 small pork shanks, each 6 to 7 ounces (170 to 200 grams) and 2 inches (5 cm) thick

Salt and freshly ground black pepper

½ cup (62 g) *tipo* 00 flour (see page 277) or all-purpose flour

¼ cup (60 ml) grapeseed oil

2 medium-size carrots, diced (1 cup/125 g)

1 medium-size yellow onion, diced (1 cup/160 g)

2 medium-size ribs celery, diced (1 cup/100 g)

¼ cup (60 ml) red wine

3 cups (720 grams) canned plum tomatoes, preferably San Marzano, cored and crushed by hand

1 sachet of 3 sprigs rosemary, 4 sprigs thyme, 10 peppercorns, 1 garlic clove, and 1 bay leaf (see page 277)

Saffron Rice Crema:

1 tablespoon (15 ml) olive oil

2 tablespoons (20 g) minced yellow onion

½ cup (100 g) Arborio or other risotto rice, rinsed

Salt and freshly ground black pepper

3 to 4 cups (0.75 to 1 L) very hot tap water or boiling water, divided

1 tablespoon (2 g) saffron

Gremolata:

2 tablespoons (7 g) chopped fresh flat-leaf parsley

1 small garlic clove, minced

Grated zest of ½ lemon

(continued on next page)

For the shanks: Preheat the oven to 350°F (175°C). Rinse the pork shanks, and then pat them dry. Season both sides with salt and pepper and dredge the shanks in flour in a shallow plate.

Heat the oil in a Dutch oven over medium-high heat. When hot, add the shanks and sear on both sides, about 5 minutes per side. Transfer the shanks to a plate and add the carrots, onion, and celery to the pan. Cook until golden brown, 5 to 8 minutes. Add the red wine, scraping the pan bottom and cooking for a minute or two. Add the shanks back to the pan, and cook until the wine reduces in volume by about three-quarters, 3 to 4 minutes. Add the tomatoes, along with enough water to cover the ingredients halfway. Add the sachet to the pan, cover, and braise in the oven until the shanks are tender, $2\frac{1}{2}$ to $3\frac{1}{2}$ hours, checking once or twice and adding water, if necessary, to keep the shanks halfway covered in liquid. Remove the shanks and pass the vegetables and braising liquid through a food mill to make a rustic puree. You can also use a food processor, pureeing the vegetables with just enough liquid to make them loose, and then mixing the puree back into the braising liquid. You should have about 3 cups (750 ml) of puree.

For the crema: Heat the oil in a medium saucepan over medium heat. Add the onion, and cook until soft but not browned, 3 to 4 minutes. Stir in the rice and season with salt and pepper. Add 2 cups (475 ml) of the hot water and bring to a gentle simmer. Cook, stirring occasionally just to make sure the rice is not sticking on the bottom. Avoid overstirring, as the more you stir the starchier and gummier the final crema will be. Cook until the rice is so tender that it starts to fall apart and most of the liquid is absorbed, 30 to 40 minutes total, adding just enough water, as needed, to prevent sticking. You will need to add about $\frac{1}{2}$ cup (120 ml) every 15 minutes after the first 20 minutes.

Meanwhile, steep the saffron in 2 tablespoons (30 ml) of hot water. Add the steeped saffron and steeping liquid to the rice, along with a final $\frac{1}{2}$ cup (120 ml) of added water. While the rice mixture is still hot, puree it quickly in a blender on high speed. The longer it purees, the gummier it will become, so keep the pureeing time short. If the puree is too thick, add a little water to thin it to a nice creamy consistency. Taste and season with salt and pepper.

For the gremolata: together the parsley, garlic, and lemon zest.

Pour the pureed braising sauce from the shanks into a medium saucepan, along with enough water to make a sauce the consistency of thick gravy. Season to taste with salt and pepper and half of the gremolata. Place the pork shanks in the sauce and heat through, 8 to 10 minutes.

Spoon the crema on individual plates, top with the shanks and some sauce, and sprinkle with the remaining gremolata.

CHOCOLATE FLAN

Everyone teases me about the name of this dish because it's basically a molten chocolate cake, but at Frosio, we called it a flan. I've made this dish hundreds and hundreds of times. It's one of the first desserts I cooked for Claudia, and I'll keep serving it to her for years to come. It's a great make-ahead dessert because you can pour the chocolate mixture into the flan molds and refrigerate it for hours or even days ahead of time. Then you take it straight from the fridge to the oven just before serving.

Whip the sugar, eggs, and egg yolks in a stand mixer on high speed until light and fluffy, about 10 minutes.

Heat the butter in a saucepan over medium heat until melted and hot. Add the chocolate and remove from the heat. Let stand until the chocolate is mostly melted, 5 minutes or so. Stir until the chocolate and butter are blended. Blend into the egg mixture on low speed. Sift in the flour on low speed.

Preheat the oven to 375°F (190°C). Butter and flour six to eight 4- to 6-ounce (125- to 175-ml) baking tins or ramekins. Fill the buttered and floured tins to just under the inside rim. Bake until set on the sides but still gooey in the center, 6 to 8 minutes. The centers should be soft to the touch and jiggle when shaken but not be really liquidy. (The flan molds can be filled, covered, and refrigerated for up to 2 days before baking. Bake uncovered straight from the refrigerator, adding a minute or two to the baking time.)

To finish, spoon a swirl of crème anglaise on each plate. Run a knife around the edge of each flan to loosen it. Turn each flan out onto the plate. Top each with confectioners' sugar and a couple of teaspoons of chopped pistachios. Place a couple of tablespoons of chopped pistachios on the plate as a bed for the gelato. Use two spoons to scoop the gelato into an oval shape (quenelle) and place the quenelle on the chopped pistachios.

MAKES 6 TO 8 SERVINGS

1½ cups (300 g) granulated sugar

4 large eggs

6 large egg yolks

8 ounces (2 sticks/227 g) unsalted butter

8¾ ounces (250 g) chocolate, preferably 58% cacao, chopped (2 cups)

1⅔ cups (208 g) *tipo* 00 flour (see page 277) or all-purpose flour

½ cup (120 ml) Crème Anglaise (page 284)

Confectioners' sugar, for dusting

¾ cup (112 g) chopped raw unsalted pistachios, preferably Sicilian

1½ cups (375 ml) Pistachio Gelato (page 286)

CHESTNUT RICE PUDDING with PERSIMMON

MAKES 4 SERVINGS

Candied Chestnuts and Puree:

10 ounces (283 g) peeled chestnuts, thawed if frozen, divided

2 cups (400 g) granulated sugar, divided

Rice Pudding:

1 teaspoon (5 ml) grapeseed oil or canola oil

1 cup (200 g) Arborio or other risotto rice

¼ cup (60 ml) sweet white dessert wine

4 cups (1 L) whole milk

2 large eggs, beaten

1¼ cups (250 g) granulated sugar

Pinch of salt

½ cup (120 ml) heavy cream

To Serve:

1 ripe persimmon (any type), sliced into half-moon shapes

Claudia's Uncle Bruno and Aunt Betty live just a mile or two from where she grew up. Betty is from Denmark and makes amazing desserts. When I was trying to perfect a rice pudding, I asked Claudia whether her aunt had a recipe. She told me about the chestnut rice pudding that Betty makes every year for the holidays. I played with the recipe a little and added some candied chestnuts to make it more special. The trick is to fold in some softly whipped cream to keep the pudding light and fluffy.

For the candied chestnuts and puree: Place 4 ounces (113 g) of the peeled chestnuts in a small saucepan. Cover with water and bring to a boil over high heat. Boil until the chestnuts are very tender but keep their shape, 10 to 15 minutes. Drain.

In another saucepan over medium-high heat, combine 1 cup (200 g) of the sugar and 1 cup (235 ml) of water. Simmer until the mixture thickens slightly but does not change color and reaches 223°F (106°C) on a candy thermometer, 5 to 7 minutes. Remove from the heat and stir in the boiled chestnuts. Let stand for 2 to 3 days in the refrigerator so the chestnuts can soak up the syrup.

Meanwhile, combine the remaining 6 ounces (170 g) of peeled chestnuts and remaining 1 cup (200 g) of sugar in a medium saucepan. Add just enough water to barely cover the chestnuts. The nuts should still poke through the top of the liquid. Bring to a simmer over medium heat, and cook, covered, until the chestnuts are tender, about 10 minutes. Strain and reserve the cooking liquid. Puree the chestnuts in a food processor or blender, adding just enough cooking liquid so that the mixture can be pureed. It will be very thick, like peanut butter. Set aside.

For the pudding: Heat the oil in a large saucepan over medium heat. Add the rice, and cook until lightly toasted, 2 to 3 minutes, stirring now and then. Add the wine without stirring, and cook until it is almost evaporated. Add the milk in four 1-cup (235 ml) additions, allowing the milk to be absorbed between each addition. Stir only to break up the rice grains and prevent a skin from forming on the surface. It should not be stirred like risotto. The rice will take 15 to 20 minutes to cook and should be tender but not mushy. When tender, stir in the eggs, sugar, salt, and chestnut puree, stirring gently to break up any clumps of rice. Return the pan to low heat and stir gently to cook the eggs without scrambling them, 2 to 3 minutes. Refrigerate until cold, at least 1 hour or up to 3 days.

Whip the cream in a cold bowl with cold beaters on medium-high speed until softly whipped (the mixture should form loose, soft peaks when the beaters are lifted), 3 to 4 minutes. Fold the whipped cream into the pudding.

To Serve: Spoon the pudding into coffee cups or dessert bowls and top with the sliced persimmons. Drain and chop the candied chestnuts and scatter them onto the pudding, along with a generous drizzle of the candied chestnut syrup.

RHUBARB TARTELLETTE with ITALIAN MERINGUE

We made a couple of rhubarb desserts at Frosio Ristorante, but none of them captured the taste of rhubarb from my youth. I grew up in Nashua, New Hampshire, right next to my mémère (my grandmother). She always had mounds of rhubarb growing in the garden. She would put stalks of raw rhubarb in little paper cups filled halfway with sugar and give it to the kids. We'd dip the raw rhubarb in the sugar and munch away. My sister and cousins didn't love it, but I couldn't get enough. It was like sweet-tart Fun Dip candy. This dessert captures some of that raw rhubarb experience. It's like a lemon meringue pie but with rhubarb marmalade as the filling and pieces of raw rhubarb dipped in lemon syrup served on top. At Osteria, I serve individual rhubarb tartelletta, but here I've done it in a single tart pan to make it easier. If you want to serve individual tarts, double the recipe and use ten individual tart pans, each about 4 inches (10 cm) in diameter.

MAKES 10 SERVINGS

Tart Dough:

8 ounces (2 sticks/227 g) unsalted butter, at room temperature

1 cup (120 g) confectioners' sugar

½ vanilla bean, split and scraped

Zest of ½ lemon

7 large egg yolks, at room temperature

2½ cups (343 g) pastry flour

Rhubarb Marmalade:

1 pound (450 g) rhubarb, chopped

1 tablespoon (15 ml) freshly squeezed lemon juice

¼ teaspoon (1 g) unsalted butter

1 cup plus 2 tablespoons (225 g) granulated sugar, divided

1¾ teaspoons (8.25 g) powdered pectin

Italian Meringue:

2¼ cups (450 g) granulated sugar

1 cup (235 ml) egg whites (from about 5 large eggs)

Pinch of salt

1 vanilla bean, split and scraped

Rhubarb Topping:

4 ounces (113 g) rhubarb, thinly sliced (1 cup)

¼ cup (60 ml) Candied Lemon Peels (page 288)

(continued on next page)

For the tart dough: Combine the butter, sugar, vanilla, and lemon zest in the bowl of a stand mixer fitted with the paddle attachment. Beat on medium speed until light, about 3 minutes. Gradually add the egg yolks, one by one, allowing each yolk to be incorporated before adding the next. Change the speed to low and slowly add the flour, mixing only until incorporated. The dough will be sticky and eggy yellow in color.

Turn the dough out onto a sheet of plastic wrap, cover with another sheet of plastic wrap, and quickly press into a disk with a rolling pin. It will be delicate, so work quickly to keep it cold. Wrap the dough in the plastic wrap and refrigerate for at least 20 minutes or up to 2 days.

Roll the dough between several sheets of overlapping plastic wrap or parchment paper to a 13-inch (33-cm)-diameter circle no thicker than ¼ inch (6 mm). Set a 10-inch (25-cm) tart pan with a removable bottom on a baking sheet. Remove the top sheet from the dough, then gently invert the dough over the tart pan. Gently fit the dough into the pan so it reaches the edges and comes up the sides, moving the dough into place yet stretching it as little as possible. Trim the dough by rolling the rolling pin over the edges of the pan so that the dough sits flush with the top of the pan. Cover loosely and refrigerate for 20 minutes.

Preheat the oven to 350°F (175°C). Line the dough with parchment paper or foil, leaving some overhanging to use as handles. Pour dried beans or pie weights onto the parchment or foil to keep the dough from puffing during baking. Bake until the edges of the dough are lightly browned, 12 to 15 minutes. Remove the parchment or foil and beans or weights and continue baking the crust until evenly golden, another 12 to 15 minutes or so. Remove from the oven and let cool.

For the marmalade: Mix the rhubarb with the lemon juice, butter, and all but 2 tablespoons (25 g) of the sugar in a nonreactive saucepan. Mix the remaining sugar with the pectin in a small bowl. Let the rhubarb stand at room temperature for 2 hours.

Bring the mixture to a boil over medium-high heat, and cook until the rhubarb starts to fall apart, about 5 minutes. When the rhubarb is fall-apart tender, whisk in the sugar and pectin mixture. Lower the heat slightly and simmer until the mixture coats the back of a spoon and the marmalade will set when cooled, 3 to 4 minutes.

Let the marmalade cool and then pour it into the baked tart shell, spreading it in an even layer. Refrigerate until set, about 30 minutes or up to 4 hours.

For the meringue: Combine the sugar and ½ cup (120 ml) of water in a small saucepan, and cook over medium heat until the mixture reaches 240°F (116°C) on a candy thermometer, 8 to 10 minutes. Meanwhile, combine the egg whites, salt, and vanilla in the bowl of a stand mixer fitted with the whisk attachment. Whip the egg whites on medium speed until soft peaks form when the beaters are lifted. Change to high speed and, with the machine running, slowly pour the sugar syrup into the egg whites. Whip until the mixture cools down to room temperature (you'll feel the sides of the bowl go from hot to luke-warm), 3 to 5 minutes. The meringue will be thick and glossy. Scrape the mixture into a pastry bag fitted with the star tip, or just cover the bowl and refrigerate for up to 4 hours.

For the rhubarb toppings: Combine the rhubarb and the candied lemon peels in a small bowl. Toss to coat.

If using a pastry bag for the meringue, pipe the meringue in small dollops or a decorative pattern over the tart. Or spoon the meringue over the tart, and then press and lift the back of the spoon repeatedly on the meringue to make small curls on the surface. Broil the meringue under a broiler 4 to 6 inches (10 to 15 cm) from the heat or with a kitchen torch until golden brown all over. Remove the ring of the tart pan by pressing the tart up through the bottom. Cut the tart into wedges and serve each wedge with a spoonful of rhubarb and candied lemon peels.

CENE AND FIOBBIO

FARM TO TABLE. . . . FIFTY FEET

OUR TOES MET UNDER THE TABLE. MATTEO AND CLAUDIA'S FRIENDS WERE DRINKING AND LAUGHING AT THE OTHER END OF THE TABLE. THEY SEEMED MILES AWAY.

We were at the Tucans, an Irish bar just down the street from Piazza Vecchia, the main square of Bergamo's medieval-looking old city on the hill. Claudia and I could barely communicate because I didn't know much Italian and she didn't know English, but I couldn't take my eyes off of her olive brown skin. We sipped Scotch across from each other and slipped off our shoes. She seemed to like me.

A few days later, Claudia left for a two-week vacation to Ireland with her friend Livia. We texted each other the whole time she was away. One night, she texted me: "*Sogni d'oro.*" The translation was "Dreams of gold," but it didn't seem quite right. The next day at work, I asked everyone in the Frosio kitchen what it meant. They made fun of me, but we figured out that it means "sweet dreams."

Claudia got home at the beginning of May, and I couldn't wait to see her. We made plans to get drinks at O'Dea's, another Irish bar in Bergamo. She picked me up around ten p.m. in her red Mini Cooper. Even with the language barrier, we got our points across, talking about our families, friends, America, and Italy. We left the bar around three a.m. and I drove her Mini back to Frosio Ristorante, where I lived upstairs. The engine quieted down, we opened the doors and stepped outside. I walked around to her side to say good night and noticed the moon in the sky. I leaned

toward her, and we kissed.

After that night, we spent a lot of time together. She lived about a half hour from the restaurant on a hilltop called Monte Bò in the village of Cene. When I first rode there on a borrowed motorcycle, it took forever to get to the top. She lived at her mother's place, a beautiful yellow house with terra-cotta roof tiles, perched on the hillside overlooking a lush, green mountain range. Claudia gave me a brief tour. The spring gardens were just starting to bloom. Outside the kitchen door, a huge rosemary bush grew near some lavender, sage, and oregano plants. The back steps led down under the pergola, and kiwifruit hung from the top of the pergola. Claudia told me that persimmons and pomegranates grew there in the fall. Their property stretched down the mountainside and was dotted with fruit trees, including figs, plums, and two kinds of cherries—amarena and bing. Wild asparagus were coming up near the edge of the forest. They had walnut trees and kept chickens.

As a chef, I was blown away. All this great food, right in their backyard! A grove of chestnut trees sloped down the hill, and when I met Claudia's brother, Alex, he told me that wild boar crawled up the hillside to eat the chestnuts in the fall. He would hang out of the window with his hunting dog, Dick, and then shoot them. Alex would butcher the boar and their mother, Pina, would braise it with rosemary, tomatoes, onions, red wine, olive oil, and butter and serve the ragù over polenta.

I learned that Pina is quite the cook. Her father, Vittorio, was a butcher with a *salumeria* in Bergamo. Her father-in-law, Giorgio, was a cattle farmer and cheese maker. So she always had fresh meat, cheese, and produce at her fingertips. When Claudia was a kid, they had a donkey named Casimiro. After the donkey died, Pina braised it with juniper, cinnamon, cloves, and black pepper, and Claudia ate it.

When I heard that, I really started to fall for her. This

was a family of food lovers. Cooks! Claudia and I spent the next several weeks sharing all of our favorite things. I showed her my favorite gelato place, Paradiso, in Alme; and she turned me on to the incredible licorice gelato at Gelateria Peccati de Gola in nearby Albino.

It didn't take long for the rest of her family to get curious about "the American boy." The first time I met them was at the end of May at Claudia's grandmother's house in Fiobbio, just a few kilometers down the hill from Cene. Everyone was gathering to celebrate the baptism of Francesca, her uncle Vittorino's new baby. When I walked in with Claudia, I heard "*L'americano è qui. Ciao. E benarrivato!*" which means, "The American is here. Hello. And welcome!" Except for her Aunt Betty, no one spoke English. They spoke Bergamascan, a dialect that barely sounds like Italian. We sat around for the next couple of hours, stumbling through various conversations about my work, family, America, and the younger President Bush (no one liked him). Without Aunt Betty translating, I would have been completely lost. I found out that the Fiobbio house was her grandmother Anna's. Anna had two daughters, Pina and Irene, and four sons, Bruno, Vittorino, Nunzio, and Piero. Most of them had children, the newest one being Vittorino's daughter, Francesca.

Her family prepared a giant meal, and we started eating around noon. Piero owned a *gastronomia* (gourmet shop) and brought shrimp in *salsa rossa*, octopus and potato salad, prosciutto cotto mousse, liver pâté in gelatin, little savory puff pastry tarts, and a mountain of salumi. Her aunt Irene made lasagne with salmon. Nonna Anna made a veal roast with vegetables from the garden. She also made this incredibly rich-tasting, mahogany-colored rabbit served on the bone over polenta. They raised the rabbits out back. To make the polenta, Nonna lifted off three metal rings from the flat-top burner of the wood stove, using a little tool that hung on the edge. That brought the polenta pot closer to the flames,

which made the polenta burn a little on the sides, giving it a smoky aroma. Nonna liked that I was interested in how to make the food.

Toward the end of the meal, six different cheeses appeared on the table, including formagella, Gorgonzola, and casolet. By five o'clock, when I had to get back to work at the restaurant, they had just started dessert. There was sponge cake with fruit and whipped cream, cookies, *piccola pasticceria* (tiny pastries), and coffee made in the Italian *moka* pot. There was a ton of food. I was in heaven!

I learned that back in the day, Claudia's family was one of the first in Fiobbio to own a car. Almost everyone in the family ran a business, and they were very proud of Claudia, a young woman running her own successful video rental store in town. They were nervous that an American was going to come and break her heart, or maybe even take her away from Italy and ruin her life. But I was less interested in going back to the States than I was in staying here as long as I could. When I thought about it, I'd only saved enough money to get me through the next couple of months. But I could feel my life changing. I needed to stay here. I was starting to feel more at home than I had felt for years.

ZUCCHINI FLOWERS STUFFED with RICOTTA and TUNA

MAKES 4 TO 6 SERVINGS

1 (8 ounce/227 g) can Italian tuna in olive oil

12 zucchini blossoms

12 ounces (340 g) fresh whole-milk ricotta cheese (1½ cups)

2 tablespoons (7 g) chopped fresh mint

2 tablespoons (30 ml) plain, dry bread-crumbs

Salt and freshly ground black pepper

6 cherry or grape tomatoes, halved lengthwise

4 baby zucchini, sliced

Extra-virgin olive oil, for drizzling

In late spring 2004, I spent more and more of my time off at Claudia's house in Cene, eating, cooking and getting to know the family. Her mother had an amazing garden filled with zucchini flowers. Those orange and green trumpets bloomed right up until the summer heat started to hit. At some point, Pina started stuffing the blossoms with tuna and ricotta. The filling was a mixture she'd been using for years; she typically breaded and fried it like meatballs. Then she thought, "Why not stuff it into all these zucchini blossoms?" She baked the stuffed zucchini blossoms with little tomatoes from her garden and it became this famous dish in town. Everyone wanted the recipe because it was so easy and so good.

Preheat the oven to 350°F (175°C).

Drain the oil from the tuna into a small bowl. Brush any dirt from the zucchini blossoms with a paper towel, but don't wash the blossoms or they'll get soggy. Gently twist and pull out the stamens from the centers of the blossoms, using tweezers, if necessary.

Add the tuna, ricotta cheese, and mint to the breadcrumbs, stirring until combined; taste and season with salt and pepper. Spoon the filling into a resealable plastic bag (the filling can be refrigerated at this point for up to 2 days). Cut off a corner of the bag and pipe the filling into the zucchini blossoms, leaving some room for the blossom to close at the end. Arrange the stuffed blossoms in a 2-quart (2-L) shallow baking dish or on a baking sheet, and top each blossom with a tomato half, cut-side down. Arrange the sliced baby zucchini around the edge of the baking dish.

Bake until the filling is set, 12 to 15 minutes. If the tomatoes are still firm, run the dish under the broiler until they wilt a little. Drizzle with a little olive oil and serve.

PEAR and TREVISO SALAD with TALEGGIO DRESSING

MAKES 4 SERVINGS

Pear and Treviso Salad:

12 ounces (340 g) Treviso radicchio (1 head)

4 ounces (113 g) Belgian endive (1 large head)

1 tablespoon (15 ml) sherry vinegar

3 tablespoons (45 ml) extra-virgin olive oil, plus more for drizzling

Salt

1 Bartlett pear, peeled, seeded and finely chopped

1 tablespoon (4 g) chopped mixed fresh herbs (parsley, rosemary, and thyme)

Taleggio Dressing:

½ cup (120 ml) whole milk

2 ounces (56 g) Taleggio cheese, grated (½ cup)

1 large egg yolk

½ cup (120 ml) extra-virgin olive oil

1 to 2 teaspoons (5 to 10 ml) sherry vinegar

Salt and freshly ground black pepper

In the fall, you find two things in every home in Bergamo: bitter greens and Taleggio cheese. Claudia made the best salads with bitter greens from their garden, and there was always a big piece of Taleggio sitting on the table. One afternoon I came over for lunch during a break from the restaurant and made a warm dressing with the Taleggio. I melted the cheese and pureed it with milk, sherry vinegar, olive oil, and an egg yolk. With the pears and radicchio, you get sweet, salty, sour, and bitter flavors in your mouth all at once.

For the pear and Treviso salad: Cut the Treviso lengthwise into quarters and the Belgian endive lengthwise in half. Then cut both crosswise on a diagonal, leaving the pieces pretty big (1 to 2 inches/2.5 to 5 cm long), and place in a large bowl.

Put the sherry vinegar in a small bowl and whisk in the 3 tablespoons (45 ml) of oil until blended. Season with salt to taste. Drizzle about half of the vinaigrette over the greens and toss until coated. Add the pear and mixed herbs to the remaining vinaigrette and toss to coat.

For the Taleggio dressing: Put the milk in a small saucepan and bring to a boil over high heat. Remove from the heat and whisk in the Taleggio until it melts and incorporates. Pour the mixture into a blender and blend in the egg yolk, then slowly drizzle in the oil and 1 teaspoon (5 ml) of the sherry vinegar. Taste and season with additional sherry vinegar, salt, and black pepper, as needed.

Divide the Treviso mixture among plates and drizzle with a generous amount of the Taleggio dressing, about 2 to 3 tablespoons (30 to 45 ml) per plate. Drizzle with some olive oil, 1 to 2 teaspoons (5 to 10 ml) per plate, then scatter the pears over the salad and serve immediately.

Note

The dressing will keep for about 3 days in the refrigerator. Return to room temperature and reblend before using. Look for Treviso radicchio, which has a long bullet-shaped head like Belgian endive. It's larger than the common round Chioggia radicchio found in most North American markets. Either radicchio will work fine here, but if you're using Chioggia, you might need two heads instead of one.

CRESPELLE DELLA MAMMA

Pina usually stuffs crêpes with marmalade made from figs, plums, cherries, or other fruit harvested from around the house. But one year, her family foraged a ton of porcini mushrooms and dried them to make them last through the winter. That Christmas, she came up with these savory *crespelle* stuffed with ricotta, fontina, ham, and spinach. She folded the crêpes around the filling like little Christmas presents, layered them in a baking dish, and topped them with two sauces: béchamel and porcini tomato. I loved the dish so much that I now have it on the menu at Alla Spina in Philadelphia. The recipe here makes enough for a big family, but if you want less, cut the amounts in half.

For the crêpes: Whisk together the milk, eggs, and butter in a small bowl. Put the flour in a large bowl and slowly whisk the milk mixture into the flour. Season with salt and pepper and strain to remove any lumps of flour. Let rest at room temperature for 1 hour or in the refrigerator up to 4 hours.

Dab a paper towel with oil, wipe a 6-inch (15-cm) nonstick pan with it, and put the pan over medium heat. Briefly whisk the batter to wake it up. Pour about ¼ cup (60 ml) of batter into the center of the pan and quickly swirl the batter by tilting the pan in large circular motions, spreading the batter to the edges of the pan to create an even circle. Cook until the top is dry but beaded with sweat, about 30 seconds. Flip the crêpe, and cook the other side for 10 to 15 seconds. You should have about twenty 6-inch/15-cm crêpes.

For the porcini sauce: Soak the porcini in the hot water until softened, about 15 minutes. Pluck the mushrooms from the soaking liquid and chop finely. Reserve the soaking liquid. Heat the oil in a medium saucepan over medium heat. When hot, add the garlic, and cook until lightly browned, 2 to 3 minutes. Add the chopped porcini and sauté for 4 to 5 minutes. Crush the tomatoes by hand, discarding the cores and adding the tomato flesh and juices to the pan as you work. Season with salt and pepper and add half of the reserved porcini soaking liquid. Cook over low heat until you have a nice thick tomato sauce, 25 to 30 minutes. If the tomato sauce gets too thick, thin it with a bit more of the reserved porcini soaking liquid.

For the crêpe filling: Combine the ricotta, Parmesan, fontina, spinach, and nutmeg in a medium bowl. Season with salt and pepper.

To assemble the dish, preheat the oven to 375°F (190°C) and spread a little béchamel over the bottom of a 3-quart (3 L) baking dish. Place one slice of ham on a crêpe and spread a heaping tablespoon of ricotta filling over the ham. Spoon on 1 tablespoon (15 ml) of béchamel and fold up the crêpe like a package, folding in two sides first, then folding over the other two sides to enclose the filling. Place the filled crêpe in the prepared baking dish and top with a spoonful of béchamel. Repeat with the remaining crêpes, ham, filling, and béchamel, layering them in the baking dish. Pour in enough porcini sauce to come half way up the baking dish. Sprinkle with Parmesan and bake until hot and bubbly, about 45 minutes.

MAKES 10 SERVINGS

Crêpes:

2 cups (475 ml) whole milk

2 large eggs

1 tablespoon (15 ml) melted unsalted butter

2 cups (250 g) *tipo* 00 flour (see page 277) or all-purpose flour

Salt and freshly ground black pepper

Oil, as needed

Porcini Sauce:

1½ ounces (43 g) dried porcini mushrooms (1 cup)

1 cup (235 ml) hot water

¼ cup (60 ml) olive oil

1 garlic clove

2 quarts (2 L) canned plum tomatoes, preferably San Marzano

Salt and freshly ground black pepper

Crêpe Filling:

2 pounds (1 kg) fresh whole-milk ricotta cheese (1 quart/1 L)

3½ ounces (100 g) Parmesan cheese, grated (1 cup)

8 ounces (227 g) fontina cheese, diced (2 cups)

1 cup (235 ml) cooked chopped spinach

2 teaspoons (4.5 g) grated nutmeg

Salt and freshly ground black pepper

2 quarts (2 kg) Béchamel Sauce (page 281)

1½ pounds (680 g) thinly sliced Prosciutto Cotto (page 242) or other cooked ham, about 20 slices

3½ ounces (100 g) Parmesan cheese, grated (1 cup)

APRICOT and CHANTERELLE SALAD with PARMESAN CRISPS

Both apricot trees and chanterelles grow in the mountains near Claudia's house. One afternoon, I walked out her back door to pick some apricots from the tree and stumbled upon some chanterelles growing in the chestnut forests down the hill. The only natural thing to do was to make a salad. Americans don't always put mushrooms and fruit together. But if you think about it, they make a great combination. Lightly cooked chanterelles have some apricot aromas to them, and gently cooked apricots have a texture similar to chanterelles. What grows together goes together.

For the Parmesan crisps: Preheat the oven to 375°F (190°C). Line a baking sheet with a silicone baking mat or parchment paper. For each crisp, spoon a heaping tablespoon of grated Parmesan into a mound on the prepared baking sheet, leaving 4 to 6 inches (10 to 15 cm) between each mound. Spread each mound to a 3- or 4-inch (7.5- to 10-cm) diameter. Bake until the cheese melts, loses its moisture, and browns slightly, about 6 minutes. Remove from the oven and let cool.

For the salad: Heat a grill to medium-high.

Halve and pit the apricots. Toss the apricots in a bowl with the grapeseed oil to coat all over. Season lightly with salt and pepper. Coat the grill grate with oil, then lay the apricots skin-side down on the grate, grilling just until marked with grill stripes but not mushy, only a minute or two per side. Return the apricots to the bowl.

Heat ¼ cup (60 ml) of the olive oil over medium-low heat in a sauté pan. Add the garlic, thyme, and mushrooms. Cook slowly until the mushrooms soften a bit but aren't limp, 5 to 7 minutes. You don't want any browning on the mushrooms. Pluck the mushrooms from the pan with tongs and add to the bowl with the apricots.

Pour the sherry vinegar into a medium bowl and whisk in the remaining ¾ cup (175 ml) of olive oil in a slow, steady stream. Add the greens and toss to coat. Season with salt and pepper.

To plate, divide the dressed greens among plates and spoon the mushrooms and apricots over the top. Serve two to three Parmesan crisps per salad.

MAKES 4 SERVINGS

Parmesan Crisps:

3½ ounces (100 g) Parmesan cheese, grated (1 cup)

Salad:

4 large apricots

¼ cup (60 ml) grapeseed oil

Salt and freshly ground black pepper

1 cup (235 ml) olive oil, divided

4 garlic cloves, smashed

20 sprigs fresh thyme

3 ounces (85 g) chanterelle mushrooms (1 cup)

3 tablespoons (45 ml) sherry vinegar

6 ounces (170 g) mixed salad greens

RABBIT ALLA CASALINGA

I first tasted this dish in Fiobbio when Claudia's family was celebrating the baptism of her niece, Francesca. It's an old family dish from her great-grandmother Virginia Zanga, who lived in nearby Villa di Serio. Everyone on her side of the family was a farmer. They raised rabbits on hay and grass. They made their own butter, cured their own pancetta, and got their corn milled for polenta by the miller in town. They used what they had to make dinner. The amazing thing here is the technique: The rabbit is cut into pieces, browned in a pan, and deglazed with white wine, and then with plain water for about forty-five minutes, which creates a dark mahogany brown glaze on the rabbit and an intense-tasting sauce. The meat and sauce are served simply over polenta.

MAKES 6 SERVINGS

1 whole rabbit (5 to 7 pounds/2.25 to 3 kg), dressed

Salt and freshly ground black pepper

8 ounces (2 sticks/227 g) unsalted butter

¼ cup (60 ml) olive oil

8 ounces (227 g) pancetta, diced

4 rosemary sprigs

10 sage sprigs

1 cup (235 ml) dry white wine

9 cups (2.25 L) Polenta (page 281)

Using a cleaver, cut up the rabbit: Remove and discard the innards and excess fat deposits. Put the rabbit on its back and remove the hind legs and forelegs by driving your cleaver right through the primary joints. Keep the forelegs whole. Cut the hind legs into two pieces each by driving your cleaver through the knee joints. Cut through the breastbone, then keep your knife against bone and cut down around the rib bones, separating the flesh from the bones. Be sure to keep the thin flap of meat attached to the loin that runs up against the ribs. Remove and discard the ribs by cutting through the ribs at the backbone. Cut the rabbit crosswise through the backbone into six pieces. You should have a total of twelve pieces. Season the pieces all over with salt and pepper.

If you have one wide braising pan big enough to hold all the rabbit pieces in a single layer, use that. Otherwise, divide the butter and oil between two braising pans and place over medium heat. When hot, divide the pancetta, rosemary, and sage sprigs between the pans, and cook until the pancetta is browned, 4 to 6 minutes. Divide the rabbit pieces between the pans, laying them in a single layer, and brown them on all sides, 15 to 20 minutes, turning as needed. Divide the wine between the pans, scraping the pan bottoms to loosen the browned-on bits, and simmer for 8 to 10 minutes, or until the wine evaporates. Add just enough water to each pan to come one-quarter of the way up the meat, and simmer until the water evaporates and the rabbit continues to brown, turning the meat once or twice. As the water evaporates, you'll see the bubbles in the pan go from large to small. When the bubbles are small and fizzy, you'll start to see smoke (from the fat) rather than steam (from the water) rising from the pan. That's the right time to add more water. Again, add just enough water to come one-quarter of the way up the meat, and simmer until the water nearly evaporates, turning the meat now and then. Repeat the process of adding water, evaporating it, and turning the rabbit until the meat is tender and dark mahogany brown, 45 to 55 minutes total. This process of continual deglazing helps to create a nice dark crust on the rabbit and a richer sauce. Season the sauce with salt and pepper.

Spoon the polenta onto warmed plates. Divide the rabbit pieces among the plates, placing them on top of the polenta. Spoon the sauce over the top.

WILD BOAR BRAISED with MORETTI BEER

In Bergamo, hunters get one of three licenses: a bird license, small-game license, or a big-game license. Claudia's father, Mario, loved to hunt birds like grouse, pheasant, partridge, and pigeon. But her brother, Alex, prefers big game, such as *capriolo* (roe deer) and wild boar. Pina usually braises game meat in red wine to stand up to the strong flavor, but one day she wanted to make the boar taste lighter, so she used beer. Moretti beer is what they had in the house. Any lager-style beer works well with the milder-tasting boar you find in America.

Preheat the oven to 350°F (175°C). Season the boar all over with salt and pepper. Heat the oil in a Dutch oven over medium-high heat. Coat the boar with flour, shaking off any excess.

Add the boar to the hot pan and sear until well browned on all sides, 10 to 15 minutes total. Transfer to a plate.

Add the carrots, onion, and celery to the pan, and cook until lightly browned, 5 to 8 minutes. Add the tomatoes, and cook for 5 minutes. Add the boar back to the pan, along with the beer, the sachet, and enough water to come three-quarters of the way up the meat. Bring to a boil over high heat, cover, and braise in the oven until the meat is fall-apart tender, 3 to 4 hours. Let the boar cool in the liquid until the boar is cool enough to handle.

Transfer the boar to a bowl. Strain the braising liquid, reserving the liquid and vegetables separately. Puree the vegetables in a food mill or blender using short pulses to create a rustic puree. Combine the reserved liquid, pureed vegetables, and boar back in the pan and simmer over medium heat until the liquid reduces in volume and thickens to the texture of gravy, 10 to 15 minutes. Season with salt and pepper, and then cut or shred the meat into four to six portions. Divide the polenta among plates and top with the boar and gravy.

MAKES 4 TO 6 SERVINGS

5 pounds (2.25 kg) wild boar shoulder

Salt and freshly ground black pepper

¼ cup (60 ml) olive oil

About 1 cup (125 g) tipo 00 flour (see page 277) or all-purpose flour, for dredging

4 medium-size carrots, chopped (2 cups/145 g)

1 large yellow onion, chopped (2 cups/320 g)

4 medium-size ribs celery, chopped (2 cups/202 g)

1 cup (240 g) canned plum tomatoes, preferably San Marzano, cored and crushed by hand

1 bottle (12 ounces) Moretti or other lager-style beer

1 sachet of 1 bay leaf, 1 garlic clove, 1 sprig rosemary, 5 juniper berries, 5 whole cloves, and 5 peppercorns (see page 277)

9 cups (2.25 L) Polenta (page 281)

SCARPINOCC

MAKES 4 TO 6 SERVINGS

Filling and Pasta:

1¾ ounces (50 g) Grana Padano or Parmesan cheese, grated (½ cup)

3 ounces (85 g) white bread, crust removed, cubed (about 4 slices sandwich bread)

1 small garlic clove, minced

¼ cup (15 g) chopped fresh flat-leaf parsley

2 teaspoons (9 g) unsalted butter, well softened

1 large egg

1 cup (235 ml) whole milk

¼ teaspoon (0.5 g) ground coriander

⅛ teaspoon (0.25 g) ground cloves

⅛ teaspoon (0.25 g) freshly grated nutmeg

Salt and freshly ground black pepper

8 ounces (227 g) Egg Pasta Dough (page 282), rolled into 2 sheets, each about 1⁄32 inch (0.8 mm) thick

Sauce:

½ cup (120 ml) Walnut Pesto (page 284)

4 teaspoons (20 ml) olive oil

1 ounce (28 g) Parmesan cheese, grated (¼ cup) for garnish

¼ cup (29 g) chopped toasted walnuts for garnish

In Val Seriana, near the Serio River, the tiny town of Parre sits beneath the western slope of Monte Bò, where Claudia grew up. Parre is famous for its scarpinocc (scar-pee-NOACH), a poor man's ravioli filled with leftover bread and cheese, made during wartime. The bread is soaked in water, milk, or broth and mixed with Grana Padano or Parmesan cheese. Then the ravioli are shaped like little pointed shoes and served simply with butter and sage (*scarpinocc* means "rustic shoes"). When Parre holds its annual *sagra* (food festival) in August, the rich aromas of melted butter and fresh sage fill the entire town.

For the filling and pasta: Combine the Parmesan, bread, garlic, parsley, butter, egg, milk, coriander, cloves, and nutmeg in a large mixing bowl. Season with salt and pepper, then mix with a wooden spoon. Let stand for 15 minutes so the bread can absorb the liquid.

Lay a pasta sheet on a lightly floured work surface. Spoon ½- to ¾-inch (1.25- to 2-cm)-diameter balls of filling at 1½-inch (3.75-cm) intervals down the center of the sheet. Spray lightly with water, then pick up the long edge and fold it over the filling to meet the long edge on the other side. Gently press down the dough around each ball of filling to seal. Using a 3-inch (7.5-cm) round cutter, cut out a series of half-moons and discard the scraps of pasta. Turn each half-moon so the filling rests on top of the curved edge of the pasta (see the illustration). Slightly pinch the pasta on either side of the filling to make "wings." Use your finger to flatten the filling slightly so the half-moon will stand up easily. The finished pasta should resemble a rustic shoe with the "wings" as the toe and heel of the shoe. Repeat with the remaining pasta dough and filling. Transfer the scarpinocc to a baking sheet lined with floured waxed paper, cover, and freeze for at least 1 hour. When frozen, transfer to a resealable plastic bag, seal, and freeze for up to 2 weeks.

Bring a large pot of salted water to a boil. Drop in the pasta, in batches, if necessary, to prevent overcrowding; quickly return the water to a boil, and cook until barely tender, 4 to 5 minutes.

For the sauce: Put the pesto and olive oil into a sauté pan over medium-low heat. Add a ladle of pasta water and simmer until the sauce is loose and creamy.

Drain the pasta and add it to the pan, gently swirling until the pasta is coated with sauce. Divide among plates and garnish with the Parmesan and chopped walnuts. Serve immediately.

WHOLE ROASTED DUCK with MUSCAT GRAPES

Claudia's nonna, Anna, kept a huge garden and raised chickens and ducks in the backyard. Anna would stuff the duck with garden vegetables and herbs and roast it in her wood oven with potatoes. Her son, Bruno, refined the recipe by replacing the potatoes with muscato grapes picked from the vines growing around their poultry coops. He peeled the grapes and added them to the roasting pan at the last minute so they would just melt in your mouth. When I first tasted the dish, Bruno joked, "*L'anatra stiamo mangiando è morto di un attacco di cuore quando vede il coltello,*" which means, "The duck we are eating died of a heart attack when it saw the knife."

Season the duck with salt and pepper inside and out. Mix together the onion, carrot, celery, garlic, bay leaf, peppercorns, thyme, and rosemary. Stuff the mixture into the bird and truss the bird with kitchen string to close the cavity and secure the legs.

Preheat the oven to 375°F (190°C). Heat the oil in a large roasting pan or Dutch oven over medium-high heat. Add the duck and sear until the skin is crisp and browned on all sides, 15 to 20 minutes total, turning a few times.

Turn the duck breast-side up and transfer the pan to the oven. Roast, uncovered, until the bird registers 155°F (68°C) when a thermometer is inserted into a thigh, about 1 hour. Remove the pan from the oven and transfer the duck to a cutting board. Pour off about half of the fat from the pan and reserve it for another use. Add the cut cabbage to the remaining fat and sauté over medium heat until tender, about 5 minutes. Add the wine and simmer until the liquid reduces in volume by about half, 5 to 6 minutes. Add the stock and the accumulated juices from the cutting board, and simmer until the liquid reduces in volume and thickens enough to coat the back of a spoon, 10 to 15 minutes. Stir in the peeled grapes, season with salt and pepper, and cook just until the grapes begin to wilt, 1 to 2 minutes.

Carve the duck into leg, thigh, and breast portions and serve with the cabbage and grapes, drizzling the sauce around the plate.

Note

To truss the stuffed duck, pierce three to four 4-inch (10-cm)-long wooden skewers through the flaps of skin on each side of the cavity opening. Weave kitchen string around the skewers like a shoelace to lace the bird shut, tying it off at the top. Position the bird breast-side up with the legs facing away from you. Loop a long piece of kitchen string beneath the ends of the drumsticks, crossing the string to make an X. Pull the remaining string down, passing it beneath the thighs and pulling tight to pull the legs toward the tail. Continue pulling the string along the body toward the neck and pass it beneath the wings. Flip the bird over so the legs are now facing toward you and cross the string over the back between the two wings, pulling tight. Loop the string beneath the backbone, pull it tight, and then tie it off with a tight knot.

MAKES 4 SERVINGS

1 large duck, trimmed of excess fat (about 5 pounds/2.25 kg)

Salt and freshly ground black pepper

½ medium-size yellow onion, chopped (¾ cup/92 g)

1 medium-size carrot, chopped (½ cup/61 g)

1 medium-size rib celery, chopped (½ cup/51 g)

1 garlic clove, smashed

1 bay leaf

10 peppercorns

2 sprigs fresh thyme

2 sprigs fresh rosemary

2 tablespoons (30 ml) olive oil

6 leaves savoy cabbage, chopped into bite-size pieces

1 cup (235 ml) white wine

3 cups (750 ml) Duck Stock or Chicken Stock (page 279)

2 cups (185 g) peeled moscato grapes

FIG STRUDEL

MAKES ABOUT 16 SERVINGS

Danish Dough:

5½ cups (753 g) bread flour

⅔ cup (133 g) granulated sugar

¾ teaspoon (4.5 g) fine sea salt

2 large eggs

1 packed tablespoon (20 g) fresh yeast, or 2½ teaspoons (10 g) active dry yeast

5⅓ tablespoons (75 g) plus 1 pound (4 sticks/450 g) unsalted butter, at room temperature

Fig Filling:

⅓ packed cup (55 g) raisins, preferably both dark and golden

2 pounds (1 kg) fresh figs

4 ounces (1 stick/113 g) unsalted butter

1 packed cup (220 g) dark brown sugar

¾ teaspoon (2 g) ground cinnamon

⅛ teaspoon (0.75 g) fine sea salt

1 large egg

About 3 tablespoons (38 g) raw or turbinado sugar, for sprinkling

About 1 cup (235 ml) apricot jam, briefly warmed, for brushing

Pina has five fig trees, and sometime in September, the fruit starts dripping with nectar. This strudel shows off the ripe figs because you just cut them in half, caramelize the cut sides in a pan, and lay them on the dough, which is then braided over the top. The dough recipe comes from my friend, Andrea Forcella, who owns Olfà pastry shop in Osio Sotto, about twenty minutes south of the old city in Bergamo. It's sort of like puff pastry but has more stretch, because you roll out the dough and let it rest several times, developing gluten and creating that light, chewy texture of classic Danish pastries. It doesn't take much hands-on time, but there is a lot of resting time, so it is a multi-day process. I like to warm up slices of the strudel in a buttered pan and serve them on a bed of toasted sliced almonds with a spoonful of Mascarpone Gelato (page 287). This recipe makes a pretty big strudel. But it keeps for several days and is so good it rarely sticks around that long.

For the Danish dough: Mix the flour, sugar, salt, eggs, yeast, 5 ⅓ tablespoons (75 g) of the butter, and 1 cup plus 1 tablespoon (265 ml total) of water in a stand mixer fitted with the dough hook on low speed until the flour gets incorporated, about 2 minutes. Change to medium speed and mix until the dough is sticky and elastic, another 4 minutes. Turn out the dough into a buttered bowl, shaping it into a ball. Cover with a kitchen towel and let rise in a warm spot until doubled in size, about 1 hour.

Line a large rimmed baking sheet with parchment. Turn the dough out onto the prepared sheet. Cover and let rest in the refrigerator overnight.

Roll the remaining pound (450 g) of butter between sheets of plastic wrap to an even 13 x 9-inch (33 x 23-cm) rectangle. Roll the dough on a lightly floured work surface to an 18 x 13-inch (46 x 33-cm) rectangle (the same width but twice as long as the butter). Transfer the rolled butter onto half of the rolled dough: remove the top sheet of plastic, invert the butter onto the dough, and then remove the remaining plastic, scraping the butter off the plastic as necessary to create an even bed of butter on the dough. Cover with the other half of dough and pinch the edges firmly to seal. Roll the dough out again to a rough 18 x 13-inch (46 x 33-cm) rectangle. Fold the dough so that the two short edges meet in the center, and then fold the dough in half (this is called a four-fold or book fold). Cover and refrigerate until the dough and butter are evenly chilled, about 30 minutes or up to 2 hours.

Position the dough on a floured work surface and roll out the dough again to an 18 x 13-inch (46 x 33-cm) rectangle. Fold the dough over itself three times to make a three-fold (like folding a letter), starting at a short edge. Cover and let rest in the refrigerator again, at least 30 minutes or up to 2 hours. Repeat rolling out the dough and folding into a three-fold two more times, positioning the seam-side away from you each time, and resting the dough in the refrigerator between each turn. Cover and let the dough rest overnight in the refrigerator. (The completed dough can also be covered and refrigerated for 2 days before assembling and baking the strudel.)

The next day, roll the dough to an 18 x 8-inch (46 x 20-cm) rectangle about ¼ inch (5 mm) thick. Gently fold the dough into a three-fold, transfer it to a large baking sheet, and unfold it on the sheet. Chill until the filling is ready.

For the fig filling: Soak the raisins in warm water until softened, about 10 minutes. Drain, chop coarsely, and set aside.

Remove the fig stems and cut the figs in half lengthwise. Melt the butter in a large sauté pan over medium heat. When the butter is foamy and hot, add the figs, and cook until the cut sides are light golden brown, 4 to 5 minutes. Add the chopped raisins, brown sugar, cinnamon, and salt. Cook until the mixture becomes very thick and lightly caramelized, 5 to 6 minutes. Remove from the heat and let cool completely. (The fig filling can be made ahead and refrigerated for 2 days before assembling the strudel. Bring the filling to room temperature before using.)

Place the filling on the rolled sheet of dough in a line about 3 inches (7.5 cm) wide, leaving about 2 inches (5 cm) on either side. Use a pizza cutter or sharp knife to cut lines about 1 inch (2.5 cm) wide diagonally through the exposed dough on both sides of the filling; it will look sort of like a Christmas tree (see pages 82 and 83). Beat the egg with 1 tablespoon (15 ml) of water. Braid the exposed strands of dough over the filling, bringing the opposite strands together and brushing the bottom strand with the egg wash before laying the opposite strand over it (this bonds the two strands together to create a seal).

Cover with a kitchen towel and let proof in a warm spot until almost doubled in size, about 1 hour.

Preheat the oven to 350°F (175°C). Brush the top and sides of the dough with the egg wash and sprinkle with the raw sugar. Bake until golden brown, 35 to 40 minutes. As soon as the strudel comes out of the oven, brush with the apricot jam.

FIG STRUDEL ASSEMBLY

CLAUDIA'S LIMONCELLO TIRAMISU

MAKES 10 TO 12 SERVINGS

Mascarpone Mousse:

8 large eggs

1½ cups (300 g) granulated sugar, divided

2 pounds (1 kg) mascarpone (about 4 ¼ cups)

2 lemons

Limoncello–Soaked Ladyfingers:

¾ cup (150 g) granulated sugar

1½ cups (375 ml) Pina's Limoncello (opposite page) or other limoncello

1 (8-ounce/227-g) package ladyfingers, about 30 ladyfingers

Tiramisu is like an Italian Tastykake (a beloved Philadelphia snack cake). You soak cookies in syrup and layer them between a creamy mascarpone filling. You can flavor the syrup and filling however you like. Coffee and chocolate is the most common combination, but Claudia always made tiramisu with fruit that grew in her backyard. Her cherry tiramisu was one of my favorites. Then she came up with this limoncello tiramisu made with Pina's Limoncello (page 85). It's my new favorite. Refreshing, rich, and ridiculously good.

For the mascarpone mousse: Separate the eggs, putting the yolks in a medium bowl and the whites in another bowl. Add 1 cup (200 g) of the sugar to the yolks and whip with an electric mixer on medium-high speed until thick and pale yellow in color, 2 to 3 minutes. Beat the mascarpone in a separate bowl with clean beaters on medium speed until softened. Add the whipped yolks and beat on medium speed until smooth. Grate the zest from the lemons and squeeze out ¼ cup (60 ml) of lemon juice. Stir the lemon zest and juice into the mascarpone mixture.

Whip the egg whites in a clean bowl with clean beaters on medium speed until frothy, 2 to 3 minutes. Add the remaining ½ cup (100 g) of sugar and whip on medium-high speed until the whites form medium-soft peaks when the beaters are lifted, another 2 to 3 minutes.

Fold the whipped whites into the mascarpone mixture to form a mousse.

For the limoncello-soaked ladyfingers: Combine the sugar and ¾ cup (175 ml) of water in a small saucepan over medium-high heat. Bring to a simmer and cook just until the sugar dissolves. Remove from the heat and set the pan in an ice bath to cool down the syrup. Stir in the limoncello.

Soak the ladyfingers in the limoncello syrup in batches for 20 seconds; the cookies should not be saturated all the way to the center or they will fall apart. As you work, lay the soaked ladyfingers in the bottom of a 2½-quart (2.5 L) baking dish, breaking up the cookies as necessary to make an even layer. Spread a layer of mousse over the ladyfingers. Continue making layers of soaked ladyfingers and mousse until the dish is filled, ending with a layer of mousse on top. Cover and refrigerate for at least 2 hours or up to 1 day.

Note

The finished tiramisu can be refrigerated for up to 1 day before serving. It's ideal after just a few hours in the fridge, as the ladyfingers will continue to soak up liquid in the tiramisu and eventually become soggy.

PINA'S LIMONCELLO

After they made wine from the grapes on their property, Pina's grandfather would make grappa from the stems, skins, and grape must. Grappa was the sipping liquor of Bergamo. You never saw limoncello because lemons didn't grow there. But in the mid-1990s, Pina went on vacation to the Amalfi coast and brought back giant lemons the size of grapefruits. These lemons have almost no juice, so the peels are used to make *mostarda* (fruit relish), *canditi* (candied fruit), and limoncello. One of her ex-boyfriends gave Pina this recipe for limoncello. She only makes it once or twice a year in twenty-liter batches, which takes about two hundred lemons. She keeps her limoncello in the freezer in tall, clear glass bottles with pieces of red cloth tied around the tops. (It doesn't actually freeze because of the alcohol.) You can use Eureka lemons (the most common grocery store variety), but keep in mind you'll only be using the peels. Squeeze all the leftover lemons and use the juice to make lemonade!

MAKES 2½ QUARTS (2.5 L)

20 Eureka lemons, 15 Sicilian lemons, or 10 Amalfitano lemons

1 quart (1 L) grain alcohol or 100-proof vodka

5 cups (1 kg) granulated sugar

Peel the lemons, using a vegetable peeler or large zester, taking care not to remove much of the bitter white membrane beneath the peel. Marinate the peels in the grain alcohol in a glass jug at room temperature for 2 weeks. Strain into a pitcher and reserve the peels.

Combine the sugar, 1½ quarts (1.5 L) of water, and the peels in a large saucepan. Bring to a simmer over medium heat, stirring just until the sugar dissolves, 5 to 8 minutes. Remove from the heat and let cool, and then strain out and discard the peels.

Let the syrup cool completely, then stir into the alcohol. Store in bottles in the freezer, sipping or using as needed.

SEX ON THE ITALIAN RIVIERA

CLAUDIA DROVE. I TOOK IN THE LANDSCAPE. TRAVELING FROM BERGAMO TO LIGURIA WAS LIKE GOING TO OCEAN CITY, MARYLAND, FROM PHILADELPHIA, EXCEPT WE PASSED THROUGH THE APENNINE MOUNTAIN RANGE. WHAT A VIEW WHEN YOU REACH THE TOP! ROLLING GREEN HILLS GIVE WAY TO ROCKY CLIFFS AND ENDLESS BLUE WATER AS THE LIGURIAN SEA SPREADS BEFORE YOU.

This was our first getaway. It was early June when we got there—a little before tourist season—so it wasn't too crowded. Pina's boyfriend, Carmine, set us up to stay at Hotel Florida in Lerici, just down the coast from the mountain villages of le Cinque Terre. We spent a little time in Lerici, then hopped a ferry up the coast. The boat took us around the tip of Porto Venere past all five villages: Riomaggiore, Manarola, Corniglia, Vernazza, and Monterosso. On the cruise, Claudia told me about the area. My Italian and her English were getting better. "This is where we spent our summer vacations," she said. "It's the closest beach and it's always warm in the summer." The rugged shores reminded me of northern Maine. But the cliffs were steeper; the water, deeper indigo; and the sloping terraces, sprouted with scraggly olive trees, lemon trees, and vineyards that looked thousands of years old. "The Cinque Terre landscape is just mountains and sea," she continued. "It's hard to grow things, but what does grow is intense with flavor." She explained how the basil is the most aromatic on earth. How the olives are small but jammed with flavor. And how currents from the Mediterranean and Tyrrhenian Seas encourage algae to grow, which feeds the local fish and gives them an incredible taste.

Explaining all this to me, Claudia looked as robust and beautiful as the olive groves on shore. We stepped off the ferry in Monterosso, and I took in the deep perfume of basil. No wonder pesto was born in this region. Fragrant basil, velvety olive oil, rich little pine nuts. . . the ingredients are all local to these seaside cliffs. It made sense. They cooked with what they had.

I knew that corzetti was the region's most famous pasta. Each circle of dough gets embossed with an intricate design stamped from a one-of-a-kind woodcut stamp. The stamps themselves are carved from olive wood or walnut wood and traditionally etched with a family crest to celebrate the birth of a child. Authentic corzetti stamps are nearly impossible to find outside of Liguria. I went into umpteen curio shops looking for them. It became the Great Corzetti Quest.

When we got to Vernazza, it was midmorning. You could smell the *farinata* throughout the whole town. *Farinata* is a local chickpea flatbread made after the morning yeast breads come out of the oven. "Oh my god," Claudia said, lifting her nose to the air, "we have to go down this street." We got lost down a half-dozen crooked, narrow streets before arriving at a nondescript back door. We went in, and it turned out to be a factory bakery, not a café or store. The workers looked at us, like, "What the hell are you doing here?" Claudia told them, "We're visiting. Jeff is a chef from America working in Italy." Ten seconds later, I had a piece of *farinata* in my mouth, seasoned with onion, rosemary, and black pepper. Claudia had one with stretchy mozzarella. Before long, we were sitting at the water's edge, tasting different *farinata* and focaccia made with fava bean flour and chestnut flour, laughing with the workers. Claudia wiped a few stray *farinata* crumbs from my chin.

In Manarola, we stopped to read a little trattoria's chalkboard sign advertising its porcini tasting. Time for lunch! The first course was *funghi porcini di Borgotaro*, summer porcini from Parma, sliced and breaded in polenta flour and fried. Delicious. Fettuccine with porcini came next. Then oven-

roasted veal breast with porcini sauce. We finished off the mushroom tasting with two straws in a goblet of *sgroppino*, a kind of frozen slushy made with lemon sorbet and grappa.

After lunch, we hit the Sentiero Azzurro (Blue Trail) that connects le Cinque Terre and has incredible views. The vivid flowers, steep terraces, sweet herbs, craggy cliffs, and gleaming blue seas hypnotized our senses at every turn. Back down in town, we sampled gelato every chance we could. The best was at 5 Terre Gelateria e Crêperia in Manarola.

With our licorice gelatos, we strolled along the Via dell'Amore from Manarola to Riomaggiore. We paused in secluded nooks along the way to kiss over our gelato: we couldn't stop looking at each other, like teenagers in love. Claudia told me that these five fishing hamlets were once completely isolated from one another by rocky hills. Boats were the only means of transportation, and villagers mostly kept to themselves. The railway came in the late 1800s, and in the 1920s, the first walking path was cut between the five villages. It allowed young lovers from different villages to find each other, so it was called *Via dell'Amore* ("Lovers' Walk").

I wondered what it would be like to live in one of these jumbled pink, blue, or yellow houses that tilt toward the sea. We later walked the main street, Via Colombo, and Claudia and I were seduced by all the little shops selling fresh-picked strawberries, cherries, lemons, *nespoli* (loquats), leeks, spiky artichokes, savoy cabbage, rainbow chard, ruddy Taggiasca olives, and little vegetable fritters and savory pies. We'd just eaten but we were hungry again.

Wandering through le Cinque Terre gave us more time to talk than we'd ever had before. We talked about our families and lives back home. Our hopes for the future. Our dreams. The idea of owning our own restaurant came up. Before we knew it, the ferry back to Lerici was about to board.

Although Liguria has some of the best seafood in Italy, we'd only had a few nibbles of fish throughout the day. Some anchovies in Monterosso. Fried *gianchetti* (whitebait) in Riomaggiore to go with an *aperitivo*. We saved our appetites for dinner that night in Lerici. Dei Pescatori on Via Doria is one of the best seafood restaurants in the region. There is no menu and platter after platter of fresh-caught fish just keeps coming. . . stuffed anchovies, grilled sardines with lemon and olive oil, fried and marinated trout, grilled swordfish, steamed mussels with white wine, sautéed *gamberi* (shrimp), langoustines, *vongole veraci* (carpet clams) with pasta. . . it was endless, uncomplicated, and beautiful. Each briny bite seemed to capture the entire glorious day in our mouths. We capped the meal with a couple of glasses of *sciacchetrà*, the sweet local white wine perfumed with apricot and honey.

The next day, we didn't leave our room at the Hotel Florida until three in the afternoon. We had a gorgeous view of the ocean. It was the first time I told Claudia that I loved her.

Cockles and Eggs with Bruschetta

•

Grilled Sardines with Taggiasca Olives
and Celery Salad

•

Grilled Stuffed Calamari with Meyer Lemon
and Beets

•

Corzetti with Clams, Tomatoes,
and Peperoncino

•

Genovese Ravioli with Capon

•

Halibut al Cartoccio with
Ligurian Olives and Oregano

•

Spaghetti al Nero di Seppia with Shrimp

•

Meyer Lemon Tortas with Poppy Seed Gelato

•

Sweet Ricotta Frittelle with Raspberry Preserves

•

Chickpea Cakes with Warm Lemon Crema

COCKLES and EGGS with BRUSCHETTA

MAKES 2 TO 4 SERVINGS

2 tablespoons (30 ml) olive oil, plus
    some for the bread

2 garlic cloves, thinly sliced

30 cockles, New Zealand clams, or small
    hard-shell clams, scrubbed (18 to 20
    ounces/510 to 570 g)

½ cup (120 ml) dry white wine

⅛ teaspoon (0.25 g) chile flakes

4 large eggs, lightly beaten

3 scallions, thinly sliced (green parts
    only)

Salt and freshly ground black pepper

4 slices rustic country bread

Scrambled eggs and clams are two ingredients I never would have thought to put together. But this makes a fantastic springtime dish. The first time I tasted it was when Brad Spence, the chef at Amis in Philadelphia, made it for me for lunch. I was blown away. It's no more difficult than making scrambled eggs. You just cook cockles in the pan first. When you scramble the eggs, they cook right inside the opened cockle shells, getting seasoned with all the briny juices. The best time I ever tasted this dish was on my last trip to le Cinque Terre. The intensely orange eggs and mineral-rich cockles in Liguria made it taste even better.

Heat the 2 tablespoons (30 ml) of oil in a large sauté pan over medium heat. Add the garlic, and cook until the garlic begins to toast and turn light brown around the edges, 3 to 4 minutes.

Remove from the heat and add the cockles, wine, and chile flakes. Return to the heat, cover, and steam until all the cockles open, 5 to 6 minutes.

Once all the cockles open, add the eggs to the pan and scramble the eggs in the cockle liquid until soft and just cooked through, 1 to 2 minutes. Stir in the scallions and season with salt and pepper.

Brush the bread with a little olive oil and grill or broil until lightly toasted. Transfer the cockles and eggs to warm plates and serve with the toasted bread. Allow your guests to scoop the eggs and cockles from the shells.

GRILLED SARDINES with TAGGIASCA OLIVES and CELERY SALAD

You find grilled sardines in trattorias all along the Ligurian coast. They usually serve them as an appetizer with a drizzle of lemon and olive oil. Cooking them on the bone releases collagen as they cook, making them moister and richer. If you fillet these little fish, they tend to dry out. I love them with the salty punch of Taggiasca olives, the heart of Liguria's prized olive oil. Serve this starter dish with a few lemon wedges for squeezing over the fish.

Heat a grill to medium-high heat.

Coat the cleaned sardines with grapeseed oil, then generously season with salt and pepper. Lightly oil the grill and grill the sardines until just grill-marked and cooked through, about 2 minutes per side. Transfer to plates.

Meanwhile, pour the lemon juice into a medium bowl. Whisk in the blended oil in a slow, steady stream until combined and thickened. Add the celery and olives, then season with salt and pepper.

Spoon the salad over the sardines. Garnish with tight bunches of the mâche and drizzle the remaining vinaigrette from the bowl around the plates. Sprinkle each serving with flake salt and serve immediately.

MAKES 4 SERVINGS

8 whole sardines, fins removed, gutted, cleaned, and rinsed under cold water

2 tablespoons (30 ml) grapeseed oil

Salt and freshly ground black pepper

1 tablespoon (15 ml) freshly squeezed lemon juice

3 tablespoons (45 ml) blended oil (page 276)

4 medium-size ribs celery, strings removed, thinly sliced on a diagonal

½ cup (60 g) Taggiasca or other Ligurian olives, pitted and chopped

4 small bunches mâche (lamb's lettuce), about 2 cups (70 g), cleaned, for garnish

Flake salt, such as Maldon sea salt, for garnish

GRILLED STUFFED CALAMARI with MEYER LEMON and BEETS

I'd always heard in cooking school—and among Italians—that you never mix cheese and fish. But it's a myth. Cheese tastes good with seafood as long as it's not overpowering. Mild squid and a creamy ricotta filling work great together. You usually see stuffed calamari braised in tomato sauce, but I wanted to give this a lighter spin to capture the romance of my first trip to le Cinque Terre. I put the grilled calamari on a bed of arugula and topped it with a lemony roasted beet salad. If you can find them, use Meyer lemons. They're sweeter and more floral, like the lemons in Liguria. If you use common Eureka lemons, add a pinch of sugar to cut the sourness.

MAKES 4 TO 6 SERVINGS

8 ounces (227 g) red or Chioggia beets

About ½ cup (68 g) kosher salt

12 small whole calamari (squid), cleaned

¾ cup (175 ml) extra-virgin olive oil, divided

6 stalks Swiss chard (8 to 10 ounces/227 to 285 g)

1 garlic clove, sliced

1 cup (235 ml) white wine

2 pounds (1 kg) fresh whole-milk ricotta cheese (1 quart)

1 ounce (28 g) Parmesan cheese, grated (¼ cup)

1 large egg

½ cup (54 g) plain, dry breadcrumbs

Salt and freshly ground black pepper

16 Meyer lemon segments

¼ cup (60 ml) freshly squeezed Meyer lemon juice

2 tablespoons (6 g) minced chives

6 ounces (170 g) arugula (about 6 cups)

Preheat the oven to 500°F (260°C). Scrub the beets well, then rinse them and leave them wet. Put the salt in a heatproof dish, add the beets, and pack a thick layer of salt around each beet. Transfer to a baking sheet and roast the beets until tender enough for a fork to slide in and out easily, 2 to 3 hours. Let cool, then rinse the beets and cut them into very small cubes. You should have about 1 cup (136 g). Set aside or refrigerate for up to 3 days.

To clean each squid, pull away the head and tentacles from the hood (tubelike body), and then reach into the hood and pull out the entrails and the plasticlike quill, taking care not to puncture the pearly ink sac. Cut off the tentacles just above the eyes, and discard the head. Squeeze the base of the tentacles to force out the hard "beak," and rinse the tentacles and the hood under cold running water. Using the back of a paring knife or your fingers, pull and scrape off the gray membrane from the hood. Cut off and discard the two small wings on either side of the hood. Refrigerate the hoods in ice water until ready to stuff. Pat dry the squid tentacles.

Heat 1 tablespoon (15 ml) of the oil in a large cast-iron skillet over high heat. When smoking hot, add the tentacles, and cook until curled, firm, and browned here and there, 4 to 5 minutes. Remove from the heat and let cool.

Separate the leaves from the stems of the chard. Trim any rough spots, then coarsely chop the stems and leaves. Heat 3 tablespoons (45 ml) of the oil in the skillet over medium heat. Add the chard stems and garlic, and cook for 2 minutes. Add the wine, and cook until the stems are almost tender, 8 to 10 minutes. Add the leaves, and cook, stirring now and then, until the liquid evaporates and the leaves wilt down a bit, 2 to 3 minutes. Let cool slightly, then transfer to a food processor, along with the seared tentacles. Mince the chard mixture using short pulses. Transfer to a bowl and whisk in the ricotta, Parmesan, egg, and breadcrumbs. Season to taste with salt and pepper. Spoon into a resealable plastic bag and refrigerate for up to 1 day.

Snip a corner off the bag and pipe the mixture into the squid bodies, stuffing them full. Close the ends of the squid with toothpicks. If you have any leftover filling, you can use it as a ravioli filling. Season the squid all over with salt and pepper and coat lightly with oil.

Heat a grill to medium heat. Brush the grill, coat with oil, and grill the stuffed squid directly over the heat until grill-marked and set in the center, turning a few times, about 8 minutes.

Gently combine the beets, lemon segments, lemon juice, chives, and remaining ½ cup (120 ml) of olive oil. Season with salt and pepper.

Divide the arugula among plates. Place two stuffed calamari on each plate and top with the beet salad. Drizzle with the remaining dressing in the bowl.

CORZETTI with CLAMS, TOMATOES, and PEPERONCINO

When my family came to Italy to meet Claudia's family, we made a special trip to Liguria to find a corzetti pasta stamp. They're pretty rare (see the Sources on page 289 for some suggestions). We first looked in a little town called Bergeggi, about an hour north of Genoa. When we got to le Cinque Terre, we looked in each of the five towns. We couldn't find a single stamp, and it started driving Claudia crazy. But I was obsessed. Finally, in Monterosso, in the last shop I looked in, I found them. Beautiful ones. I bought four of them. The traditional sauce for corzetti is a spin on basil pesto made with only pureed pine nuts, marjoram, and milk. But to remind me of the amazing Ligurian seafood, I like to serve corzetti with clams and little summer tomatoes.

MAKES 6 SERVINGS

Corzetti Dough:

4¾ cups (595 g) *tipo* 00 flour (see page 277) or all-purpose flour

2 large eggs

¼ cup (60 ml) olive oil

Clams and Tomatoes:

5 pounds (2.25 kg) small hard-shell clams, such as littlenecks

10 tablespoons (155 ml) olive oil, divided

1 medium-size yellow onion, finely chopped (1¼ cups/200 g)

1 small garlic clove, smashed

½ bunch fresh flat-leaf parsley, stems and all

1 quart (1 L) white wine

1 quart (1 L) Fish Stock (page 279) or water

2 cups (340 g) grape tomatoes or small early summer tomatoes, halved

1 long hot pepper or peperoncino, minced (about ¾ cup/112 g)

(continued on next page)

For the corzetti dough: Combine the flour and eggs in the bowl of a stand mixer fitted with the dough hook and mix on low speed. With the machine running, gradually add the oil until incorporated, then gradually add 1 cup (235 ml) of water until incorporated. Turn the mixer to medium-high speed and mix until the dough holds together. Separate the dough into three pieces and gently knead each piece in your hands until the dough looks smooth. Shape each piece into a rectangle the width of your pasta roller. Roll each piece of dough into a long rectangle about $\frac{1}{8}$ inch (3 mm) thick (setting #2 or #3 on the KitchenAid attachment) onto a floured work surface. Using a lightly floured corzetti stamp or 2½-inch (6.25-cm) cookie cutter, cut out circles of dough; you should get fifty to sixty circles from all three pieces of dough with no rerolling. Lightly flour the woodcut corzetti stamp and then stamp each circle to imprint the design. If you don't have a corzetti stamp, leave the circles plain or use a lightly floured cookie stamp or butter stamp. Place the corzetti in single layers between sheets of floured parchment paper, cover, and freeze for up to 2 days.

For the clams and tomatoes: Scrub the clams and rinse under cold running water.

Heat ¼ cup (60 ml) of the oil in a large, deep sauté pan. Add the onion, garlic, and parsley, and cook until the onion is soft but not browned, 4 to 6 minutes. Add the white wine and boil over high heat until the liquid has reduced in volume by half, 10 to 15 minutes. Add the clams and fish stock. Cover and steam until the clams open, 10 to 12 minutes. Remove from the heat as soon as the clams open, then transfer the clams to a plate. Line a mesh strainer with cheesecloth and strain the clam liquid through the cheesecloth; set aside. Pick out the meat from the clams and refrigerate it in the strained clam stock for up to 4 days.

When ready to serve, bring two large pots of salted water to a boil. Add half of the corzetti, one by one, to each pot, stirring gently to help prevent sticking. Partially cover the pots and cook just until the corzetti are tender, about 5 minutes. Reserve about 1½ cups (375 ml) of pasta water, then drain.

Meanwhile, heat 2 tablespoons (30 ml) of the olive oil in a deep sauté pan over medium heat. Add the tomatoes, and cook until they start to break down, 4 to 5 minutes. Add the hot pepper, and cook until soft, 6 to 8 minutes. Add the clams, 1¼ cups (310 ml) of the clam stock, 1 cup (235 ml) of pasta water, and the remaining ¼ cup (60 ml) of olive oil to the pan. Bring to a simmer over medium-high heat and cook until the liquid reduces in volume by about half, 5 to 8 minutes. Add the cooked pasta and toss gently in the sauce.

Using tongs, overlap eight corzetti in a circle on each plate. Simmer the sauce in the pan until slightly reduced and thickened, and then spoon over the corzetti.

GENOVESE RAVIOLI with CAPON

Genoa sits in the center of Liguria, slightly closer to the mountains bordering Piedmont. It's Italy's largest seaport, but the food there includes more land animals, such as chicken and veal calves, because of the landscape. You see this ravioli in all the Genovese restaurants. It's usually stuffed with veal organ meats, such as brains or sweetbreads. I added the capon as a little twist. Some of the capon meat gets pureed to make a rich, creamy sauce that tastes sort of like chicken soup but thicker. You'll need one small capon (4 to 5 pounds/1.75 to 2.25 kg) for this recipe, or you can use one large or two small chickens. Cut off the legs and wings and leave the bones in for the sauce. For the ravioli filling, remove the skin and bones from the breast.

MAKES 6 TO 8 SERVINGS

Genovese Sauce:

1½ pounds (680 g) capon legs and wings

Salt and freshly ground black pepper

About 1 cup (125 g) *tipo* 00 flour (see page 277) or all-purpose flour

2 tablespoons (30 ml) grapeseed oil

1 medium-size yellow onion, coarsely chopped (1 cup/160 g)

1 large carrot, coarsely chopped (1 cup/122 g)

2 medium-size ribs celery, coarsely chopped (1 cup/101 g)

2 cups (475 ml) white wine

1¼ quarts (1.25 L) Chicken Stock (page 279)

1 sachet of 1 sprig parsley, 1 sprig rosemary, 1 sprig thyme, 1 bay leaf, and 6 black peppercorns (see page 277)

About ¾ cup (175 ml) olive oil

About ¼ cup (60 ml) sherry vinegar

3½ ounces (100 g) Parmesan cheese, grated (1 cup)

Ravioli Filling:

20 ounces (567 g) boneless, skinless capon breast, cubed

2 ounces (57 g) chicken livers

20 ounces (567 g) veal or calf's brains

Salt and freshly ground black pepper

½ cup (62 g) *tipo* 00 flour (see page 277) or all-purpose flour, for dredging

4 tablespoons (57 g) unsalted butter

¼ cup (60 ml) olive oil

5 sage leaves

1 pound (450 g) Egg Pasta Dough (page 282), rolled into 4 sheets, each about 1/32 inch (0.8 mm) thick

For the Genovese sauce: Rinse the capon legs and wings and pat dry. Season the capon all over with salt and pepper. Dredge the pieces in the flour, shaking off the excess.

Heat the grapeseed oil in a large Dutch oven (or two) over medium-high heat. When hot, add the capon pieces in batches to prevent crowding and sear until golden brown on both sides, 5 to 6 minutes per side. Transfer the pieces to a platter as they are browned.

Preheat the oven to 350°F (175°C). Add the onion, carrots, and celery to the pan and cook, stirring now and then, until nicely browned, 6 to 8 minutes. Stir in the white wine and simmer until the liquid is reduced in volume by about one third. Pour in the chicken stock and bring to a simmer, then add the capon back to pan, along with the sachet. Cover, transfer to the oven, and braise until the meat falls easily off the bone, $2\frac{1}{2}$ to 3 hours.

Remove and discard the sachet. Transfer the meat to a platter and let cool slightly. Pick the meat and skin from the bones, discarding the bones. Be sure to remove all of the bones because the sauce will be pureed. Puree the meat, skin, vegetables, and braising liquid in a blender in batches, adding enough olive oil to each batch to create a slightly thickened sauce. Pour into a large, deep sauté pan, and season to taste with sherry vinegar, salt, and pepper.

For the ravioli filling: Put all parts of a meat grinder and the cubed capon breast and chicken livers in the freezer until ice cold, about 15 minutes. Grind the capon breast and chicken livers in the meat grinder with the small die. Cover and refrigerate.

Season the brains with salt and pepper and dredge them in flour, shaking off the excess.

Heat the butter, olive oil, and sage in a large sauté pan. When the butter is foamy and hot, add the brains and sear them in the pan until nice and golden brown all over, 8 to 10 minutes. Drain on paper towels and let cool.

Puree the cooled brains in a food processor. Add to the ground capon and liver mixture, season with salt and pepper, and mix until thoroughly combined. Spoon into a large resealable plastic bag and refrigerate until ready to use or up to 3 days.

Lay a pasta sheet on a lightly floured work surface and dust with flour. Trim the ends of the sheet to make them square, then fold the dough in half lengthwise and make a small notch at the center to mark it. Open the sheet so it lies flat again and spritz with water.

Cut off a small corner of the resealable plastic bag so you can pipe the filling on the pasta. Beginning at the left-hand side, pipe two rows of $\frac{1}{2}$-inch (1.25-cm)-diameter balls of filling along the length of the pasta, leaving a $\frac{1}{2}$-inch (1.25-cm) margin around each ball and stopping at the center of the sheet. Lift up the right-hand side of the pasta sheet and fold it over to cover the balls of filling. Gently press the pasta around each ball of filling to seal. Use a $2\frac{1}{2}$-inch (6.25-cm) round, fluted ravioli cutter or a similar size biscuit cutter to cut the ravioli. Repeat with the remaining pasta dough and filling. You should have about ninety-six ravioli.

When ready to serve: Bring a large pot of salted water to a boil. Drop in the ravioli in batches, quickly return the water to a boil, and cook until tender yet firm, 2 to 3 minutes. Drain the pasta, reserving about 1 cup of the pasta water.

Heat the Genovese sauce in a large, deep sauté pan over medium heat. When hot, add the cooked ravioli, in batches, if necessary, to prevent crowding, and simmer until the sauce coats the pasta, 3 to 4 minutes. Add some of the reserved pasta water, if necessary, to create a creamy sauce. Divide among plates and top with Parmesan.

HALIBUT AL CARTOCCIO
with LIGURIAN OLIVES AND OREGANO

MAKES 4 SERVINGS

Potatoes:

8 fingerling potatoes, scrubbed

4 teaspoons (20 ml) grapeseed or olive oil

Salt and freshly ground black pepper

4 teaspoons (5 g) unsalted butter

4 teaspoons (1 g) chopped fresh flat-leaf parsley

Halibut:

¼ cup (60 ml) olive oil, plus a little extra for drizzling

1½ pounds (680 g) halibut fillets, cut into 4 pieces

Salt and freshly ground black pepper

12 pitted Ligurian or Niçoise olives, halved lengthwise

24 fresh oregano leaves

12 thin slices of lemon

¼ cup (60 ml) freshly squeezed lemon juice

3 tablespoons (42 g) unsalted butter, cut into small pieces

Al cartoccio is the Italian equivalent of French cooking *en papillote,* or in parchment paper. It's one of my favorite ways to cook fish because it's gentle, like a combination of steaming and poaching. Just be sure to pick a fish that's tender enough to cook all the way through in five to ten minutes. A dense fish, such as mako shark, wouldn't work so well, but halibut is perfect. I serve the cartoccio with some fingerling potatoes on the side and have guests slit open their own packages. Each package comes to the table like a gift from the kitchen. You open the paper and a burst of steamy aroma bathes you in the scents of the Italian Riviera... fresh lemon, olives, and oregano.

For the potatoes: Put the potatoes in a pot and cover with cold water. Bring to a boil over high heat and boil until the potatoes are tender, 6 to 8 minutes. Let the potatoes cool until warm, then cut in half lengthwise.

Heat the grapeseed oil in a sauté pan over medium-high heat and fry the potatoes, cut-side down, until golden brown, 4 to 5 minutes. Drain any excess oil, then season the potatoes with salt and pepper and toss with the butter and chopped parsley.

For the halibut: Meanwhile, preheat the oven to 450°F (230°C). Cut four 10-inch (25 cm) squares of parchment paper and grease each with a thin film of olive oil. Season the halibut all over with salt and pepper, then divide them among the parchment squares. Mix together the olives, oregano, and 2 tablespoons (30 ml) of the olive oil and arrange over the halibut. Overlap two to three lemon slices on each portion, then drizzle with the lemon juice. Divide the cut-up butter among the portions, scattering it over the lemons, and drizzle with the remaining 2 tablespoons (30 ml) of olive oil.

To make each package, fold the parchment corner to corner over the fish to make a triangle. You'll have to nudge the fish slightly off center to make the corners meet. Starting at one of the other corners, begin rolling the paper toward the fish; continue making a series of small double folds all the way around the fish until you reach the opposite corner and the paper is folded tight against the fish. Twist the final corner several times to seal it tight, then fold it under the paper package.

Put the packages on a large rimmed baking sheet and drizzle each with a little olive oil. Bake until the fish is about 120°F (49°C) on an instant-read thermometer stuck through one of the packages, 5 to 7 minutes.

Using a spatula, transfer each cartoccio to a plate. Slit open the package, arrange the potatoes around the fish, and serve immediately.

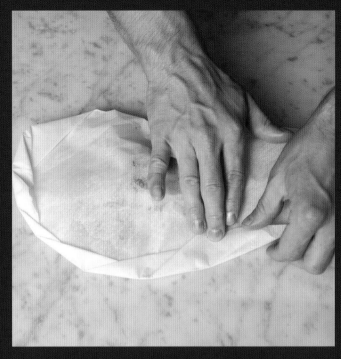

SPAGHETTI al NERO di SEPPIA with SHRIMP

MAKES 4 SERVINGS

1 pound (450 g) Squid Ink Spaghetti (page 283)

1 cup (235 ml) extra-virgin olive oil, divided

1 leek, cleaned and trimmed and cut into long thin strips

1 quart (1 L) Shrimp Stock (page 280)

1 pound (450 g) shrimp, peeled and cut into ½-inch (2.5-cm) pieces

½ cup (60 g) chopped fresh flat-leaf parsley

Salt and freshly ground black pepper

The best squid ink actually comes from *seppia* (cuttlefish). The ink sacs are larger and have a stronger taste. I've seen squid ink used to flavor everything from pastas and sauces to breads and ricotta cheese. It's one of my all-time favorite pastas. I use plenty of ink to make sure the pasta dough gets completely black. Be careful, though, the ink gets everywhere, just as with a busted ballpoint pen. To make the spaghetti, follow the directions on page 283 for making squid ink pasta, then extrude the pasta through the spaghetti attachment of your pasta machine. If you buy dried squid ink spaghetti, add a few minutes to the cooking time here.

Bring a large pot of salted water to a boil. Drop in the spaghetti, quickly return the water to a boil, and cook until tender yet firm, 2 to 7 minutes, depending on how long the spaghetti has been refrigerated. Drain the pasta, reserving the pasta water.

Heat ¾ cup (178 ml) of the oil in a large, deep sauté pan over medium heat. Add the leek, and cook until soft but not browned, 4 to 5 minutes. Raise the heat to medium-high, add the shrimp stock, and simmer it down a little, 4 to 5 minutes. Add the cooked pasta, shrimp, parsley, and the remaining ¼ cup (59 ml) of oil, cooking and tossing until the shrimp is no longer pink and the sauce is creamy, 3 to 4 minutes. Season with salt and pepper, divide among bowls, and serve.

MEYER LEMON TORTAS with POPPY SEED GELATO

I've always loved lemon poppy seed pound cake. And I used to make a cold lemon cake that was soft and airy like a creamy soufflé. I wanted to put all those flavors together and came up with this dessert. It makes the perfect ending to a springtime meal. Poppy seeds are used here in the form of a gelato. Lemons appear in both the cake and the sauce, which features the peels of Meyer lemons. Meyer lemons taste closer to Ligurian lemons than your typical American Eureka lemons do. But if you can't find Meyers, you can use regular lemons here. Just taste the lemons and add some sugar to balance the acidity.

Preheat the oven to 375°F (190°C). Boil a kettle of water for a hot water bath.

For the torta: In a stand mixer on medium speed, cream the butter and ⅔ cup (133 g) of the sugar until light and fluffy, 3 to 5 minutes. Add the egg yolks, one at a time, mixing until they are incorporated, scraping down the bowl frequently. Grate the zest from the lemon into the bowl and squeeze the juice into the bowl. Mix until combined.

Combine the flour and salt. Alternate between adding the flour mixture and milk to the batter in three additions, ending with the milk.

Meanwhile, whip the egg whites on medium speed, slowly adding the remaining 2½ tablespoons (32 g) of sugar until medium peaks form when the beaters are lifted, about 5 minutes. Gently fold the whites into the egg yolk mixture in three additions.

Butter and flour eight 4-ounce (120-ml) ramekins or baking tins and place them in a 15 x 10-inch (38 x 25-cm) baking dish or a rimmed baking sheet. Pour the batter into the ramekins to just under the inside rim. Slide the baking dish into the oven and carefully pour boiling water into the dish or sheet to come about ½ inch (1.25 cm) up the sides of the ramekins. Bake until just set, 13 to 15 minutes. Remove the tortas from the water bath, and let the tortas cool in the ramekins. Refrigerate for at least 1 hour or up to 2 days.

For the lemon peel sauce: Fill a bowl with ice water. Put the lemon peels in a pot with cold water to cover by 1 inch (2.5 cm). Bring to a boil, drain immediately, and transfer the peels to the ice water to stop the cooking. Repeat this process of boiling, draining, and cooling in ice water three times.

Combine the lemon juice, ¼ cup (60 ml) of water, and the lemon peel in a medium saucepan. Bring to a boil over medium-high heat. Stir together the sugar and pectin in a small bowl and then add to the pan. Bring the mixture to 217°F (103°C) on a candy thermometer. Remove from the heat and let cool to room temperature. Cover and refrigerate for at least 1 hour or up to 1 week.

To serve: Spoon a pool of sauce on each plate. Run a knife around each torta and then invert over the plate to unmold. Drizzle more sauce on top and then spoon the poppy seed gelato on the side.

MAKES 8 SERVINGS

Torta:

5⅓ tablespoons (75 g) unsalted butter, at room temperature

⅔ cup plus 2½ (180 g) tablespoons granulated sugar, divided

3 large eggs, at room temperature, separated

1 Meyer lemon

¾ cup plus 1 tablespoon (101 g) *tipo* 00 flour (see page 277) or all-purpose flour

Pinch of salt

⅓ cup (90 ml) whole milk

Lemon Peel Sauce:

1¼ cups (120 g) Meyer lemon peel

¾ cup (175 ml) freshly squeezed Meyer lemon juice

1¼ cups (250 g) granulated sugar

½ teaspoon (2.25 g) powdered pectin

To Serve:

1½ cups (375 ml) Poppy Seed Gelato (page 287)

SWEET RICOTTA FRITTELLE
with RASPBERRY PRESERVES

MAKES 6 TO 8 SERVINGS

Raspberry Preserves:

¼ cup (60 ml) glucose syrup or light corn syrup

¾ cup plus 2 tablespoons (175 g) granulated sugar, divided

1 pound (450 g) raspberries (about 3¾ cups)

1½ teaspoons (7 g) powdered pectin

Frittelle:

14 ounces (400 g) fresh whole-milk ricotta cheese (1¾ cups)

2 large eggs

¼ cup (50 g) granulated sugar

Zest of 1 lemon

1 vanilla bean, split and scraped

¾ cup (94 g) *tipo* 00 flour (see page 277) or all-purpose flour

1 teaspoon (4.5 g) baking powder

Oil, for frying

To Serve:

Confectioners' sugar, for dusting

Italians will make fritters out of anything. Meat, fish, vegetables, and fruit. They're the ultimate snack when paired with something creamy. I was looking through some old Italian cookbooks and kept coming across this ricotta fritter with lemon curd. I thought it would be fun to use raspberries instead of lemon. The fritter ends up tasting sort of like a jelly doughnut but with the raspberry preserves on the side. The fruit marries well with the cheese.

For the raspberry preserves: Combine the glucose syrup, ½ cup plus 2 tablespoons (125 g) of the sugar, and 1 tablespoon (15 ml) of water in a medium saucepan. Bring to a boil over medium heat. Gently stir in the raspberries, and cook until heated through, 1 to 2 minutes. Combine the pectin and the remaining ¼ cup (50 g) of sugar in a small bowl and gradually whisk into the berries. Return the mixture to a boil, and cook until slightly thickened, 4 to 5 minutes. The preserves will set further upon cooling. Scrape into a heatproof bowl and let cool. Use immediately or refrigerate for up to 2 weeks.

For the frittelle: Combine the ricotta, eggs, sugar, lemon zest, and vanilla in a stand mixer on low speed until blended. Combine the flour and baking powder in a small bowl and gradually add to the ricotta mixture on low speed. Scoop the mixture into 2-inch (5-cm)-diameter balls onto a parchment-lined baking sheet. (Or cover and refrigerate for up to 1 day, scooping out balls of dough as needed.) You should have 20 to 24 balls.

Heat the oil in a deep fryer or heavy pot to 375°F (190°C). Fry the balls in batches without crowding until set in the center and deep golden brown, 2 to 3 minutes, adjusting the heat to maintain the frying temperature at all times. Drain on paper towels.

To serve: Spoon a pool of preserves on the bottom of each plate. Top with two or three *fritelle* and a dusting of confectioners' sugar.

CHICKPEA CAKES with WARM LEMON CREMA

Every town in le Cinque Terre uses chickpeas and chickpea flour in a variety of dishes. You can smell the *farinata* (chickpea flatbreads) cooking in the streets during lunchtime. After my first visit, I researched how the residents used chickpeas and was surprised to hear how popular they were in desserts. What makes this dessert special is that you coat the cake molds with sugar, so they get a little crunchy on the outside. The insides of the cakes stay moist and complement the buttery lemon sauce. I like the cakes so much, I always make a big batch. But if you want less, you can halve this recipe.

For the chickpea cakes: Preheat the oven to 375°F (190°C). Butter and sugar eight 4-ounce (120-ml) ramekins or baking tins and place on a baking sheet.

Puree the chickpeas in a food processor or blender until relatively smooth, scraping down the sides once or twice. You should have 2 cups (475 ml) of thick chickpea puree. Transfer the puree to a large bowl and add the sugar, lemon zest, flour, salt, whole egg, and egg yolks. Gently whisk until smooth. Whip the egg whites in a stand mixer on high speed until medium-stiff peaks form when the beaters are lifted. Gently fold the whites into the puree mixture. Spoon the batter into the prepared ramekins and bake until the cakes are set and golden brown, 12 to 15 minutes.

For the lemon sauce: Whisk together the lemon juice, sugar, and egg yolks in a heatproof bowl until light and pale yellow. Heat the butter and cream in a heavy saucepan over medium heat until it begins to simmer, and then remove from the heat. Whisk half of the hot cream mixture into the yolk mixture until incorporated, and then return the combined mixture to the pan. Return the pan to low heat and stir constantly but gently until the sauce thickens slightly and registers a temperature of 165°F (74°C) on a candy thermometer, about 5 minutes. Remove from the heat and stir for about 2 minutes, or until the sauce thickens to the consistency of heavy cream. Strain through a fine-mesh sieve into a bowl and let stand a few minutes, stirring occasionally. You should have about 2 cups (475 ml) of sauce.

To serve: Spoon a pool of warm lemon sauce on each plate. Turn out a warm cake onto each plate. Drizzle a little olive oil around the plate, then dust the cakes with confectioners' sugar.

MAKES 8 SERVINGS

Chickpea Cakes:

3 cups (600 g) cooked or canned chickpeas (drain and rinse if using canned)

10 tablespoons (125 g) granulated sugar

Zest of 1 lemon

2 tablespoons (16 g) *tipo* 00 flour (see page 277) or all-purpose flour

Pinch of salt

1 large whole egg, plus 4 large eggs, separated

Lemon Sauce:

Juice of 3 lemons

1 cup plus 2 tablespoons (225 g) granulated sugar

4 large egg yolks

4 ounces (1 stick/113 g) unsalted butter

½ cup (120 ml) heavy cream

To Serve:

Olive oil, for drizzling

Confectioners' sugar, for dusting

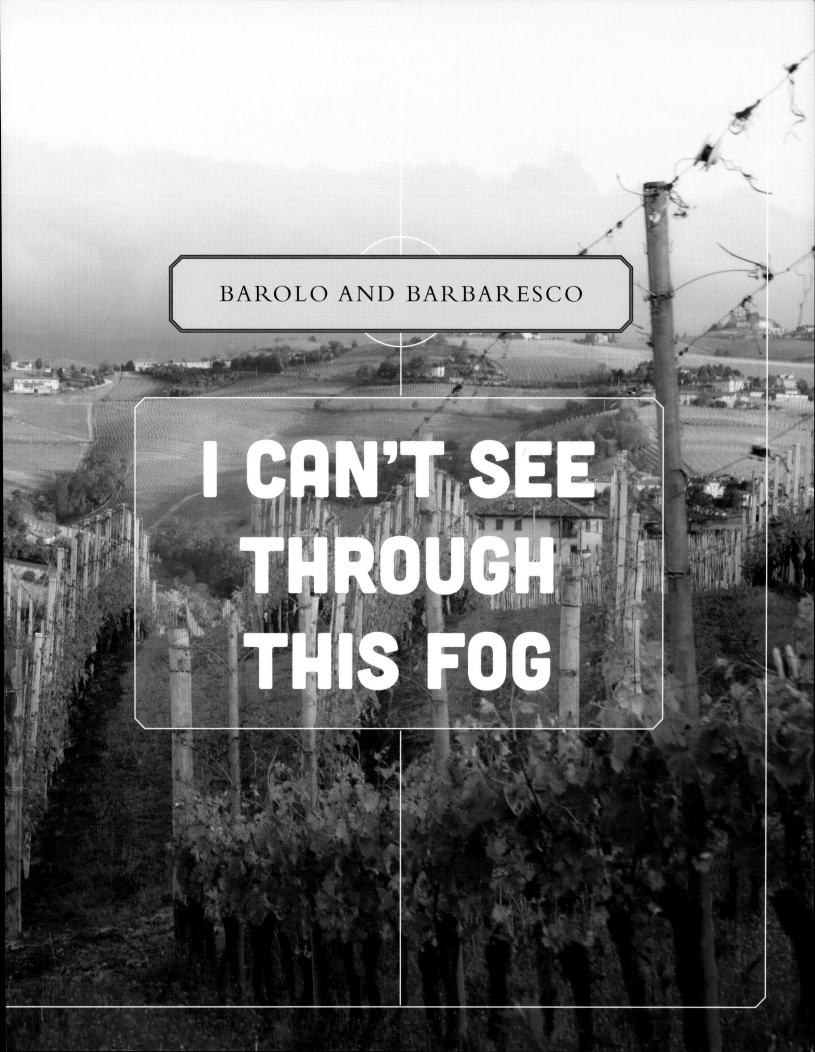

BAROLO AND BARBARESCO

I CAN'T SEE THROUGH THIS FOG

"BAROLO HAS BEEN CALLED 'THE KING OF WINES AND THE WINE OF KINGS,'" SAID CAMILLO. HE TOLD ME BAROLO HAS SO MUCH TANNIN THAT IT IS BEST AGED FOR AT LEAST TEN YEARS TO MELLOW IT.

But in the 1980s, new producers wanted to start selling the wine sooner. So they shortened the traditional fermentation time to less than two weeks and aged the wine for only a few years in smaller French oak barrels instead of in big Slovenian casks. "For Barolo traditionalists, this meant war," said Camillo. "It was a fight over what could legally be called Barolo wine."

This was my first trip to Piedmont, about a two-hour drive southwest of Bergamo. As the birthplace of the slow food movement, the first Eataly megastore, the world's best white truffles, and some of Italy's finest wines, Piedmont is a culinary mecca. Camillo wanted to show me some of the wineries that helped Frosio Ristorante earn its Michelin star. It was 2004 and Matteo Donadoni (nicknamed "Jack") was driving. Jack worked the front of the house at Frosio, along with Camillo.

We left Bergamo at six in the morning and drank wine all day from eight thirty to five o'clock. Camillo took us to both modern and traditional Barolo and Barbaresco wineries, including Scavino, Clerico, Ceretto, Rocche dei Manzoni, and Marchesi di Grésy. In the center of Barbaresco, we stopped for lunch at Trattoria Antica Torre, just down the street from the famous Gaja winery. Antica Torre serves classic Piedmont dishes, such as Fassone beef carpaccio, *vitello tonnato,* tajarin egg noodles, and *bonèt,* a rich chocolate-amaretti pudding cake. We ended the meal with some Bra and Castelmagno cheeses.

On the drive back to Bergamo, Jack pontificated about the food. "Everything is a little richer and more refined in Piemont," he said. Jack explained how the region borders France and was under French control a few times. Even the traditional Barolo winemaking methods were originated by a Frenchman. The truffles and chocolate are finer than anywhere else in Italy. They fatten up the local Fassone cattle with sugar beets and zabaglione to make *bue grasso* and hold a Fat Ox festival every year in Carrù. Even such peasant dishes as risotto get the royal treatment up here, with a finish of truffles, butter, or cheese. "We have a saying in Bergamo," Jack went on: "'*La boca l'è mia straca se la sa mia de aca.*' It means, 'Your mouth is not tired if it doesn't taste like milk.'" In other words, always finish a meal with some satisfying cheese, no matter how full you might be.

I think Jack was a little drunk, but I got the picture. And I totally agreed about the lavish food in Piedmont. It made me want to come back.

In the fall of that year, I drove there with Claudia for a weekend getaway. We had GPS but it didn't do us any good. As the nights get cooler in Piedmont, a dense fog settles into the hills, making it impossible to find your way. Factor in the steep, twisty, one-car roads, and you're lost in no time. We started driving around ten in the morning for a lunch reservation at Da Cesare, a tiny restaurant in Albaretto Della Torre, about twenty minutes from Barolo. But a thick fog led us so far astray, we didn't make it to Da Cesare until two in the afternoon! It didn't matter. When you make a lunch reservation at Da Cesare, that could mean anywhere from noon to three p.m. Chef Cesare Giaccone cooks when you show up. There is no menu because it changes every day.

Except for the *capretto* and *zabaione*. Cesare always spit-roasts a baby goat over a wood fire outside the kitchen. And he always serves *zabaione* tableside from a big copper bowl with his famous hazelnut cookies, baked and served right in the hazelnut shells. I've tried to make those cookies a hundred times and still can't get them right.

That fall, he started us off with his signature porcini and white peaches, thinly sliced and sautéed with a pan sauce of chicken stock, sherry vinegar, and cream. Next came a warm salad of duck breast with orange vinaigrette and local lettuces. Claudia licked her fork, and I could hear Cesare chopping the goat on his butcher block. The meat came to the table crispy but tender and drizzled only with herbed olive oil. It was outstanding. Cesare is one of Piedmont's most well known *personaggi*. He makes his own Barolo salt and Barolo wine vinegar, ages cheese in his cellar, and paints in his spare time. In his cellar, he showed us a wheel of Castelmagno cheese that he'd been aging for a year; his bottle of 1955 Gaja Barbaresco; and a dust-covered bottle of 1906 Barolo from Mascarello, one of the region's oldest winemakers. "When are you going to retire?" I asked him, trying to wrap my head around my own future as a chef. Cesare was already seventy. "Never," he said. "I'll be cooking for the rest of my life."

Claudia and I thanked him, and then drove to Ca' du Rabajà, a B&B about twenty minutes away, in Barbaresco. It's a beautiful brick red inn and winery that overlooks the vineyards. Ca' du Rabajà is a member of the Produttori del Barbaresco, a consortium of winemakers that pools its grapes and expertise to produce consistent Barbaresco wine. Barolo wine has a loftier reputation than Barbaresco, but Barolo wines are notoriously inconsistent. Both wines are made from 100 percent nebbiolo grapes, the local grape named after the local fog (*nebbia,* in Italian). But Barolo's wider growing zone and changes to the winemaking methods over the years have made Barolo something of a crapshoot. It's true that Barbarescos don't bottle-age as gracefully. And they don't get nearly as big and aromatic. But Barbarescos are more drinkable when young and more reliable, thanks in part to the consortium.

We checked in, showered, changed, and drove to Osteria dei Catari for dinner that night, in the medieval village of Monforte d'Alba. The restaurant is super-rustic with exposed wooden beams inside, brick showing through the stucco here and there, and a dark wooden staircase leading to the second floor where colorful murals line the walls. For a first course, I had *tajarin*, the region's thin handmade egg noodles, and they were insanely good. The shaved fresh truffles helped, of course. Claudia had veal-stuffed *raviolini del plin* draped in a buttery sage sauce. She ordered veal breast with Barolo sauce for an entrée, and I had rustic, "hunter-style" braised rabbit. We couldn't resist the *torrone semifreddo* with chocolate sauce for dessert.

Eating different versions of the same food in both Barolo and Barbaresco, I started to realize something: Italian cooking is intimately tied to the place that it comes from and the people who make it. It's hyperlocal. The people in each region, and even each town, depend on their local food and local wine for their unique sense of identity. There is no single, standard *tajarin* or *vitello tonnato*. The dish changes from town to town. This fundamental idea is no more evident than in Barolo and Barbaresco, two famous Italian wines that are made within ten miles (16 km) of each other and use the exact same grapes, yet employ different wine-making methods that result in two distinct wines, each with its own distinguished and celebrated characteristics.

Panfried Veal Tongue with
Bagna Cauda and Leeks

•

Red Bell Pepper Tonnato
with Caper Berries

•

Rabbit Agnolotti with Pistachio Sauce

•

Robiola and Fava Bean Francobolli

•

Polenta Gnocchi Stuffed
with Taleggio Cheese

•

Whole Roasted Pheasant
with Barbaresco Sauce

•

Veal on a Stone

•

Warm Quince Tortini
with Cranberry and Orange

•

Zabaione with Moscato and Fresh Figs

PAN-FRIED VEAL TONGUE
with BAGNA CAUDA AND LEEKS

The first time I ever tried tongue, it was on a taco in Basalt, Colorado. This was years before I lived in Italy. Then in Piedmont, I had it over and over as part of the famous *bollito misto* (boiled mixed meats) served with *salsa verde* and *salsa rossa*. I love the idea of fish and meat together, so I thought the region's creamy anchovy sauce (*bagna cauda*) would go great with soft, crispy veal tongue. I boil the tongue until tender and then slice it and bread and fry each slice only on side, for crunch. Sometimes I add a bitter edge by garnishing the dish with pieces of radicchio and a few grindings of black pepper.

MAKES 4 TO 6 SERVINGS

Veal Tongue:

1½ quarts (1.5 L) 3-2-1 Brine (page 280)

⅛ teaspoon (0.75 g) curing salt #1 (see page 277)

1 veal tongue (about 1½ pounds/680 g)

Bagna Cauda and Leeks:

1 cup (235 ml) whole milk

1 cup (235 ml) heavy cream

4 garlic cloves, smashed

1 cup (235 ml) blended oil (page 276)

2 ounces (57 g) salt-packed anchovies (about 5), rinsed and filleted (see note)

Salt and freshly ground black pepper

2 leeks, cleaned and trimmed

4 ounces (1 stick/113 g) unsalted butter

Leaves from 1 sprig fresh rosemary

Breading and Garnish:

About ½ cup (62 g) *tipo* 00 flour (see page 277) or all-purpose flour

1 large egg, beaten

About ½ cup (54 g) plain, dry breadcrumbs

4 tablespoons (57 g) unsalted butter

¼ cup (60 ml) olive oil, plus some for drizzling

1 tablespoon (4 g) chopped fresh flat-leaf parsley for garnish

Note

To prepare salt-packed anchovies, rinse them well, brushing off the salt with your fingers, or soak them for a few hours in several changes of cold water to help remove the salt. Remove the heads, tails, and fins. Place the blade of your knife perpendicular to the fish just below where the head was and cut along the body, holding the blade against the backbone as you go. This will remove the top fillet. Put the tip of your knife under the backbone and then pull out and remove the backbone to expose the bottom fillet.

For the veal tongue: Combine the brine and curing salt in a large resealable plastic bag. Add the veal tongue, press out the air, seal, and refrigerate for 3 days.

Transfer the tongue to a medium saucepan. Add one-quarter of the brine and enough water to cover the tongue by about 1 inch (2.5 cm). Cover and bring to a simmer over medium heat, then adjust the heat so that the liquid simmers gently. Simmer until the tongue is tender (about 190°F/88°C internal temperature), 1 to 1½ hours. Remove the pan from the heat and let the tongue cool down in the liquid.

When cool, remove and discard the skin. Cut the tongue crosswise into slabs about ¼ inch (6 mm) wide. Refrigerate for up to 2 days.

For the bagna cauda and leeks: Combine the milk, cream, and garlic in a medium saucepan over medium-high heat. Bring to a simmer, then lower the heat to medium and cook until the liquid reduces in volume by about half, 6 to 8 minutes, taking care not to let the milk boil over. Meanwhile, heat the oil and anchovies in a sauté pan over medium heat until the anchovies break down, 3 to 4 minutes. Let cool slightly, then slowly scrape the oil mixture into the cream mixture; it may bubble up some. Simmer until the liquid reduces in volume by about one-third, thickens, and gets creamy, another 6 to 8 minutes. Let cool slightly, then puree in a blender. Season with salt and pepper.

Cut the leeks into pieces about 1½ inches (3.8 cm) long and 1 inch (2.5 cm) wide, and transfer them to the same sauté pan used for the anchovies. Add the butter and rosemary, and cook over medium heat, stirring a few times to break up the leek layers, until the leeks become super-soft and nearly melted but not browned, about 10 minutes. If necessary, stir in a little water so that the liquid remains creamy and not separated. Scrape into the pureed bagna cauda and keep warm over low heat.

Pour the flour, beaten egg, and breadcrumbs into three separate shallow bowls. Dredge one flat side of each piece of veal tongue in the flour, then the egg, then the breadcrumbs. Heat the butter and oil in a skillet over medium-high heat. When hot, add the tongue in batches, breaded-side down, and fry until golden brown on that side only, 3 to 4 minutes. Then flip, and cook the other side for 1 to 2 minutes. Transfer to paper towels to drain.

Spoon the bagna cauda mixture down the middle of small plates. Place a few pieces of tongue, breaded-side up, in the center of each plate. Drizzle with olive oil and garnish with chopped parsley.

RED BELL PEPPER TONNATO with CAPER BERRIES

MAKES 4 SERVINGS

4 roasted red bell peppers (page 278)

1¼ teaspoons (3 g) powdered gelatin

4 anchovy fillets

1 tablespoon (15 ml) white wine vinegar

½ ounce capers (about 2 table-
spoons/14 g), plus a few for garnish,
preferably salted instead of soaked

7 ounces (200 g) canned Italian tuna
packed in olive oil

Salt and freshly ground black pepper

½ cup (120 ml) mayonnaise

Zest from 2 lemons

2 tablespoons (8 g) chopped fresh flat-
leaf parsley

½ cup (120 ml) olive oil

I'm always looking for new variations of *vitello tonnato*, Piedmont's classic dish of braised and sliced veal leg served cold with a creamy olive oil, egg yolk, and tuna sauce. At Osteria, we serve sliced porchetta with tonnato sauce. But at Alla Spina, I wanted to do a lighter snack and decided on this mousse of tuna wrapped in roasted pepper to form a sort of savory cannoli. Caper berries and lemon bring out the traditional tonnato flavors.

Cut the roasted peppers into eight rectangles, each about 4 to 5 inches (10 to 13 cm) long and 2 to 3 inches (5 to 8 cm) wide.

Mix the gelatin with 1 tablespoon (15 ml) of water in a medium heatproof bowl and let stand until bloomed (plump, soft, and hydrated), 5 minutes. Meanwhile, puree the anchovies, vinegar, and capers in a food processor. With the machine running, slowly add the tuna a little at a time, stopping to scrape down the sides of the bowl once or twice. Season with salt and pepper.

Put the bowl of bloomed gelatin over a pan of gently simmering water and heat until melted and smooth, 3 to 4 minutes, stirring a few times. Slowly stir the tuna mixture into the gelatin a little at a time, until fully incorporated. Remove the bowl from the heat and let cool for 5 minutes. Cover and refrigerate until very firm, at least 2 hours or up to 2 days. When the mixture has chilled, fold in the mayonnaise and keep cold.

Combine the lemon zest, parsley, and olive oil in a small bowl.

Lay the pepper rectangles out flat and spread about 2 teaspoons (10 ml) of cold filling over each one. Roll up the peppers like little jelly rolls to make a tube shape. The stuffed, rolled peppers can be refrigerated for up to 4 hours before serving. Top each with a caper berry (or more if you're using small capers) and drizzle the flavored oil over the top.

RABBIT AGNOLOTTI with PISTACHIO SAUCE

I'm a big fan of combining meat and nuts—especially rabbit and pistachios. Rabbit is delicate meat, but when roasted over wood, it takes in a ton of flavor that stands up to pistachios. I like to spit-roast a whole rabbit over wood for this ravioli filling, and then grind it with mortadella and bind the filling with egg and Parmesan. You can also grill rabbit pieces as described in the recipe. Add some water-soaked wood chips to the fire for more smoke flavor. I call for rabbit legs instead of a whole rabbit, to make a reasonable number of servings for home cooks. But if you want to cook a whole rabbit, double the recipe. You'll get about twenty servings, which can be frozen for a week or two, so you get a few meals out of it.

MAKES 8 TO 10 SERVINGS

Rabbit and Mortadella Filling:

1¾ pounds (794 g) rabbit legs

Salt and freshly ground black pepper

2 tablespoons (30 ml) grapeseed oil

5 ounces (142 g) mortadella, cubed

1 large egg

1¾ ounces (50 g) Parmesan cheese, grated (½ cup)

1 pound (450 g) Egg Pasta Dough (page 282), rolled into 4 sheets, each about ¹⁄₃₂ inch (0.8 mm) thick

Pistachio Sauce:

2 cups (300 g) raw unsalted pistachios, preferably Sicilian

1 cup (235 ml) blended oil (page 276)

1 tablespoon (15 ml) sherry vinegar

5 large basil leaves

½ small garlic clove

Salt and freshly ground black pepper

To Serve:

2 tablespoons (30 ml) white truffle paste (see Sources, page 289)

1 cup (150 g) chopped raw unsalted pistachios, preferably Sicilian

3½ ounces (100 g) Parmesan cheese, grated (1 cup)

¼ cup (60 ml) extra-virgin olive oil

For the rabbit and mortadella filling: Light a grill for indirect medium heat, about 350°F (175°C); on a charcoal grill, bank all the hot coals to one side of the grill; on a gas grill, light the burners on only one side of the grill and leave the other burners off.

Season the rabbit legs with salt and pepper and coat all over with oil. Coat the grill grate with oil. Grill directly over the heat until browned on both sides, about 5 minutes per side. Move the rabbit to the unheated part of the grill, and cook until the juices run clear, about 140°F (60°C) on an instant-read thermometer, 30 to 35 minutes. While cooking, turn the rabbit a few times and baste it with oil to keep it moist.

Transfer the rabbit to a platter, and when cool enough to handle, remove and discard all the bones, reserving the meat and skin. You should have about 1¼ pounds (570 g) of rabbit meat. Grind the rabbit meat and mortadella together on the small (¼-inch/6.2-cm) die of a meat grinder into a large bowl. Using the paddle attachment of an electric mixer or a wooden spoon, mix in the egg and Parmesan until incorporated and the mixture looks somewhat pasty. Spoon the mixture into a resealable plastic bag, seal, and refrigerate for at least 1 hour or up to 2 days.

Lay a pasta sheet on a lightly floured work surface. Form two rows of ½-inch (1.25-cm)-diameter balls of filling along the length of the sheet, leaving a 1½-inch (6 mm) margin around each ball. Spritz the dough with water to keep it from drying out as you work. Cut the pasta sheet in half lengthwise between the rows of filling to make two long sheets. Lightly moisten the long edges of the sheets with a spritz or a finger dipped in water. Starting from the outside edges in, fold the dough over just to cover the filling and roll the sheet of pasta over itself again. Next, pinch the dough in between the balls of filling to remove the air, starting at one end and working your way to the other. Place a finger gently on the stuffing to create a dimple, then cut between the balls of filling to create the ravioli. Repeat with the remaining pasta dough and filling. You should have 175 to 200 agnolotti. You may have some leftover filling; use it like you would use any other sausage. Place the agnolotti in single layers between sheets of waxed or parchment paper, cover, and freeze for up to 2 days. Take the pasta right from the freezer to the pasta water to cook.

For the pistachio sauce: Buzz the pistachios, blended oil, sherry vinegar, 1 tablespoon (15 ml) of water, and the basil and garlic in a blender or food processor until smooth, 2 to 3 minutes. Season with salt and black pepper, and then refrigerate in a sealed container for up to 3 days or freeze for up to 1 month. Makes about 3 cups (750 ml).

Bring a large pot of salted water to a boil. Drop in the pasta in batches, and cook just until tender, 2 to 4 minutes. Drain, reserving the pasta water.

To serve: Meanwhile, combine the pistachio sauce, truffle paste, and 2 cups (475 ml) of pasta water in a large, deep sauté pan over medium heat. Add the drained pasta and toss gently until the sauce is creamy, 2 to 3 minutes. Divide the pasta and sauce among plates and top with chopped pistachios, Parmesan cheese, and a drizzle of extra-virgin olive oil.

ROBIOLA and FAVA BEAN FRANCOBOLLI

The first time I made francobolli ravioli was out of Mario Batali's *Babbo Cookbook*. They look like postage stamps on the plate (*francobolli* is Italian for "postage stamps"). I love the small, delicate shape. Mario's francobolli were filled with lamb's brain, but I like a more colorful filling. Fava beans came right to mind. They blend up nice and creamy, and you can see the bright green color right through the pasta. A simple butter sauce with mint is all that's needed to finish the dish.

Bring a large pot of water to a boil and fill a large bowl with ice water. Add the whole fava pods to the boiling water and blanch for 1 minute. Transfer to the ice water to stop the cooking. When cool, pluck the favas from the pods, then pinch open the pale green skin on each bean and pop out the bright green favas into a bowl. You should have about 1 cup (188 g).

Heat 1 tablespoon (15 ml) of the olive oil in a sauté pan over medium heat. Add the onion, and cook until soft but not browned, 3 to 4 minutes. Add ½ cup (94 g) of the fava beans and just enough water to cover the beans (about ½ cup/120 ml). Cook just until the beans are tender, 4 to 5 minutes. Using a slotted spoon or spider strainer, scoop the beans and onion from the liquid and transfer them to a blender, reserving the liquid. Puree the beans and onion, adding just enough of the cooking liquid to make a smooth puree. Transfer to a mixing bowl and add the robiola, 2 tablespoons (12.5 g) of the Parmesan, and the egg. Season with salt and pepper and whisk until smooth. Spoon into a resealable plastic bag and refrigerate for at least 1 hour or up to 1 day.

Lay a pasta sheet on a lightly floured work surface and dust with flour. Trim the ends to make them square, then fold the dough in half lengthwise and make a small notch at the center to mark it. Open the sheet so it lies flat again and spritz with water. Beginning on the left-hand side, place two rows of ½-inch (1.25-cm)-diameter balls of filling along the length of the pasta, leaving a ½-inch (1.25-cm) margin around each ball and stopping at the center of the sheet. Lift up the right-hand side of the pasta sheet and fold it over to cover the balls of filling. Gently press the pasta around each ball of filling to seal. With a knife or fluted pasta wheel, cut into 1-inch (2.5 cm) squares, trimming off any excess. Repeat with the remaining pasta dough and filling. You should have about 125 francobolli. If you're not going to cook them immediately, toss the francobolli with a little bit of flour and freeze in an airtight container.

Bring a large pot of salted water to a boil. Drop in the francobolli, quickly return the water to a boil, and cook until tender yet firm, 3 to 4 minutes. Drain the pasta, reserving the pasta water.

Put the butter, remaining ¼ cup (60 ml) of olive oil, and smashed garlic in a deep sauté pan over medium heat. When the butter melts and the oil is hot, whisk in 1 cup of pasta water until blended. Add the remaining ½ cup (94 g) of fava beans, the cooked pasta, and the mint. Cook until the sauce becomes thick and creamy, 1 to 2 minutes.

Divide among plates and garnish with the remaining ½ cup (50 g) of Parmesan and the mint chiffonade.

MAKES 6 TO 8 SERVINGS

1 pound (450 g) fava beans in the pods

5 tablespoons (75 ml) olive oil, divided

2 tablespoons (20 g) minced yellow onion

5 ounces (141 g) robiola cheese (⅔ cup)

2¼ ounces (64 g) Parmesan cheese, grated (2 tablespoons plus ½ cup), divided

1 large egg

Salt and freshly ground black pepper

8 ounces (227 g) Egg Pasta Dough (page 282), rolled into 2 sheets, each about 1/32 inch (0.8 mm) thick

12 ounces (3 sticks/340 g) unsalted butter

4 garlic cloves, smashed

¼ cup (15 g) chopped fresh mint, plus a few leaves of mint cut in chiffonade, for garnish

POLENTA GNOCCHI STUFFED with TALEGGIO CHEESE

MAKES 4 TO 6 SERVINGS

1 pound (about 2½ cups/450 g) cooked Polenta (page 281), at room temperature

½ cup (62 g) *tipo* 00 flour (see page 277) or all-purpose flour, plus about 2 cups (250 g) for dusting

2¼ ounces (64 g) Parmesan cheese, grated (⅔ cup), divided

2 tablespoons (14 g) plain, dry bread-crumbs, sifted

1 large egg

Salt and freshly ground black pepper

8 ounces (227 g) Taleggio cheese, cut into ¼- to ½-inch (about 1 cm) cubes (about 2 cups)

8 ounces (2 sticks/227 g) unsalted butter

As a cook, you always want to try to use up every ingredient without throwing anything away. Polenta lasts for a few days in the fridge, so why not use leftovers to make gnocchi? Stuffed with Taleggio cheese, they're fantastic. The dumplings will seem wet when you make them. That's okay. The wetter they are, the more tender they'll be. Just handle them gently and roll them lightly in flour. If you like, add a few leaves of fresh sage to the brown butter in the sauce.

Put the polenta in the bowl of a stand mixer fitted with a paddle attachment and mix on medium speed until smooth, 2 to 3 minutes. Add ½ cup of flour, ⅓ cup (33 g) of the Parmesan, and the breadcrumbs and egg, and season to taste with salt and pepper. Mix on medium-low speed just until combined, 30 seconds or so, scraping down the sides once to incorporate all the ingredients. Spoon the filling into a resealable plastic bag, seal, and refrigerate for at least 1 hour or up to 1 day.

Pour about 1 cup (125 g) of flour into a large bowl. Snip a corner from the bag and squeeze the gnocchi mixture from the bag into the flour in ¾-inch (2 cm)-diameter balls. Coat your hands with flour, make a small dimple in each ball with your pinky tip, and then insert a piece of Taleggio inside each dimple, gently pinching the dough around the cheese and rolling the ball between your hands to completely enclose the cheese. Repeat with all of the gnocchi and roll in flour to coat them. You should have fifty to sixty gnocchi.

Bring a large pot of salted water to a boil. Drop in the gnocchi in batches to prevent overcrowding, and cook until the polenta firms up and the cheese begins to melt, 5 to 6 minutes (test one to make sure the cheese is melting).

Meanwhile, melt the butter in a sauté pan over medium-low heat and continue cooking until the milk solids begin to brown and fall to the bottom of the pan, 10 to 15 minutes.

Divide the gnocchi among plates and sprinkle with the remaining Parmesan. Pour the browned butter over the top.

WHOLE ROASTED PHEASANT
with BARBARESCO SAUCE

I grew up in southern New Hampshire and started hunting at the age of twelve. We mostly hunted game birds, such as pheasant, around the apple orchards in Wilton. My dad would rub mayonnaise under the skin and roast the birds, but they always got dry and tough. I learned that you have to undercook them a little. Now, I stuff the pheasants with herbs and garlic, tie them up, and pan-roast them to about 140°F (60°C). Then I cut the meat off the carcass and squeeze the carcass into the pan to enrich the sauce. A little truffle paste helps, too. If you can't get pheasant, you could make this dish with chicken.

Preheat the oven to 450°F (230°C). Remove and discard any remaining feathers from the pheasants, then pull out the innards and set aside. Season the birds inside and out with salt and pepper. Stuff the garlic, thyme, and bay leaf into the cavities and truss the birds by tying the legs together (see note for trussing instructions).

Heat 1 tablespoon (15 ml) each of the butter and oil in each of two oven-proof sauté pans (or use one giant pan if you have one). Set them over medium-high heat and, when hot, add a pheasant breast-side down to each pan and sear on all sides until nicely browned, 8 to 10 minutes total, taking care not to tear the skin when turning the birds. Turn the birds breast-side up, transfer the pans to the oven, and cook until an instant-read thermometer registers 140° to 145°F (60° to 63°C) when inserted into a leg, about 25 minutes. Remove the pans from the oven and transfer the pheasants to a cutting board. Let rest for 10 to 15 minutes.

Meanwhile, return the pans to medium heat. Finely chop the pheasant livers and hearts, add to the pans, and sauté for 2 to 3 minutes. Add the wine, scraping the pan bottom, and simmer until the liquid reduces in volume by about half, 4 to 6 minutes. Add the stock, and cook until the liquid thickens enough to start coating the back of a spoon, another 5 minutes or so.

Cut each pheasant into six pieces, removing the legs, wings, and breast from the carcass. Scrape any juices from the cutting board into the pan and squeeze the carcass over the pan to release all its juices. Simmer for 2 to 3 minutes, then strain out the liver and heart, if you like, or leave them in. Stir in the remaining 2 tablespoons (30 ml) of butter and 2 tablespoons (30 ml) of olive oil, along with the vinegar and truffle paste, stirring like mad until the sauce blends together and emulsifies. Season to taste with salt and pepper.

Serve the pheasant pieces with the Barbaresco sauce.

MAKES 4 SERVINGS

2 female pheasants (with innards), each 2½ to 3 pounds (1.1 to 1.3 kg)

Salt and freshly ground black pepper

1 garlic clove, halved

8 sprigs thyme

1 bay leaf, torn in half

4 tablespoons (57 g) unsalted butter, divided

¼ cup (60 ml) extra-virgin olive oil, divided

1 cup (235 ml) Barbaresco or another dry red wine

1 cup (235 ml) Chicken Stock (page 279)

1 tablespoon (15 ml) red wine vinegar, preferably Barbaresco or Barolo

1 tablespoon (15 ml) white truffle paste or shaved fresh white truffles

Note

To truss the stuffed pheasants, pierce three or four 4-inch (10 cm)-long wooden skewers through the flaps of skin on each side of the cavity openings. Weave kitchen string around the skewers like a shoelace to lace the bird shut, tying it off at the top. Position the bird breast-side up with the legs facing away from you. Loop a long piece of kitchen string beneath the ends of the drumsticks, crossing the string to make an X. Pull the remaining string down, passing it beneath the thighs and pulling tight to pull the legs toward the tail. Continue pulling the string along the body toward the neck and pass it beneath the wings. Flip the bird over so the legs are now facing toward you and cross the string over the back between the two wings, pulling tight. Loop the string beneath the backbone, pull it tight, and then tie it off with a tight knot.

VEAL ON A STONE

The food at Da Cesare in Piedmont is the most simple and elegant you will ever experience. In 2004, out from the kitchen came this piping hot stone with a veal loin cooked rare and sliced thin, so you could use the stone to finish cooking the veal to your liking. You could smell fresh rosemary and thyme sprigs searing beneath the hot stone. The dish was served with an heirloom tomato and basil salad and a little rock salt. Perfection! You can use any flat, heavy stone that will retain heat. I like Pennsylvania bluestone, but salt blocks also work well. Look for bluestone at landscaping stores or salt blocks at the Meadow (see Sources, page 289). You can get away with using only two stones if everyone shares.

MAKES 4 SERVINGS

Four 6-inch (15-cm) square Pennsylvania bluestones, salt blocks, unglazed quarry tiles, or other dense, heavy stones

4 heirloom tomatoes

3 tablespoons (45 ml) olive oil, plus a few tablespoons for searing

1 tablespoon (15 ml) red wine vinegar, preferably Barolo

6 basil leaves, cut into chiffonade

Salt and freshly ground black pepper

2 pounds (1 kg) boneless veal loin

8 sprigs rosemary

8 sprigs thyme

Maldon sea salt

If using bluestones, rinse the stones clean, dry them, and place them in a cold oven. Heat the oven to 500°F (260°C) and let the stones preheat in the oven until very hot (about 400°F/205°C surface temperature), about 6 hours. If using salt blocks, heat them over a gas burner on the lowest heat for 15 minutes, then raise the heat from low to medium to high every 10 to 15 minutes until very hot (about 600°F/315°C), about 45 minutes. For electric burners, prop the salt blocks on a wok ring or other rack to avoid direct contact with the heating element.

Meanwhile, bring a large pot of water to a boil and fill a large bowl with ice water. Score an X into the bottom of each tomato with a sharp knife and blanch the tomatoes in the boiling water until the skins start to curl back a little from the X, 30 seconds to 1 minute. Immediately transfer the tomatoes to the ice water and let them stand until cooled, a minute or two. Starting at the X, peel the skin from the tomatoes and discard. Cut them in half through their equator and gently squeeze them upended over a bowl or trash can to remove and discard the seeds and gel (you can use your fingers or the tip of a knife to help dig out the seeds and gel). Cut out the core and then finely dice the tomatoes. Transfer them to a bowl and mix in the oil, vinegar, and basil. Season with salt and pepper and let stand at room temperature for 30 minutes.

About a half-hour before you are ready to serve, cut the veal crosswise into four equal portions (8 ounces/227 g each), season with salt and pepper, and let stand at room temperature for 20 minutes.

Heat a few tablespoons (about 45 ml) of the olive oil in a large sauté pan over medium-high heat. When hot, add the veal and sear until golden brown on both sides but nice and rare and still cool to the touch in the middle, about 4 minutes per side.

Slice the veal through the side into slabs about ¼ inch (6 mm) thick and place the slabs on a plate or another wooden board. Place the rosemary and thyme on wooden boards that can hold the hot stones (the stones will go on top of the herbs). Using heatproof silicone gloves or thick, insulated grill gloves, carefully remove the hot stones from the oven or stovetop and place them on the herbs on the wooden board. Allow guests to use their forks to transfer the slabs of veal to the hot stones, and cook the veal to their liking (it only takes about a minute per side). Serve with the tomato salad, allowing guests to season the stone-seared veal to taste with Maldon sea salt. If using salt blocks, you may not need the finishing salt because some salt will be released into the veal from the block.

WARM QUINCE TORTINI
with CRANBERRY and ORANGE

Tortino means "small tart." Mixing choux pastry with pastry cream is what makes the tart special. It creates an unbelievably light and flaky crust. You could put whatever you want inside—cherries, pears, bananas—and the tart would taste awesome. This version is my Italian twist on American apple pie, using quince as the filling and cranberry compote as the sauce. The recipe is written for individual pies, the way we serve them at Osteria. You'll need eight fluted three- to four-inch (7.5- to 10-cm) brioche molds (any extras can be frozen and then reheated). Or for one large tart, use a single deep-dish pie pan, rolling the dough for both top and bottom crusts.

MAKES 8 SERVINGS

Pastry Cream:

¾ cup (150 g) granulated sugar, divided

¼ cup (32 g) cornstarch

9 large egg yolks

1⅔ cups (400 ml) whole milk

6 tablespoons (90 ml) heavy cream

½ vanilla bean, split and scraped

Pâte à Choux Dough:

7 ounces (200 g) unsalted butter

1½ cups (205 g) pastry flour

¼ teaspoon (1.5 g) salt

6 large egg yolks

Quince Filling:

2¼ pounds (1.1 kg) quinces, peeled, cored, and coarsely chopped

1 tablespoon (14 g) unsalted butter

Juice of 1 lemon

2½ cups (500 g) granulated sugar

1½ teaspoons (4 g) ground cinnamon

¼ teaspoon (0.6 g) ground mace

⅛ teaspoon (0.3 g) ground cloves

⅛ teaspoon (0.3 g) ground allspice

⅛ teaspoon (0.3 g) ground ginger

1 cup (235 ml) apple cider

Cranberry and Orange Sauce:

Peel from ½ orange

9 ounces (about 2¼ cups/255 g) fresh cranberries

1 cup (200 g) granulated sugar

3 tablespoons (45 ml) brandy

To Serve:

1 cup (235 ml) Crème Anglaise (page 284)

For the pastry cream: Combine the sugar, cornstarch, and egg yolks in the bowl of a stand mixer fitted with the whisk attachment. Mix on medium speed until smooth, about 2 minutes.

Bring the milk, cream, and vanilla to a boil in a medium saucepan over medium heat. Remove from the heat and mix about ½ cup (120 ml) of the hot milk mixture into the egg mixture. Scrape all of the egg mixture into the pot of hot milk, and cook over medium heat until thick and creamy. Transfer the mixture to the mixer bowl and whip on low speed until cool, 4 to 5 minutes.

For the pâte à choux dough: Melt the butter with ⅞ cup (210 ml) of water in a large saucepan, and bring it to a rolling boil. Stir in the flour and salt, cooking and stirring vigorously until the flour absorbs the water and a film forms on the bottom of the pan, 2 to 3 minutes. When the dough comes together and pulls away from the sides of the pan, about a minute later, transfer the dough to the bowl of a stand mixer fitted with the paddle attachment. Mix on medium speed for 1 minute to cool the dough. Add the eggs one or two at a time, allowing each addition to become fully incorporated before adding the next and scraping down the bowl as necessary.

Add the cooled pastry cream to the pâte à choux, and mix on low speed until combined to make the final tart dough. It will be sticky. Cover and refrigerate until ready to use or up to 4 hours.

For the quince filling: Combine the chopped quinces, butter, lemon juice, sugar, cinnamon, mace, cloves, allspice, ginger, and cider in a large saucepan. Bring to a boil over medium-high heat, and then lower the heat to medium-low and simmer until the quince breaks down and thickens the entire mixture into a jam, 30 to 40 minutes.

For the cranberry and orange sauce: Cut the orange peel into very thin strips about 3 inches (7.5 cm) long (julienne). Reserve the rest of the orange for another use. Set up three small pots of boiling water and fill a bowl with ice water. Blanch the orange peels in the first pot for 30 seconds, then transfer with a slotted spoon to the ice water to cool. When cool, blanch the peels in the second pot for 30 seconds and transfer to the ice water to cool again. When cool, blanch the peels in the third pot for 30 seconds and transfer to the ice water to cool.

Combine the blanched orange peel, cranberries, sugar, and brandy in a medium saucepan over medium heat. Simmer until the cranberries break down some and the mixture thickens (about 215°F/102°C on a candy thermometer), 20 to 25 minutes.

Preheat the oven to 375°F (190°C) and butter eight fluted 3- to 4-inch (7.5- to 10-cm) brioche molds.

On a lightly floured work surface, roll out half of the dough to an even ¼-inch (6-mm) thickness; the dough will be sticky and you will need a lot of flour to roll it out. Cut eight circles out of the dough, each about 4½ inches (11.5 cm) in diameter, and line the prepared molds with the dough, easing it into all the flutes of the molds. Fill halfway with the quince filling.

Roll the remaining half of the dough on the work surface, adding flour as needed, to an even ¼-inch (6-mm) thickness. Cut eight circles out of the dough to fit over the top of the tortini. Lay the top crust on each tortino and crimp the edges to seal. Place the tortini on a rimmed baking sheet and bake until golden brown, 15 to 20 minutes. Let cool on a rack for 10 minutes.

To serve: Spoon a pool of Crème Anglaise on each plate and top with a warm tortino. Spoon on some of the cranberry and orange sauce.

ZABAIONE with MOSCATO AND FRESH FIGS

Listening from the dining room of Da Cesare, you can hear the clang of the whisk in Cesare's copper bowl as he makes his famous zabaione. It's never too thick or too soupy or too sweet. It's perfect. He doesn't cook it in a double boiler but in a copper bowl right over a burner, whisking like hell. It takes skill to keep from scrambling the eggs. I wrote this recipe using the safer method of whisking the zabaione in a bowl over gently simmering water.

MAKES 2 SERVINGS

6 ripe fresh figs

2 large egg yolks

Two half-eggshells of granulated sugar

Two half-eggshells of Marsala or muscat wine

2 hazelnut biscotti cookies or other biscotti

Quarter the figs and divide them among small serving bowls.

Combine the egg yolks, sugar, and wine in a heatproof bowl or the top of a double boiler. Whisk vigorously until the mixture is thick and pale yellow, 2 to 3 minutes. Set the bowl over a saucepan of barely simmering water. You don't want the water at a rolling boil or it will cook the eggs too quickly. Whisk constantly until the mixture takes on enough air to triple in volume, thicken slightly, and fall in sheets when the whisk is lifted. It should register 145°F to 150°F (63°C to 66°C) on an instant-read thermometer and take about 5 minutes of whisking over the hot water.

Spoon the zabaione over the figs at the table and garnish the bowls with hazelnut biscotti.

BAROLO

 BANDIERA ARANCIONE
Marchio di qualità turistico ambientale per l'entroterra

SIMPLE ITALIAN COOKING AT ITS BEST

THE 7 CLUB WAS FULL OF GORGEOUS ITALIAN WOMEN WORKING OUT. WITHIN WALKING DISTANCE OF FROSIO, THE GYM WAS MY SAFE HAVEN BETWEEN SHIFTS AT THE RESTAURANT. BUT SINCE CLAUDIA AND I STARTED DATING, I HADN'T WORKED OUT IN WEEKS. IT WAS GOOD TO GET BACK IN THE GYM.

When I got back to work, I finished icing the last of the *piccola pasticceria* (petit fours), one of my specialties. During lunch, Jack Donadoni came into the kitchen and told me that Stefano Arrigoni was in the dining room and wanted to know who was making them. Stefano was the owner of Osteria della Brughiera, another Michelin-starred restaurant just down the road from us in Villa d'Almè. Tall and artistic, Stefano came for lunch at Frosio once a week and was impressed with my desserts. When I came out to talk with him, we hit it off right away, and he said I should come to La Brughiera for dinner.

"You should definitely go," said Jack. "The food is incredible. La Brughiera is one of Bergamo's thirty Michelin restaurants." Jack was always bragging about Bergamo being called "*la città più stellata*," "the city with the most stars," and Lombardy having the most Michelin-starred restaurants in all of Italy. I'd already eaten at several of them and felt lucky to have cooked at two of them—Frosio and Loro. It was time to check out another.

La Brughiera opened in 1991. Over the years, Mario Batali, Michael Schlow, and other Italian restaurateurs in America have eaten there. It's a shining example of simple, refined Italian food. Stefano also owns an art gallery in Bergamo, and the physical spaces of La Brughiera are impeccably designed—a perfect blend of contemporary and rustic. You enter the restaurant through an iron gate leading up a pebbled walkway past a minimally decorated patio with umbrella-covered tables. In the foyer, stunning paintings—

both modern and classic—adorn the walls. The dining rooms are to the left. The *cantina,* to the right. When Claudia and I came for dinner, Stefano's father, Walter, was in the cantina, slicing dark red prosciutto and deeply marbled coppa on a gleaming antique Berkel meat slicer. Guests are invited to linger in this dimly lit wine cellar with some Franciacorta and hand-carved salumi before heading to their tables for dinner. Hundreds of wine bottles line the old stone walls, and a green marble table offers all manner of homemade pickles, cheeses, breads, and salumi. Stefano brought Claudia and me past the meat slicers, through a brick archway, to the cavernous curing room, where pancetta, guanciale, prosciutto, culatello, culaccia, and other sausages hung on meat hooks from a wet ceiling. Kneeling on the floor, he pushed the lid off a chilly tomb of Carrara marble to show us thick slabs of rosemary-rubbed *lardo* curing, layer upon layer, inside. For a moment, I was transported back to the Mangili butcher shop by the salty smell of aging meat and fat.

As we reentered the cantina, Stefano told me that his chef, Paolo Begnini, started in 1996, just a few years after they opened. Paolo is a tall, broad-chested guy with thin eyebrows. Paolo handed Claudia and me each a piece of unsalted bread rubbed with tomato and two-day-old fresh sausage. Suddenly, it seemed that all of my culinary experiences of the past year, from butchering to baking to dining to home cooking, were captured in that one bite of bread and meat.

Claudia and I sat down for dinner and the dishes came to the table without a single order. Treviso with shaved arti-

chokes, fried egg and fresh local cheese. Veal and truffle pâté on toast with a salad of guinea fowl, cipolline onions, and hazelnuts. Squash gnocchi stuffed with porcini and topped with Parmesan fonduta and shaved white truffles. Bavette pasta with baby octopus and sage. Scampi with caramelized citrus. Panfried veal brains with green beans and mustard vinaigrette. Pan-seared duck breast with citrus, cauliflower butter, and duck liver pâté.

This was the kind of food I wanted to cook more of! The ingredients were impeccable; the techniques, flawless. Paolo's pasta was ethereal and perfectly married with the sauce. His flavor combinations were concise. Presentations were uncluttered. Every dish rang true. Even desserts were a revelation. Passion fruit soufflé with pineapple-ginger sorbet. Light and crispy apple fritters with cream and cinnamon. Molten hot chocolate puffs with bourbon vanilla crema.

I felt like I'd been given a great big bear hug by the chef.

For the Italians, when you walk into their restaurant, it's like walking into their home. Even though we'd just met, both Paolo and Stefano welcomed us like old friends. That dinner lasted until two in the morning as Stefano sat with us, pouring vin santo and nibbling *cantucci* (almond cookies). He asked me about America, how Claudia and I met, and what we hoped for in the future.

Over the next several months, we went back to La Brughiera again and again. It became our favorite restaurant. By this time, I'd eaten all over Italy in various restaurants in various regions. But I still found Paolo Begnini's cooking to be the most inspiring. Every time I ate there, I learned something new. His taste was slightly more Tuscan than Bergamascan yet unlimited by allegiance to any one Italian region. He employed ingredients and techniques from all over Italy and the world, using the full range of his talents as a chef. He traveled to Tuscany to get the best coppa, sought out the best prosciutto in Parma, and bought the best local produce from Bergamo, putting most of it on the menu and preserving the rest. He made use of every culinary technique he had mastered and constantly researched and tested new ones.

By the end of that year, I was full of inspiration but completely out of money. As an American, I didn't have a work visa and couldn't get a legal job. Luckily, Frosio offered to keep me on at the restaurant and pay me under the table. I had told my dad I would send home money to pay off my school loans from the Culinary Institute of America. It wasn't easy to stay in Bergamo, but I had to. Important things were happening. With Claudia, it wasn't just another crush. And with my cooking, it wasn't just another chef job. I was maturing as a chef and as a person. I was falling in deep.

That winter, I moved in with Claudia and her mom.

Smoked Cod Salad with Frisée
and Soft-Cooked Egg

•

Ribollita Ravioli with Borlotti Beans
and Tuscan Kale

•

Squash Gnocchi with Amaretti
and Mostarda

•

Swordfish Pancetta with Fennel Zeppole

•

Veal Liver Raviolini with Figs
and Caramelized Onions

•

Oil-Poached Black Bass with Fresh Peas
and Baby Tomatoes

•

Vanilla Crespelle with Caramelized
Pineapple Sauce

•

Bomboloni with Vin Santo Crema

•

Cherry Shortcake with Cherry Meringata

Smoked Cod Salad with Frisée and
Soft-Cooked Egg (next page)

SMOKED COD SALAD with
FRISÉE and SOFT-COOKED EGG

MAKES 6 SERVINGS

1½ pounds (680 g) skinless cod fillet, cut into 4 to 5 pieces of equal thickness

2 tablespoons (6 g) minced chives

3 tablespoons (45 ml) olive oil

3 tablespoons (42 g) unsalted butter, melted

Juice and zest of ½ lemon

Salt and freshly ground black pepper

6 large eggs

2 ounces (57 g) pancetta, cut into ⅛-inch (3-mm) cubes

1 tablespoon sherry vinegar

2 small heads frisée (about 3 ounces/ 85 g total), cleaned and torn into bite-size pieces

Maldon sea salt for garnish

Marco Pierre White used to serve a sunny-side up egg on panfried whitefish. I loved that. The idea here is similar, but the egg is soft-cooked in the shell. You peel off the top third of the cooked white to expose the egg yolk. When you slide your fork into it, the yolk flows out onto the fish, enriching it like a ready-made sauce. With some pancetta in the frisée salad, it makes a salty, crunchy, sharp, sweet, bitter, creamy start to a meal.

Set up a smoker by putting 1 cup (50 g) of wood shavings or small chips, preferably oak or apple, in the bottom of a roasting pan and setting the pan on the stovetop so that the chips sit directly over the heat of the burner but the rest of the pan is not over the heat. Put a rack in the pan and line the rack with parchment paper. Heat the wood shavings over medium heat until they start to smoke. Set the fish on the paper away from the heat, cover the pan tightly with foil, and smoke until no longer translucent in the center, 15 to 20 minutes, making sure the wood shavings emit smoke the entire time.

Transfer the cod and its juices to a mixing bowl and add the chives, oil, butter, and lemon juice and zest. Season with salt and pepper and mix gently, adding more oil, if necessary, to make the mixture moist and glistening.

Bring 2 quarts (2 L) of water to a boil in a medium saucepan and fill a large bowl with ice water. Carefully add the eggs to the boiling water and boil for exactly 5 minutes. Immediately transfer with a slotted spoon to the ice water and let stand until cooled, about 3 minutes. When cooled, carefully remove the shell from each egg. Using a paring knife, lightly score the white around the more narrowly pointed end of the egg, and carefully peel off the white with your fingers just enough to expose the top one-quarter of the yolk without breaking it.

Cook the pancetta in a sauté pan over medium heat until lightly browned, 5 to 7 minutes. Pour the rendered fat into a measuring cup and measure out 3 tablespoons (45 ml). Discard the rest. Put the vinegar in a medium bowl and whisk in the rendered fat in a slow, steady steam until incorporated and thickened. Season with salt and pepper and then add the frisée and pancetta, reserving a few pancetta bits for garnish. Toss to coat.

For each serving, put a 6-inch (15 cm) ring mold on a small salad plate. Fill half of the ring mold with the cod mixture, forming a semicircle. Fill the other half of the mold with the frisée salad. Unmold the mixtures and place an egg directly on top. Sprinkle with the remaining pancetta bits, black pepper, and Maldon sea salt. For a more casual presentation, divide the salad and cod among plates and top each serving with an egg.

RIBOLLITA RAVIOLI with BORLOTTI BEANS and TUSCAN KALE

At La Brughiera, I noticed that Paolo Begnini would do the unexpected, riffing on classic preparations with a little twist of his own. I did the same thing here. *Ribollita* is a classic Tuscan soup made from scraps of meat, "reboiled" the next day with vegetables, and served in ceramic bowls. I simply made pasta out of the same ingredients. The beans are simmered, mashed, and simply seasoned for the pasta filling. Vegetables are stewed in their own broth, with some extra olive oil to thicken the broth. I didn't introduce any new flavors. This is just ribollita in a different form. The ravioli freeze well, so you can enjoy them again, or just cut the recipe in half to make less.

MAKES 10 TO 12 SERVINGS

Ravioli and Filling:

2 cups (12 ounces/340 g) dried borlotti (cranberry) beans, soaked overnight in water to cover

1 ounce chopped prosciutto scraps or pieces

1 medium-size yellow onion, chopped (1¼ cups/200 g)

2 medium-size carrots, chopped (1¼ cups/150 g)

2 large ribs celery, chopped (1¼ cups/125 g)

Salt and freshly ground black pepper

1 large egg

1¾ ounces (50 g) Parmesan cheese, grated (½ cup)

1 pound (450 g) Egg Pasta Dough (page 282), rolled into 4 sheets, each about ¹⁄₃₂ inch (0.8 mm) thick

Tuscan Kale:

3 tablespoons (45 ml) extra-virgin olive oil

1 large yellow onion, minced (2 cups/320 g)

4 medium-size carrots, minced (2 cups/250 g)

4 medium-size ribs celery, minced (2 cups/200 g)

1 garlic clove, smashed

2 bunches Tuscan kale (about 8 ounces/227 g total), trimmed of thick stems and chopped

2 cups (475 ml) dry white wine

1¼ cups (300 g) canned plum tomatoes, preferably San Marzano, cored and crushed by hand

1 ounce (28 g) chopped prosciutto scraps or pieces

Leaves from 2 sprigs fresh rosemary

Salt and freshly ground black pepper

4 tablespoons (57 g) unsalted butter

¼ cup (60 ml) extra-virgin olive oil

3½ ounces (100 g) Parmesan cheese, grated (1 cup), plus some for garnish

(continued on next page)

For the ravioli and filling: Drain the soaked beans and cover by 1 inch (2.5 cm) with fresh water in a medium saucepan. Wrap the prosciutto, onion, carrots, and celery in a large piece of cheesecloth and submerge in the pot. Cover and bring to a boil over high heat, and then lower the heat to medium, uncover, and cook until the beans are tender, 45 to 55 minutes. Let cool slightly, and then squeeze the cheesecloth bundle to press the liquid from the vegetables, discarding the bundle. Use a slotted spoon to transfer the beans to a blender in batches, pureeing them until smooth and adding just enough of the cooking liquid so that the beans will puree. The mixture should be thick like hummus and stick to a spoon turned upside down. Transfer to a bowl and stir in the egg and Parmesan. Season to taste with salt and pepper and mix well. Spoon the mixture into a resealable plastic bag and refrigerate for at least 1 hour or up to 2 days.

Lay a pasta sheet on a lightly floured work surface and dust with flour. Trim the ends to make them square, then fold the dough in half lengthwise and make a small notch at the center to mark it. Open the sheet so it lies flat again and spritz with water. Cut a corner from the bag of filling and squeeze the filling in ¾-inch (2-cm)-diameter balls in two rows along the length of the pasta, leaving a 1-inch (2.5-cm) margin around each ball and stopping at the middle of the sheet. Lift up the empty side of the pasta sheet and fold it over to cover the balls of filling. Gently press the pasta around each ball of filling to seal. Use a 2½-inch (6-cm) round, fluted ravioli cutter or a similar size biscuit cutter to cut the ravioli. Repeat with the remaining pasta dough and filling. Place the ravioli in a single layer on parchment paper and freeze until firm, then keep frozen in a resealable plastic bag for up to 1 week before cooking. You should have about 120 ravioli.

For the Tuscan kale: Heat the oil in a large saucepan over medium heat. Add the onion, carrots, celery, and garlic, and cook until the carrots are soft but not browned, 6 to 8 minutes. Add the kale, wine, tomatoes, prosciutto, rosemary, and just enough water to cover the kale. Stew over low heat until the kale is very tender, 12 to 15 minutes. Season to taste with salt and pepper.

To finish: Bring a large pot of salted water to a boil. Add ten to twelve ravioli per serving, and cook just until tender, 4 to 5 minutes. Work in batches, if necessary, to prevent overcrowding.

Meanwhile, heat the butter and oil in a large, deep sauté pan over medium heat. Add the kale mixture and ¾ cup (175 ml) of pasta water. Stir the ingredients until the sauce is creamy and then add the Parmesan and cooked pasta in batches. Swirl the pasta and sauce together in the pan until the sauce coats the pasta. Divide among plates and garnish with Parmesan.

SQUASH GNOCCHI with AMARETTI and MOSTARDA

Claudia's favorite dish at La Brughiera is porcini-stuffed squash gnocchi with Parmigiano fonduta. They use almond flour in the gnocchi dough, roll it out, and then stuff it with porcini. Whenever we eat there, she asks me to call ahead and request the dish. I've tried numerous times but I just can't replicate it. So I came up with my own squash gnocchi flavored with crushed amaretti cookies and *mostarda* (mustard-flavored fruit relish). I like them both.

Melt 4 tablespoons (57 g) of the butter in a large deep sauté pan over medium heat. Lower the heat to medium-low and add the diced squash. Season with salt and pepper, cover, and cook for 1 hour, stirring every 10 minutes or so to make sure the squash does not brown. Uncover and cook until the pan goes dry and the squash is tender but not browned, 10 to 15 minutes more. The squash should be very dry. Transfer it to the bowl of a stand mixer fitted with the paddle attachment, and mix on medium speed until the squash is fairly smooth, 2 to 3 minutes. Mix in the egg, flour, breadcrumbs, amaretti crumbs, and ½ cup (50 g) of the Parmesan on low speed, scraping down the bowl as necessary. The mixture should be moist like wet cookie dough. Flour your hands, pinch off chunks the size of large marbles, coat them in flour, and then roll into balls between your palms.

Bring a large pot of salted water to a boil. Add the gnocchi, and cook until they are tender and float, 5 to 6 minutes.

Meanwhile, combine the remaining 4 tablespoons (57 g) of butter and sage in a sauté pan over medium heat. Cook until the sage is lightly fried, 2 to 3 minutes. Add about ½ cup (120 ml) of gnocchi cooking water and simmer, shaking the pan vigorously, until slightly thickened, about 5 minutes. Stir in the mostarda.

Drain the gnocchi and divide among plates. Pour on the sauce and sprinkle with the remaining Parmesan.

MAKES 4 TO 6 SERVINGS

4 ounces (1 stick/113 g) unsalted butter, divided

1 medium-size butternut or longneck squash (about 2 pounds/1 kg), peeled, seeded, and diced (about 6 cups)

Salt and freshly ground black pepper

1 large egg

1 cup (125 g) *tipo* 00 flour (see page 277) or all-purpose flour, plus about 1 cup (125 g) for dusting

½ cup (54 g) plain, dry breadcrumbs

3 tablespoons (22 g) amaretti cookie crumbs

2¾ ounces (75 g) Parmesan cheese, grated (¾ cup), divided

8 large sage leaves

¼ cup (60 ml) minced mostarda

SWORDFISH PANCETTA with FENNEL ZEPPOLE

Traditional Italian bacon, pancetta, is made with pork belly. But why not use other bellies? Most animals store enough fat in their bellies to stand up to the curing process. When swordfish belly is cured, it slices up into these beautiful pale pink ribbons with a rich mouthfeel like lardo. Some shaved fennel and a golden citrus vinaigrette make it a gorgeous plate. Ask for swordfish belly at any fishmonger's. It's usually a throwaway part of the fish, so they'll be happy to sell it to you. Just call your fish market ahead of time and ask them to save the swordfish belly for you. If they don't have any swordfish in, try tuna belly or salmon belly.

For the swordfish pancetta: Rinse the swordfish belly and pat it dry. Combine the kosher salt, sugar, curing salt, fennel seeds, coriander, red pepper, and garlic in a medium bowl. Add to the swordfish to the bowl, patting in the cure to completely cover the fish on all sides. Cover the bowl and refrigerate for 36 hours. Remove the fish from the bowl, rinse it, and pat it dry. Refrigerate in a covered container for up to 1 month.

For the fennel zeppole: Combine 1 cup (235 ml) of water with the milk, sugar, fennel seeds, salt, and pepper, and butter in a medium saucepan and bring up to a boil over medium-high heat. Whisk in the flour until incorporated, and stir with a wooden spoon until the dough forms a ball and a skin forms on the inside of the pot. Transfer the dough to a mixer fitted with the paddle attachment and add the eggs, one at a time, mixing on low speed until each egg is incorporated. On a floured work surface with floured hands, pinch up golf ball–size balls of dough. You should get about thirty-two. Roll each ball into a log and gently twist each log in opposite directions from the center into a twisted log 5 to 6 inches (13 to 15 cm) long. Form the twisted log into a circle, but overlap the ends of the circle to make an X, pinching the dough gently at the X. Each zeppola should look like a loop with an X, kind of like a pretzel that hasn't been twisted at the X. The zeppole can be transferred to a shallow, parchment-lined container, covered, and refrigerated for up to 2 hours.

Heat the oil to 350°F (175°C) in a deep fryer or large, heavy pot. Deep-fry the zeppole until golden brown, 2 to 3 minutes, adjusting the heat to maintain a constant 350°F (175°C) temperature. Drain on paper towels and immediately season with salt.

To serve: Pour the citrus vinaigrette into a bowl. Trim the fennel, discarding the tough white core but reserving the fronds. Shave the fennel lengthwise on a mandoline into thin strips. Add to the vinaigrette, along with the parsley, and season with salt. Toss to combine.

Arrange the shaved fennel in a single layer on a wooden platter or plates. Very thinly slice the swordfish and drape over the fennel. Place the zeppole in the center and garnish the plate with small fennel fronds. Drizzle the swordfish with the remaining vinaigrette in the bowl.

Note

If you want to make eight servings instead of sixteen, just cut the zeppole recipe in half. But leave the pancetta as is. Trust me. You'll be slicing off ribbons of swordfish pancetta almost every day and dipping them in the citrus vinaigrette.

MAKES 16 SERVINGS

Swordfish Pancetta:

1 pound (450 g) swordfish belly

5 teaspoons (14 g) kosher salt

½ teaspoon (2 g) granulated sugar

¼ teaspoon (1.5 g) curing salt #2 (see page 277)

¼ teaspoon (0.5 g) toasted and ground fennel seeds

¼ teaspoon (0.5 g) ground coriander

⅛ teaspoon (0.25 g) ground red pepper

½ small garlic clove, pressed into a paste

Fennel Zeppole:

1 cup (235 ml) whole milk

¼ cup (50 g) granulated sugar

1 tablespoon (6 g) toasted and coarsely ground fennel seeds

½ teaspoon (3 g) salt

¼ teaspoon (0.5 g) freshly ground black pepper

4 ounces (1 stick/113 g) unsalted butter

2¼ cups (280 g) *tipo* 00 flour (see page 277) or all-purpose flour

4 large eggs

Oil, for frying

To Serve:

1 cup (235 ml) citrus vinaigrette (page 277)

2 fennel bulbs, with fronds

¼ cup (15 g) chopped fresh flat-leaf parsley

Salt

VEAL LIVER RAVIOLINI with FIGS and CARAMELIZED ONIONS

I had been making liver pâtés for a while and always folded in butter to help them keep their shape. It seemed like it would make an awesome pasta filling, so I heated some pâté in a pan and it melted nice and slow. Perfect. When you put a fork into this raviolini, it's super-creamy, plus you get some sweetness from the onions and figs. You could make this with duck liver or chicken liver if you can't find veal.

MAKES 4 TO 6 SERVINGS

Veal Liver Raviolini:

1¼ pounds (567 g) veal liver

1 ounce (28 g) pancetta, cut into ½-inch (1.25-cm) cubes

1 small yellow onion, chopped (⅔ cup/106 g)

Leaves from 1 large sprig fresh rosemary

1½ tablespoons (22 ml) brandy

8 ounces (2 sticks/227 g) cold unsalted butter, cut into cubes

1¾ ounces (50 g) Parmesan cheese, grated (½ cup)

Salt and freshly ground black pepper

8 ounces (227 g) Egg Pasta Dough (page 282), rolled into 2 sheets, each about ¹⁄₃₂ inch (0.8 mm) thick

Figs and Caramelized Onions:

¼ cup (60 ml) olive oil

5 medium-size yellow onions, cut into half-moon slices (6½ cups/1 kg)

2 ounces (57 g) lardo, cut into strips

4 tablespoons (57 g) unsalted butter

1 pound (450 g) small fresh figs

1½ teaspoons (7 ml) balsamic vinegar

2 tablespoons (8 g) chopped fresh rosemary

Salt and freshly ground black pepper

1 ounce (28 g) Parmesan cheese, grated (⅓ cup) for garnish

For the veal liver raviolini: Cut the veal liver into pieces about two fingers wide and set aside. Cook the pancetta in a large sauté pan over medium heat until some of the fat renders and the pancetta looks translucent, 3 to 4 minutes. Transfer the pancetta to a bowl. Raise the heat to medium-high and when the rendered fat is hot, add the veal liver and sear until nicely browned on all sides, 6 to 8 minutes total. Return the pancetta to the pan, along with the onion and rosemary, and cook until the onion is translucent and the liver is cooked through, 3 to 4 minutes more. Pour in the brandy, lower the heat to medium, and cook until the liquid reduces in volume by about three-quarters, 4 to 5 minutes. Remove from the heat and transfer the mixture to a bowl; cover and refrigerate until very cold, at least 1 hour.

Combine the veal liver mixture and cold butter cubes in a food processor, and puree until very smooth, stopping to scrape down the sides a few times. For the smoothest texture, pass the mixture through a tammy cloth (woolen strainer), triple layer of cheesecloth, or fine-mesh sieve. Add the Parmesan, season with salt and pepper, and pulse briefly to combine. Spoon the filling into a resealable plastic bag and refrigerate for at least 1 hour or up to 1 day.

Lay a pasta sheet on a lightly floured work surface and dust with flour. Trim the ends to make them square, then fold the dough in half lengthwise and make a small notch at the center to mark it. Open the sheet so it lies flat again and spritz with water. Cut off a small corner of the resealable plastic bag so you can pipe the filling on the pasta. Beginning at the left-hand side, pipe two rows of filling along the length of the pasta, stopping at the center of the sheet. For each row, pipe rectangular strips of filling about 1½ inches (4 cm) long by ½ inch (1 cm) wide with a ½-inch (1 cm) margin around each strip. Lift up the right-hand side of the pasta sheet and fold it over to cover the strips of filling. Gently press the pasta around each strip of filling to seal. Use a fluted ravioli cutter or sharp knife to cut the ravioli into rectangles about 2½ inches (6 cm) long by 1½ inches (4 cm) wide. Repeat with the remaining pasta dough and filling. You should have about thirty-two raviolini.

For the figs and caramelized onions: Heat the olive oil in a large sauté pan over medium-high heat. When hot, add the onions, shaking the pan to distribute the hot oil. Lower the heat to medium and cook, stirring frequently, until the onions shed their water and go from translucent to light golden to deep caramel brown, 30 to 40 minutes total. To keep the onions from browning unevenly, stir in a little water now and then. Scrape into a bowl and set aside.

Put the lardo and butter in the pan, and cook over medium heat until the lardo renders its fat and the butter turns golden brown, 10 to 12 minutes. Cut the figs length-wise into quarters (or eighths if the figs are large) and add to the pan, along with the caramelized onions, vinegar, and rosemary. Season with salt and pepper to taste and keep warm over very low heat.

When ready to serve, bring a large pot of salted water to a boil. Drop in the raviolini, quickly return the water to a boil, and cook the pasta until tender yet firm, about 2 minutes. Use a spider strainer or slotted spoon to transfer the raviolini to plates.

Spoon some warm sauce over each plate and sprinkle with Parmesan.

OIL-POACHED BLACK BASS with FRESH PEAS and BABY TOMATOES

MAKES 4 SERVINGS

Bass and Poaching Oil:

4 black bass fillets, skin on, about 6 ounces (170 g) each

3 cups (750 ml) grapeseed oil

1½ cups (375 ml) extra-virgin olive oil

10 to 15 sprigs fresh thyme

3 bay leaves

Peas and Tomatoes:

1½ pounds (680 g) English peas, shelled

2 cups (340 g) baby grape or pear tomatoes

1 cup (235 ml) extra-virgin olive oil, divided

4 to 6 spring onions, trimmed and julienned

Salt and freshly ground black pepper

¼ cup (60 ml) freshly squeezed lemon juice

2 teaspoons (2.5 g) torn fresh tarragon

2 teaspoons (2. 5 g) torn fresh chervil

Maldon sea salt for garnish

Poaching fish in olive oil is a genius technique. It's something Paolo Begnini did all the time. The oil keeps the fish moist but doesn't make it taste watery, as poaching in water sometimes does. When I got back to the States and started cooking at Osteria, we were getting in these big, beautiful black bass in the spring. They had gorgeous, clear flesh and a clean, briny aroma. I knew exactly what to do with them. With spring onions, peas, and first-of-the-season tomatoes, this is very much a springtime dish. But if you can't find black bass, you could also make it with branzino, wild striped bass, or even snapper. It helps to start heating both the oil and the blanching water at the same time, so the overall timing of the dish works out.

For the bass and poaching oil: Rinse the bass, and pour the oils into a deep sauté pan big enough to hold all of the fish. Roll the thyme and bay in cheesecloth and wrap and tie with kitchen string. Add the sachet to the poaching oil and bring the mixture to 220°F (105°C) over medium heat. Add the bass; the oil temperature will drop. Adjust the heat so that the oil temperature stays at 190°F (88°C). Poach the bass at 190°F until just a little moist and translucent in the center, about 130°F (54°C) internal temperature, 7 minutes or so. Carefully transfer the fish to paper towels to drain.

For the peas and tomatoes: Meanwhile, bring a medium pot of salted water to a boil and fill a large bowl with ice water. Add the peas and blanch for 1½ minutes. Transfer to the ice water to stop the cooking. When cool, use your fingers to slip the peas from their skins. You should have about 1½ cups (218 g) shelled peas.

Drop the tomatoes into the boiling water and blanch for 10 seconds. Transfer to the ice water to stop the cooking. When cool, slip the tomatoes from their skins. Set aside.

Heat ¼ cup (60 ml) of the oil in a medium sauté pan over medium heat. Add the onions, and cook until soft but not browned, 3 to 4 minutes. Add the skinned tomatoes and warm through, 1 to 2 minutes. Season with salt and pepper.

In another pan, heat the remaining ¾ cup (175 ml) of oil and the lemon juice over medium heat. Add the peas and herbs and warm through, 1 to 2 minutes. Season with salt and pepper.

Spread the onions in the center of each plate. Place the fish on top and the tomatoes around the fish. Spoon the peas over the top and garnish with sea salt and black pepper.

VANILLA CRESPELLE with
CARAMELIZED PINEAPPLE SAUCE

MAKES 12 TO 14 SERVINGS

Crespelle:

8 large eggs

2 vanilla beans, split and scraped

4 cups (500 g) *tipo* 00 flour (see page 277) or all-purpose flour

4 cups (1 L) whole milk

Grapeseed oil, for cooking the crespelle

Caramelized Pineapple Sauce:

8 ounces (2 sticks/227 g) unsalted butter

1 pineapple, peeled, cored, and diced small

2 cups (400 g) granulated sugar

½ cup (120 ml) dark rum

1½ cups (375 ml) heavy cream

Confectioners' sugar, for dusting

My wife is the queen of crêpes. She can make them with her eyes closed. In culinary school, I was taught to make crêpes with barely any color. But she gets the pan nice and hot and the crêpes get beautifully browned all over. When I tasted her crêpes (called *crespelle* in Italy), they had so much more character than the ones I was used to making. The real star here is the sauce, made from diced pineapple cooked in butter until the juice evaporates and the pineapple turns deep amber. The caramelized flavor is unreal. Just watch your eyebrows: when you add the rum; it will flambé. I made a generous yield here because the crespelle and sauce both keep well—and they're so good you might have two servings.

For the crespelle: In a medium bowl, whisk together the eggs and vanilla. Whisk in the flour to make a very thick batter that is difficult to whisk. Gradually whisk in the milk so that the batter is thin enough to just barely coat the back of a spoon. Let stand for 5 minutes.

Heat an 8-inch (20-cm)-diameter pan with a little grapeseed oil over medium heat until it's almost smoking. If you have two pans, you can cook two crespelle at once. Pour out any excess oil, and then, holding the pan handle, pour in 3 to 4 tablespoons (45 to 60 ml) of batter, and quickly tilt the pan in a circle to spread the batter as thinly as possible across the bottom of the pan. Cook until the crespelle is set on top and the edges are lightly browned and starting to curl, 1 to 2 minutes. Flip, and cook the other side for 1 minute. If using immediately, stack the crespelle on a plate. If you are making the crespelle ahead of time, stack them between sheets of waxed paper, let cool, then refrigerate for up to 4 days or freeze for up to 4 weeks.

For the caramelized pineapple sauce: Melt the butter in a large saucepan over medium-high heat. Add the pineapple, and cook until most of the juice evaporates and the pineapple turns light golden brown, about 15 minutes. Stir in the sugar, and cook until it turns a light amber color (355°F/180°C on a candy thermometer), about 5 minutes. Stand back and add the rum; it will sputter, may well ignite, and the sugar will be extremely hot. When the sputtering or flames die down, carefully stir in the cream, remove the pan from the heat, and let cool.

For each serving, heat about ⅓ cup (90 ml) of sauce in a sauté pan. Add two crespelle, and cook until heated through, about a minute. The crespelle will fold over themselves in the pan, which is fine. Use tongs to fold the crêpes into quarters and transfer to a plate. Pour the sauce over the top and dust with confectioners' sugar.

BOMBOLONI with VIN SANTO CREMA

Vin santo is a Tuscan dessert wine that ranges in sweetness from bone dry to sherry-like to Madeira-like. It's usually enjoyed with *cantucci* (almond cookies similar to biscotti) for dipping into the wine to soak it up. When I did a dinner in Philadelphia for a regular Tuscan customer named Paolo Paoletti, this was the dessert. I stuffed the doughnuts with vin santo *crema*. He loved it. But if you don't want to go through the trouble of stuffing the doughnuts, you could serve them with the crema on the side.

For the starter: Use a wooden spoon to stir together the fresh yeast, sugar, flour, and milk in the bowl of a stand mixer, breaking up the yeast. If using active dry yeast, sprinkle it over the warm milk in the bowl, let stand for 5 minutes or until foamy, then stir in the remaining starter ingredients. Cover loosely and let stand at room temperature for 30 to 35 minutes.

For the dough: Add the sugar, eggs, and butter to the starter and fit the dough hook onto the mixer. Mix on medium speed until combined, 1 to 2 minutes. With the mixer running, gradually add the flour and salt and mix until the dough is sticky and stretchy, 5 to 6 minutes. Transfer the dough to a lightly buttered bowl, cover, and let rise in a warm spot until doubled in size, about 1½ hours.

Turn the dough out onto a floured work surface and pat or roll the dough to an even ½-inch (1.25-cm) thickness. Use a 2-inch (5-cm) round cookie cutter to punch out eighteen to twenty disks. Set them on a parchment-lined sheet pan, cover loosely, and refrigerate until partially risen, about 1 hour.

For the vin santo crema: Sift together the flour and sugar into a small bowl. Whisk in the egg yolks until smooth. Fill a bowl with ice water.

Combine the milk, vin santo, and vanilla in a medium saucepan and bring to a boil over medium-high heat. Don't worry if the mixture looks curdled; it will become smooth when you whisk in the eggs. Temper in the egg mixture by whisking about ¼ cup (60 ml) of the milk into the eggs until incorporated, then another ¼ cup (60 ml). Pour the mixture back into the saucepan and set over low heat, whisking to combine everything and cooking gently until thickened, 5 to 7 minutes, whisking constantly.

Cool the pan bottom by setting it into the ice water, whisking the crema to cool it down. When barely warm, press plastic wrap onto the top of the crema and refrigerate until cold, at least 1 hour or up to 2 days. When cold, spoon the crema into a pastry bag or resealable plastic bag.

To serve: Heat the oil to 350°F (175°C) in a deep fryer or deep pot. Add the dough disks in batches to prevent overcrowding and fry until golden brown, 3 to 4 minutes, flipping the doughnuts to fry all sides and adjusting the heat to maintain a constant 350°F (175°C) oil temperature. Use a spider strainer or slotted spoon to transfer the doughnuts to paper towels to drain.

When cool enough to handle, poke a ¼-inch (6-mm) hole into the side of each bombolone, snip a corner from the bag, and pipe the crema into the bomboloni until stuffed. Roll the stuffed bomboloni in sugar and serve.

MAKES 6 TO 8 SERVINGS

Starter:

1½ packed tablespoons fresh yeast (28 g), or 1 tablespoon plus ¾ teaspoon (15 g) active dry yeast

2½ teaspoons (10 g) granulated sugar

2½ tablespoons (21 g) bread flour

⅓ cup plus 2 tablespoons (110 g) warm whole milk

Dough:

½ cup (100 g) granulated sugar

3 large eggs

⅓ cup (90 ml) unsalted butter, melted and cooled

3⅔ cups (500 g) bread flour

1¼ teaspoons (7.5 g) salt

Vin Santo Crema:

7 tablespoons (54 g) *tipo* 00 flour (see page 277) or all-purpose flour

6 tablespoons (75 g) granulated sugar

6 large egg yolks

1½ cups (375 ml) whole milk

½ cup (120 ml) vin santo

½ vanilla bean, split and scraped

To Serve:

Oil, for frying

¾ cup (175 ml) granulated sugar, for dusting

CHERRY SHORTCAKE with CHERRY MERINGATA

Every pizza place in Italy serves meringata. It's usually something they buy premade from a company called Bindi. *Meringata* is a crunchy cake of meringue stuffed with *fiordilatte* gelato (basic white gelato) and *frutti di bosco* (mixed berries). The first time I had it was in Villa d'Almè and it has since become a favorite dessert that my wife and I share. We usually order two of them! I don't know what kind of preservatives they add to make the cake and ice cream last. My meringue cake kept melting in the freezer! So now I chop up most of the meringue and crumble it over the dessert. There are several components here but they can all be made ahead and the final result is absolutely fantastic.

For the cherry meringata: Heat the oven to 190°F (88°C) and line a baking sheet with parchment paper. Whisk together the egg whites, sugar, salt, and vanilla in the top of a double boiler or in a heatproof bowl set over a saucepan of simmering water. Gently heat the ingredients to 140°F (60°C), beating with a whisk or electric mixer on medium-low speed, 4 to 5 minutes. Then whisk or whip the mixture in the bowl on high speed until medium-stiff peaks form when the beater or whisk is lifted, 2 to 4 minutes. Remove the bowl from the heat and beat on high speed until light and fluffy, 2 minutes more. Spoon the mixture into a resealable plastic bag. Press out the air, then twist the bag around the mixture, snip off a corner, and pipe the mixture into 2-inch (5-cm)-diameter mounds on the prepared baking sheet. Bake for 8 hours or overnight until the meringue is crisp and dry. Remove from the oven and let cool completely. Store in a covered container in a cool, dry place for up to 2 days. (Avoid making the meringue in a humid environment, as it will become sticky during cooling.)

Make the Fiordilatte Gelato as directed. When the ice cream mixture is almost finished churning and nearly firm, chop up the oven-dried meringue. Add 2 cups (475 ml) of the chopped meringue to the ice cream mixture, letting it become incorporated into the mixture. Continue freezing according to the manufacturer's directions, then store the gelato in the freezer until firm, at least 2 hours.

For the polenta shortcake: Preheat the oven to 350°F (175°C). Cream the butter, sugar, and vanilla in a stand mixer on medium speed until light and fluffy, 3 to 4 minutes. Add the eggs and egg yolks, one at a time, letting each become incorporated before adding the next. Whisk together the flour, polenta, baking powder, and salt in a small bowl. Change to low speed and slowly beat the flour mixture into the egg mixture just until it is incorporated.

Spread the batter on a half sheet pan (17 x 12 inches/43 x 30 cm) and bake until set and golden brown, 12 to 14 minutes. Remove from the oven and let cool in the pan on a rack.

For the cherry sauce: Pit the cherries and place them in a medium saucepan. Add the glucose syrup, sugar, and ½ cup (120 ml) of water. Bring to a boil over high heat and boil until the mixture thickens slightly and reaches 220°F (104°C) on a candy thermometer, 10 to 12 minutes.

To assemble, cut the shortcake into 3-inch (7.5-cm) circles or squares with a biscuit cutter or knife. You should have twelve to sixteen pieces. Set one piece on each plate. Add a generous layer of the gelato, a spoonful of the cherry sauce, and some of the remaining chopped meringue. Top with another piece of shortcake, compressing gently, and a generous spoonful of cherry sauce. Scatter some of the remaining chopped meringue over the top and around the plate.

MAKES 6 TO 8 SERVINGS

Cherry Meringata:

7 large egg whites

2¼ cups (450 g) granulated sugar

Pinch of salt

1 vanilla bean, split and scraped

5 cups (1.25 L) Fiordilatte Gelato (page 287), ready to churn

Polenta Shortcake:

6 ounces (1½ sticks/170 g) unsalted butter, softened

¾ cup plus 2 tablespoons (175 g) granulated sugar

½ vanilla bean, split and scraped

3 large eggs, at room temperature

10 large egg yolks, at room temperature

¾ cup plus 1 tablespoon (100 g) *tipo* 00 flour (see page 277) or all-purpose flour

⅔ cup (105 g) coarse yellow cornmeal (polenta)

1 teaspoon (4.5 g) baking powder

½ teaspoon (3 g) salt

Cherry Sauce:

1 pound (450 g) fresh cherries

¾ cup (175 ml) glucose syrup or light corn syrup

½ cup (100 g) granulated sugar

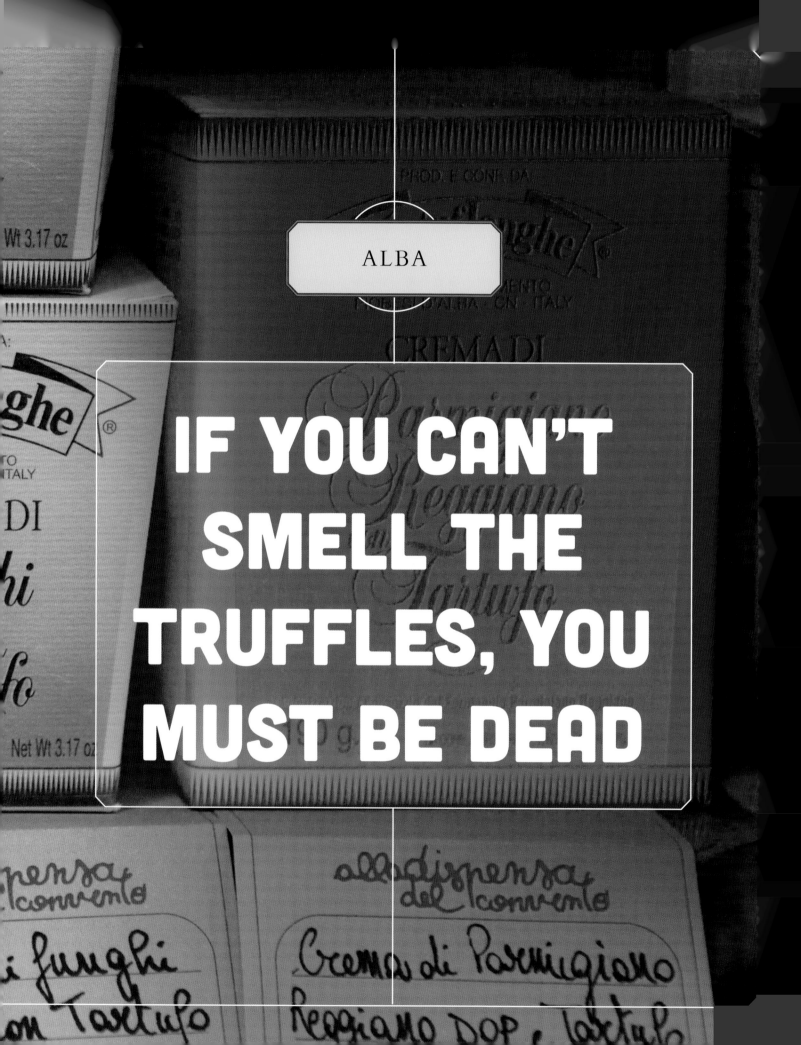

EARTHY, RICH HAZELNUTS FROM PIEMONTE. COARSE GROUND POLENTA FROM LOMBARDY. DARK ROASTED COFFEE FROM SICILY. BRACING BLACK LICORICE FROM PUGLIA. AT THE SALONE DEL GUSTO, A BIANNUAL SLOW FOOD FESTIVAL IN TURIN, EVERY REGION OF ITALY HAS ITS OWN SECTION. IT'S LIKE AN ITALIAN VERSION OF DISNEY'S EPCOT THEME PARK BUT LIGHT-YEARS BETTER WITH FOOD PRODUCERS WHO ACTUALLY LIVE AND WORK IN THAT REGION.

Claudia schooled me in each region. "Taste this," she said, holding out a slab of glistening, fatty porchetta from Lazio. And later, a shard of savory pecorino from Sardinia. And then a sip of Jermann Vintage Tunina, a golden, honey-scented wine from Fruili. She wanted me to taste how Sardinian pecorino is less salty than Pecorino Romano. How olive oils from different parts of the country have completely different aromas. Every two years in October, thousands of people from all over the globe come to the Salone del Gusto, a worldwide celebration of traditional, local foods that's open to the public. The first year I went was also the first year of Terra Madre (literally, "Mother Earth"), an off-shoot of Slow Food International that promotes sustainable food communities around the world.

Tasting, sharing, and talking about amazing food for half a day was a mind-blowing, palate-bending experience. But we hadn't even had lunch yet. Claudia and I met up with Jeff Benjamin, a partner at Vetri Ristorante in Philadelphia, who was attending some wine classes at Slow Food that year. We'd planned to have lunch together in Alba sometime in the afternoon. Why Alba? Because it was truffle season, and white truffles are the epitome of slow food: a rare find, difficult to capture as convenience food, and prized from only a few places around the world, most of all, Alba.

I drove Claudia's red Mini Cooper south from the bustling city of Turin through the vineyard-laden hills of Piemont to the tiny medieval town of Alba. During the fall, you can tell you're close just by opening the windows. The unmistakable musk of truffles seeps into the car and captivates your senses. Alba holds truffle fairs every weekend from late September to mid-November. When you step outside your car and into Piazza Garibaldi, the truffle aroma completely engulfs you. The "white diamonds of the kitchen" are everywhere, displayed on cloth-covered tables, and ranging in size from marbles to golf balls to grapefruits. All the vendors have scales. The goods are handled with care. And even a tiny amount is very expensive—about $115 (85 euros) per ounce (28 g). There's almost something illicit about it, as if they're selling some kind of drug.

During truffle season, the Alba streets also fill up with aromas of wood smoke, grilled sausages, pungent cheeses such as Castelmagno, roasting chestnuts in iron pans, and steaming cinnamon-scented wine. Just an hour earlier, we'd gorged ourselves at Salone del Gusto, but thank God we had a lunch reservation. During festival weekends, you won't get in anywhere without one.

We walked further into the old city, up Via Cavour, a V-shaped cobblestone street that leads to Piazza Risorgimento, the main town square. In the square, dozens more vendors sold torrone, porcini, salame, pears, and more truffles in one place than I had ever seen in my life. We finally arrived at Osteria dell'Arco through a stone archway in Piazza Savona.

The glass door proudly displayed a Slow Food snail logo, a good sign.

To start, I ordered veal tartare. It came mixed with olive oil and black pepper, rock salt, and, of course, white truffles. Jeff ordered vitello tonnato and Claudia had warm bagna cauda. Our pasta course was tajarin, a Piedmont specialty hand cut into little strands slightly wider than angel hair. The pasta was yellow-orange like the morning sun, and I asked the waiter how it was made. "We use forty egg yolks per kilo of flour," he said. No wonder. The Alba chickens feed only on insects and grass, so the yolks become bright orange—sometimes red. They toss the tajarin with nothing but pasta water, olive oil, butter, and cheese. Simple. The waiter came to the table with a scale, a few fresh white truffles, and a truffle slicer. He weighed the truffle and started slicing it over the tajarin until I said, "Stop." I was so hungry for truffles I didn't want him to stop at all! In Alba, the cost is about half of what it is in the United States, so we splurged and kept the truffles coming. We had roasted rabbit with polenta and truffles. Sliced roast duck with radicchio and truffles. It was a truffle orgy! We drank a bottle of La Spinetta Barbaresco, one of my favorite Piedmont wines, and watched the festival through the restaurant window. "They use dogs to hunt truffles in Italy," Jeff told me. "In France, they use pigs. But in Italy, the pigs just eat the truffles when they find them." I laughed and added, "That's because Italian truffles taste better!" Nods of agreement all around.

Back out on the streets, vendors held their prize specimens to the nose of customers as they've been doing for decades. Watching them and thinking about all the incredible foods we'd eaten that day, I came to respect the local products of Italy more than ever. Nowhere else in the world can you experience white truffles like those in Alba. Nowhere else in the world can you experience farinata as you do in Genoa. Nowhere do you find culatello quite as rich and moist as that in the town of Zibello.

Every village in Italy, no matter how small, holds an annual food festival, or *sagra*, to celebrate these foods. Alba has held its truffle sagra every year since 1930. It's how the community pays homage to what grows in the area and displays its local pride, whether it's peaches in Canale, hazelnuts in Cortemilia, rabbits in Brembio, radicchio in Treviso, torrone in Cremona, gnocchi in Castel del Rio, or bilberries in Piazzatorre. It's at the sagre that Italian food really comes to life. Turin's slow food festival is like a mega-sagra for the whole country. So is the cheese festival held in nearby Bra on alternating years. At these food festivals, Italians share what's good and delicious in their little corner of world.

Italy's food festivals helped me understand that food is woven into the cultural fabric of every town, every region, and every country around the world. Sagre are not only a source of pride but also a lifeline to other communities in faraway places. Food is common ground. It's one of the best ways to get to know someone you've never met or somewhere you've never been. As Slow Food's founder, Carlo Petrini, wrote, "Eating someone's food is easier and more immediate than speaking his language."

Truffles and Eggs

•

Veal Tartare with Shaved Artichokes
and White Truffle

•

Porcini Zuppa with Bra Cheese Fonduta

•

Polenta Caramelle with Raschera Fonduta
and Black Truffle

•

Potato Gnocchi with Castelmagno Fonduta
and White Truffle

•

Cotechino-Stuffed Quail with Warm Fig Salad

•

Oven-Roasted Rabbit Porchetta
with Peperonata

•

Bonèt

•

Pistachio Flan

•

Torrone Semifreddo with Candied Chestnuts
and Chocolate Sauce

TRUFFLES and EGGS

If you like scrambled eggs, then you have to try this dish. The truffles send it over the top. And the eggs themselves are the softest, creamiest, most custardy eggs you'll ever taste. They're mixed with fresh truffles and cooked very slowly over the lowest possible heat, while stirred constantly to keep them from scrambling. They come out soft as pudding. It's the best open-face breakfast sandwich ever.

MAKES 2 SERVINGS

2 tablespoons (28 g) unsalted butter

4 large eggs

1 ounce (28 g) finely chopped fresh white truffles, 2 tablespoons (30 ml) white truffle paste, or 2 teaspoons (10 ml) white truffle oil

Salt and freshly ground black pepper

2 slices rustic bread, toasted (preferably on a wood grill)

Melt the butter in a medium nonstick pan over the lowest possible heat. Beat the eggs, truffles, and salt and pepper in a small bowl, and then pour into the pan. Cook very slowly, stirring gently and constantly with a rubber spatula until the eggs get creamy, 8 to 10 minutes. It will take a lot of patience because the eggs should not form large curds. When they are done, they should coat a spoon and look loose and creamy like custard.

Spoon the custard over the toasted bread, and if you want to go crazy, shave on some more fresh truffles.

VEAL TARTARE with SHAVED ARTICHOKES
and WHITE TRUFFLE

Most veal in Italy is called *vitellone* and tastes a little different than US veal. *Vitellone* comes from calves eighteen to twenty months old and the meat is darker and more flavorful than American milk-fed veal—somewhere between US veal and beef. But any type of veal works here. They all taste great with truffles. During truffle season in Alba, you'll find some version of this dish on every trattoria menu.

For the truffle vinaigrette: Combine the oil, lemon juice, and truffle paste in a small blender or food processor and blend until combined (or vigorously whisk together the ingredients in a medium bowl). Season to taste with salt and pepper. Use immediately or refrigerate for up to 2 days.

For the veal tartare and shaved artichokes: Chill four plates in the freezer. Put a small bowl and all the parts of a meat grinder in the freezer for 20 minutes. When the meat grinder is cold, grind the veal in the meat grinder, using the medium (¼-inch/6-mm) die, and catching it in the chilled bowl. Cover tightly with plastic wrap and refrigerate for up to 1 hour.

Snap off and discard all of the fibrous outer leaves from the artichokes. Using a paring knife, peel the artichokes so you are left with only the tender white hearts, which will be about 1 x ½ inch (2.5 x 1.25 cm) in size. Combine the lemon juice with 2 cups (475 ml) of water in a medium bowl. Immediately drop each artichoke heart into the acidulated water to keep them from discoloring. Removing one artichoke heart at a time, thinly slice each lengthwise on a mandoline (an inexpensive handheld one works fine). As you work, put the shaved artichokes back in the acidulated water to prevent discoloration.

Drain the shaved artichokes, pat them dry, and then add the parsley and ½ cup (120 ml) of the truffle vinaigrette, stirring to combine. Season to taste with salt and pepper.

Stir the olive oil into the chilled ground veal and season to taste with salt and pepper.

For each serving, place a 4-inch (10-cm) ring mold on a cold plate and add one-quarter of the veal mixture, pressing gently to spread through the mold. If you don't have a ring mold, create a 4-inch (10-cm) round, ¼-inch (6-mm) thick circle of veal with a table knife. Spoon one-quarter of the artichoke mixture over the top of each veal circle. Use a vegetable peeler to shave a few pieces of Parmesan from the block over the artichokes. Remove the ring mold and drizzle some truffle vinaigrette around the plate. Serve immediately.

MAKES 4 SERVINGS

Truffle Vinaigrette:

¾ cup (175 ml) blended oil (page 276)

3 tablespoons (45 ml) freshly squeezed lemon juice

1 teaspoon (5 ml) white truffle paste, or ¼ teaspoon (1 ml) white truffle oil

Salt and freshly ground black pepper

Veal Tartare and Shaved Artichokes:

8 ounces (227 g) veal shoulder

4 baby artichokes, trimmed

2 tablespoons (30 ml) freshly squeezed lemon juice

¼ cup (15 g) chopped fresh flat-leaf parsley

Salt and freshly ground black pepper

¾ cup (175 ml) olive oil

1 small block of Parmesan cheese, for shaving

PORCINI ZUPPA with BRA CHEESE FONDUTA

When porcini are in season, there are a thousand and one ways to prepare them. After cleaning and slicing pounds and pounds of them one fall, I had leftover mushroom scraps and decided to make soup. The broth is just leeks, celery, garlic, chicken stock, and herbs pureed with the cooked mushrooms. The porcini flavor is so strong, you don't need much else. But a little Bra cheese *fonduta* with truffle pâté makes this soup even better. Porcini and truffles grow in Bra, so using the local cheese makes sense. If you can't find Bra cheese, use any other good melting cheese, such as fontina or Taleggio. And don't feel the need to use all fresh porcini in the soup. When I get a bumper crop of porcini, I freeze them. A mix of frozen and fresh mushrooms works fine here.

Heat 2 tablespoons (28 g) of the butter and 2 tablespoons (30 ml) of the oil in a large soup pot over medium-high heat. Add the 10 ounces (283 g) of mushroom pieces, toss to mix, and sear the mushrooms until lightly browned, 4 to 5 minutes, stirring now and then.

Add the celery and leek, lower the heat to medium, and sweat the vegetables until tender but not browned, 5 to 7 minutes. Pour in the chicken stock and submerge the sachet in the liquid. Bring to a simmer and simmer gently for 30 minutes. Remove and discard the sachet and then blend the soup in batches with a blender or stick blender until completely smooth. Season with salt and pepper to taste and cover the soup in the pan to keep it warm. (Or let cool and refrigerate for up to 4 days; gently reheat the soup before serving.)

Bring the cream to a boil in a small saucepan over medium-high heat, and then remove the pan from the heat and stir in the cheese until smooth. Stir in the truffle paste and season to taste with salt and pepper. Keep warm over very low heat to keep it from thickening too much.

Melt the remaining 1 tablespoon (14 g) of butter and 1 tablespoon (15 ml) of olive oil in a medium sauté pan over medium heat. Slice the four fresh porcini caps and sauté them in the butter and oil until heated through, 2 to 3 minutes. Add the garlic and parsley, and cook for 1 minute (this is called *porcini trifolati*).

Divide the soup among warm bowls and spoon a couple of tablespoons of *porcini trifolati* over each bowl. Drizzle with a generous amount of fonduta.

MAKES 4 SERVINGS

3 tablespoons (42 g) unsalted butter, divided

3 tablespoons (45 ml) olive oil, divided

10 ounces (283 g) fresh or frozen porcini mushroom pieces (3 cups), plus 4 fresh porcini caps

2 medium-size ribs celery, thinly sliced (1 cup)

1 large leek, cleaned and thinly sliced (1 cup)

1 quart (1 L) Chicken Stock (page 279)

1 sachet of 2 sprigs thyme, 1 bay leaf, 1 garlic clove, 4 peppercorns, and one 3-inch/7.5-cm Parmesan cheese rind (see page 277)

Salt and freshly ground black pepper

½ cup (120 ml) heavy cream

2 ounces (57 g) Bra cheese, grated (½ cup)

½ teaspoon (2 ml) white truffle paste (see Sources, page 290)

1 small garlic clove, minced

¼ cup (15 g) chopped fresh flat-leaf parsley

POLENTA CARAMELLE with RASCHERA FONDUTA and BLACK TRUFFLE

MAKES 4 TO 6 SERVINGS

1 cup (235 ml) cooked Polenta (page 281), cooled

1 large egg

1 ounce (28 g) Parmesan cheese, grated (¼ cup)

Freshly ground black pepper

12 ounces (340 g) Egg Pasta Dough (page 282), rolled into 3 sheets, each about 1/32 inch (0.8 mm) thick

Tipo 00 flour (see page 277) or all-purpose flour, for dusting

1 cup (235 ml) whole milk

6 ounces (170 g) Raschera cheese

2 tablespoons (30 ml) black truffle paste

2 tablespoons (20 g) uncooked coarse yellow cornmeal (polenta)

Extra-virgin olive oil, for drizzling

Caramelle means "candies," and this ravioli is stuffed with polenta, then twisted like a candy wrapper. I got the stuffing idea from Claudio Sadler, a Michelin two-star chef in Milan. One of his cookbooks had a recipe for polenta ravioli, and I started playing around with polenta as a filling. After a few different tries, a simple mixture of cooked polenta, Parmesan, and a little egg turned out to be the best. The sauce is made with Raschera, a soft cow's milk cheese I first discovered on one of my fall trips to Alba. It's mild and creamy like formagella, which could stand in here. Or, in a pinch, use any other creamy melting cheese.

Combine the cooled polenta, egg, and Parmesan in a food processor. Season to taste with pepper and buzz until smooth, about 1 minute. Spoon into a resealable plastic bag and refrigerate until ready to use or up to 1 day.

Lay a pasta sheet on a lightly floured work surface and dust with flour. Trim the ends to make them square, then cut the dough into 2-inch (5-cm) squares and spritz with water to keep the dough from drying out. Cut a corner from the bag and squeeze the filling into ¾-inch (2-cm)-diameter balls in the center of each square. Wet your fingers and moisten the corners of a square. Fold the pasta so the edge just covers the filling, then continue folding so that the filling is enclosed and the pasta forms a small rectangle (see page 162). Gently twist the dough around the filling like a candy wrapper and pinch the edges to seal. Dust the ravioli with flour and place on a parchment-lined baking sheet. Refrigerate for up to 2 hours or freeze until solid, then transfer to a resealable plastic bag and freeze for up to 3 days. You should have about one hundred ravioli.

Bring the milk to a boil in a small saucepan over medium-high heat. Remove from the heat and add the Raschera, whisking until melted and smooth. If the sauce is lumpy, strain it through a fine-mesh strainer into a small saucepan. Stir in the truffle paste and keep warm over very low heat.

Toast the uncooked polenta in a hot, dry skillet until fragrant and lightly browned, 2 to 3 minutes, shaking the pan often. Remove from the heat.

Bring a large pot of salted water to a boil. Drop the pasta in the boiling water in batches, if necessary, to prevent overcrowding; quickly return the water to a boil, and cook until tender yet firm, 3 to 5 minutes.

Drain and divide among warm pasta plates. Spoon some fonduta over the pasta, scatter on some toasted polenta, and drizzle some olive oil around the plate.

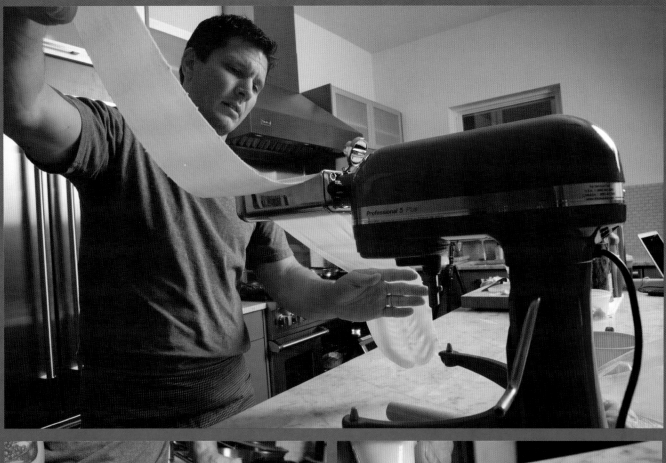

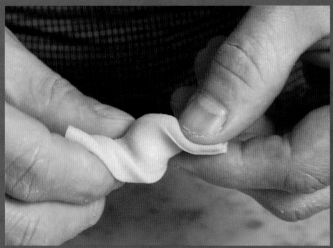

POTATO GNOCCHI with
CASTELMAGNO FONDUTA and WHITE TRUFFLE

Castelmagno is a Piedmont cow's milk cheese aged for no less than sixty days. It's crumbly, stinky, and full of rich flavor. The first time I had it was in Bra during the 2005 cheese festival. We had lunch at Boccondivino, a slow food restaurant in town, and our second course was a plate of light, fluffy pillows floating in creamy Castelmagno *fonduta*. The waiter came over and grated fresh white truffles over the top until I told him to stop. It was one of the best pasta dishes I've ever eaten.

MAKES 4 TO 6 SERVINGS

2 russet potatoes, scrubbed clean

¼ ounce (7 g) Parmesan cheese, grated (1 tablespoon)

Pinch of grated nutmeg

Salt and freshly ground black pepper

1 small egg, beaten

7 tablespoons (54 g) *tipo* 00 flour (see page 277) or all-purpose flour, sifted, plus a little more for dusting

½ cup (120 ml) heavy cream

1 tablespoon (15 ml) white rum

8 ounces (227 g) Castelmagno cheese, grated (about 2 cups)

2 tablespoons (30 ml) white truffle paste

Extra-virgin olive oil, for drizzling

Put the potatoes in a medium saucepan and cover with cold salted water by 1 inch (2.5 cm). Bring to a boil over high heat and boil until a knife slides in and out of the potatoes easily, 25 to 30 minutes. Drain, and when cool enough to handle, peel the potatoes, discarding the skins. Pass the potatoes through a food mill or potato ricer into a medium bowl. Stir in the Parmesan and nutmeg, and season with salt and pepper. Taste, adjust the seasonings, and then stir in the egg. Gently stir in the flour just until the dough comes together.

Turn the dough out onto a floured work surface and knead gently for 4 minutes. Using a floured bench knife or sharp knife, cut the dough in half and roll each piece on the floured surface into a long rope about ½ inch (1.25 cm) in diameter. Use the floured knife to cut the rope crosswise into ½-inch (1.25-cm) pieces, and dust the gnocchi with flour. Line one or two baking sheets with parchment paper and dust with flour. Transfer the gnocchi to the sheets, shake the pan to coat with flour, and refrigerate until ready to use.

Bring the cream and rum to a boil in a medium saucepan over medium-high heat. Remove from the heat and stir in the grated Castelmagno until melted and smooth. Stir in the truffle paste and salt and pepper to taste. Keep warm over very low heat.

Meanwhile, bring a large pot of salted water to a boil. Add the gnocchi in batches, if necessary, to prevent overcrowding; quickly return the water to a boil, and cook until the gnocchi float, 5 to 6 minutes. Remove with a spider strainer or slotted spoon and toss gently in the fondue.

Divide among plates and drizzle with olive oil.

COTECHINO-STUFFED QUAIL with WARM FIG SALAD

MAKES 4 SERVINGS

4 whole quail, innards removed

Salt and freshly ground black pepper

4 slices white bread

½ cup (120 ml) Chicken Stock (page 279)

6 ounces (170 g) Cotechino (page 244) or other Italian sausage

2 ounces (56 g) mortadella, ground in a food processor

1 large egg

1 ounce (28 g) Parmesan cheese, grated (¼ cup)

2 tablespoons (7 g) chopped fresh flat-leaf parsley

2 tablespoons (28 g) unsalted butter

5 tablespoons (75 ml) extra-virgin olive oil, divided

8 large fresh figs, quartered lengthwise

½ shallot, julienned

1 tablespoon (15 ml) balsamic vinegar

Walk around any Piedmont town in November, and you'll eventually hear gunshots. It's hunting season and they're shooting pheasant, quail, squab, and boar. I thought about what else grows in the fall, and figs seemed like the perfect complement to quail. I stuff the birds with *cotechino*, a coarse northern Italian fresh sausage, pan-roast the birds, and then serve them with a warm salad of figs and shallots. For the stuffing, you can use the same cotechino described in the Ciareghi recipe (page 244). Or use another coarse fresh Italian sausage.

Rinse the quail, pat dry, and season inside and out with salt and pepper.

Soak the white bread in the stock in a medium bowl for 10 minutes. Drain off any excess stock, then break up the bread and mix in the sausage, mortadella, egg, Parmesan, and parsley. Season with salt and pepper. To test the seasoning, pinch off a small piece of the stuffing mixture and fry it in a small sauté pan and then taste. Adjust the seasoning as necessary.

Preheat the oven to 375°F (190°C). Divide the stuffing between the birds, stuffing it generously into the cavities until they are very plump. Heat the butter and 2 tablespoons (30 ml) of the oil in a large heavy sauté pan (or two smaller ones) over medium-high heat. When hot, add the quail breast-side down, and cook until golden brown on both sides, 3 to 4 minutes per side. Turn the quail breast-side up, transfer the pan(s) to the oven, and cook until an instant-read thermometer registers 145° to 150°F (63° to 66°C) when inserted into the center, 6 to 8 minutes.

Transfer the quail to a cutting board and put the pan(s) over medium heat. Add the figs, cut-side down, then add the shallots and sauté until the shallots are lightly golden, 3 to 4 minutes. Pour in the vinegar to deglaze the pans, shaking the pan back and forth, and then pour in the remaining 3 tablespoons (45 ml) of olive oil, shaking the pans to combine the ingredients. Season with salt and pepper.

Cut each quail in half lengthwise to expose the stuffing. Spoon the sauce over and around each half and serve.

OVEN-ROASTED RABBIT PORCHETTA
with PEPERONATA

Porchetta is the belly of a pig wrapped around the loin and roasted. Here, I do the same thing but with rabbit. I debone a whole rabbit, pound it flat, make sausage with some of the trimmed meat, roll the rabbit around the sausage, and then pan-roast the whole thing. You could make this dish with almost any animal, but rabbit has got to be the most underrated meat in the United States. We should be eating more of it. It's lean, easy to raise, and delicious! Make this dish a few days ahead if you like. It can be served warm or cold, as can the accompanying sauté of peppers, tomatoes, and onions.

MAKES 6 TO 8 SERVINGS

Rabbit Porchetta:

1 rabbit, about 3½ pounds (1.5 kg), deboned, liver and heart reserved (see note)

3 ounces (85 g) pork fatback, cut into ½-inch (1.25-cm) cubes

About 1 pound (450 g) caul fat, for wrapping

1 teaspoon (6 g) salt, plus more for seasoning

Freshly ground black pepper

¾ teaspoon (1.75 g) dextrose powder, or ¼ teaspoon (1 g) superfine sugar

¼ teaspoon (0.5 g) cracked black peppercorns

1 large egg, beaten

2 teaspoons (10 ml) heavy cream

2 tablespoons (30 ml) grapeseed oil

1 garlic clove, smashed

2 sprigs fresh rosemary

Peperonata:

2 ripe tomatoes

1 small yellow onion

¼ cup (60 ml) olive oil

6 mixed roasted peppers (page 278), green, red, and yellow, cut into 1½-inch (3.75-cm) squares

1 garlic clove, smashed

3 sprigs fresh rosemary

½ cup (30 g) chopped fresh flat-leaf parsley

1 tablespoon (15 ml) sherry wine vinegar

Salt and freshly ground black pepper

(continued on next page)

For the rabbit porchetta: Spread the deboned rabbit on its back on a work surface. Trim 12 ounces (340 g) of the leg meat. Cut the trimmed meat into cubes and place it on a baking sheet or cutting board that will fit in your freezer. Cut 1¼ ounces (35 g) of the liver and heart into cubes and add it to the sheet or board, along with the pork fatback. (If you prefer, you can skip the organs and add an additional 1 ounce of fatback.) Spread everything in a single layer and freeze until firm and partially frozen, 20 to 30 minutes. Also freeze all parts of a meat grinder or the metal blade of a food processor.

The remaining rabbit should be roughly rectangular. Place it on a large sheet of plastic wrap, cover with another sheet of plastic, and pound the meat to an even 1/4-inch (6-mm) thickness. Lay down another large sheet of plastic (optional, to help with rolling), and stretch out enough caul fat on it to clear the pounded-out rabbit by 2 inches (5 cm) all around. Roll up the rabbit meat and then unroll it on the caul fat, shaping it into a rectangle with no holes in the meat. Season lightly with salt and pepper.

Scatter the 1 teaspoon of salt, dextrose, and peppercorns evenly over the partially frozen trimmed meat. Gently mix by hand. Grind the meat mixture in the cold meat grinder fitted with the medium plate. If using a food processor, process the mixture with short pulses until very finely chopped but not completely pureed. It should look like hamburger. Transfer to a large bowl and add the egg and cream. Gently stir until blended and then use immediately or cover and refrigerate for up to 2 hours.

Place the meat mixture on the rabbit and form it into a cylinder, leaving an inch or two of space on each end. Use the plastic and caul fat to roll the rabbit over the filling, rolling it tight until you get two-thirds of the way to the other side. Fold the excess caul fat from the edges inward, like a burrito, and continue rolling into a tight, thick cylinder. Tie the porchetta with kitchen string in four or five places to help it hold its shape. Season lightly with salt and pepper. The porchetta can be refrigerated for up to 2 hours or frozen for up to 2 weeks before cooking and serving.

Preheat the oven to 400°F (260°C). Heat the grapeseed oil, garlic, and rosemary in a large, ovenproof sauté pan over medium-high heat. When hot and sizzling, push the garlic and rosemary to the sides of the pan. Add the porchetta to the pan and sear until all sides are golden brown, 4 to 5 minutes per side. Remove and discard the garlic and rosemary before they burn. Transfer the pan to the oven and cook until the internal temperature registers 145° to 150°F (63° to 66°C) on an instant-read thermometer, 35 to 45 minutes. Transfer the porchetta to a cutting board and let rest for 15 to 20 minutes.

For the peperonata: Bring a medium pot of water to a boil, and fill a bowl with ice water. Score an X on the bottom of each tomato and drop into the boiling water until the skin near the X starts to curl, 30 seconds to 1 minute. Transfer to the ice water and swish the tomatoes until they are cool. Peel and discard the skins of the tomatoes. Cut the tomatoes in half crosswise, along their equator, and dig out the seeds and gel. Cut out and discard the core, and then cut the remaining tomato flesh into 1½-inch (3.75-cm) squares. Cut the onion into 1½-inch (3.75-cm) pieces as well.

Heat the oil in a sauté pan over medium heat. Add the onion and sweat until soft but not browned, 5 to 8 minutes. Add the tomato, peppers, garlic, and rosemary, lower the heat to low, and cook gently for 12 to 15 minutes. Remove and discard the garlic and rosemary and then season the peperonata with the parsley, vinegar, salt and pepper. Taste and add more vinegar or olive oil as necessary. The peperonata can be made up to 3 days ahead, refrigerated, and then gently reheated before serving.

Slice the porchetta into ½-inch (1.25-cm)-thick medallions and serve with the peperonata, warm or cold.

Note

To debone the rabbit, cut through the breastbone, spread open the rib cage, and set aside the heart and liver. Discard any large deposits of fat. Scrape the blade of a boning knife over the inside of the ribs to thin out the membrane. Grab the side of the rabbit and poke the ribs through the membrane, then cut down around the ribs, holding the knife against bone, to remove the meat from the bone. Take care not to cut any holes in the meat. Make long slits down the center of the inside of the backbone to loosen it from the meat. When you get to the legs, cut down to the hip joints, then break the joints in two. Using short strokes and holding the blade against bone, gradually cut along the length of the backbone and underneath it to loosen the bone from the meat. The goal is to remove the entire backbone and rib cage from neck to tail, leaving the meat intact. The legs will still be attached. To debone them, cut down the length of each bone and scrape the meat from the bones, then break the joints and pull the bones from the meat like pulling a foot out of a sock. Scrape as much meat as possible from the bones, keeping a piling of trimmed meat as you work.

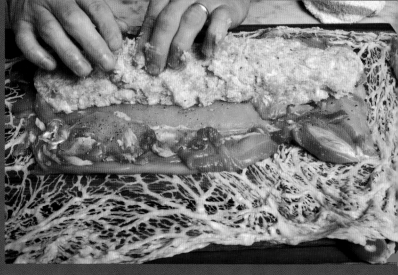

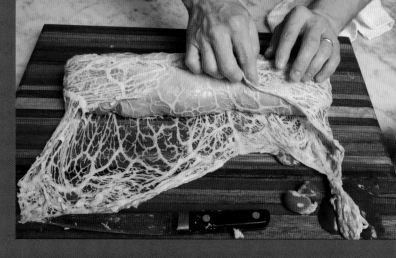

BONÈT

3 cups (600 g) granulated sugar, divided

6 large eggs

3 tablespoons (45 ml) white rum

1⅓ cups (115 g) unsweetened Dutch-process cocoa powder

1⅓ cups (160 g) finely ground amaretti cookie crumbs, plus a little extra for sprinkling

3 cups plus 2 tablespoons (780 ml) whole milk

Most restaurants in Piedmont serve some version of this dessert. It's like a chocolate flan made with crushed amaretti cookies and rum. The cookies separate out, making a soft crust, the custard stays rich and creamy, and the crème caramel forms its own syrupy sauce to drizzle over the top. The best version I've ever eaten was at Cesare Giaccone's restaurant just a half hour south of Alba. It's his mother's recipe and he hasn't changed a thing since he started making it fifty years ago. I modeled this version on that one.

Using an electric mixer on high speed or a sturdy whisk, whip together 1 cup (200 g) of the sugar with the eggs and rum until smooth, about 2 minutes. Sift the cocoa powder and cookie crumbs into the egg mixture, and then whisk until smooth. Gradually add the milk in stages, stirring until smooth between additions to prevent lumps. Cover and let stand in the refrigerator overnight.

Pour the remaining 2 cups (400 g) of sugar into a heavy sauté pan (not nonstick). Add just enough warm tap water to wet the sugar, about ¼ cup (60 ml), and cook over medium-high heat, swirling the pan but not stirring, until the sugar begins to turn medium amber in color, 6 to 8 minutes. Gently swirl the sugar in the pan to create an even-colored caramel. When the sugar is evenly golden, lower the heat to medium, stand back, and gradually add ⅓ cup (90 ml) of warm water; it will steam and spit. Cook the caramel just enough for it to remelt and become a thick, pourable syrup.

Carefully pour the caramel into a metal or ceramic 8-cup (2-L) terrine mold or 9 x 5-inch (23 x 13-cm) loaf pan; the bottom should be covered with a ¼- to ½-inch (6- to 12-mm)-thick layer of caramel that will feel tacky when cool enough to touch. Refrigerate until completely cooled, at least 1 hour or up to 4 hours.

Preheat the oven to 300°F (150°C). Set a kettle of water to boil.

Give the refrigerated bonèt mixture a stir, and then pour it into the pan over the caramel. If using a loaf pan, you may have a small amount left over; discard it. Set the pan in a larger, deeper pan (such as a roasting pan) and pour boiling water into the deeper pan to come about halfway up the bonèt pan. Bake until slightly puffed yet wobbly in the center like a firm custard, 60 to 70 minutes. Remove the bonèt pan from the water bath and let cool on a rack for 15 minutes. Refrigerate in the pan until completely cool or up to 4 days.

Run a wet knife around the edge of the bonèt and unmold it onto a large platter. Cut into ¾-inch (2-cm)-thick slices and lay a slice on each plate. Sprinkle with some cookie crumbs and a drizzle of the liquid caramel from the platter.

PISTACHIO FLAN

During the 2010 Slow Food festival, I made a point to eat at Da Guido in Pollenza. I'd heard so much about the place, I had to check it out. It's a stunning restaurant situated inside an old castle in town. Every dish in our meal was completely delicious, so for dessert, we ordered everything on the menu. This dessert floored me more than anything else. It's a small green pistachio cake enrobed in melted chocolate. When you cut into the cake, a river of creamy filling oozes out like a molten chocolate cake, but it's a gorgeous green color. The black and green colors make a striking presentation on a white plate. It took me two weeks to replicate this recipe, but I finally got it right. I ended up making my own pistachio paste in a Vitamix blender. Be sure to blend the pistachios until they're as smooth as silk. That's what makes the filling so creamy.

Preheat the oven to 350°F (175°C). Butter and flour ten 4-ounce (120-ml) baking tins or ramekins and place on a baking sheet.

Combine the sugar, egg yolks, and eggs in a stand mixer fitted with the whisk attachment. Whip on medium-high speed until pale yellow and thick enough to drip in ribbons when the whisk is lifted, 2 to 3 minutes. With the machine running, gradually add the melted butter.

Combine the pistachios and milk in a blender and puree on high speed until super-smooth and thick, 6 to 8 minutes, stopping to scrape down the side a few times. Fold the pistachio mixture into the egg mixture. Fold in the flour.

Pour the mixture into the prepared tins or ramekins and bake until very lightly browned and set around the edges but a little wobbly in the middle, 10 to 12 minutes.

Immediately invert and unmold the dishes onto plates. Spoon the warm chocolate sauce over each flan to coat it completely. Garnish with some chopped pistachios and serve hot.

MAKES 8 TO 10

1¾ cups (350 g) granulated sugar

4 large egg yolks

3 large eggs

9 tablespoons (125 g) unsalted butter, melted

1 cup (150 g) raw unsalted pistachios, preferably Sicilian, plus some chopped for garnish

¾ cup (175 g) whole milk

½ cup (62 g) *tipo* 00 flour (see page 277) or all-purpose flour, sifted

3 cups (750 ml) Chocolate Sauce (page 285)

TORRONE SEMIFREDDO with
CANDIED CHESTNUTS and CHOCOLATE SAUCE

The first time I went to Alba, I fell in love with torrone, the Italian almond nougat candy. You see mounds and mounds of it on display during the annual truffle festival. At Frosio, we made a torrone semifreddo that I always thought would be great with chocolate and chestnuts. So here it is, all the sweet flavors of Piedmont in one dish. The recipe yields a lot because each component can be kept for a week or two before serving. And it's so good, you'll want to serve it again and again.

MAKES 14 TO 16 SERVINGS

Torrone:

1 teaspoon (2.25 g) powdered egg whites

¾ cup plus 3 tablespoons (190 g) granulated sugar, divided

1 small egg white

2½ tablespoons (37 ml) glucose syrup or light corn syrup

¼ vanilla bean, split and scraped

⅓ cup (90 ml) honey

2¼ teaspoons (10 g) food-grade cocoa butter, melted

1¾ cups (250 g) whole almonds, toasted

Semifreddo:

8 large egg yolks

⅔ cup (133 g) granulated sugar

4 large egg whites

2 cups (475 ml) heavy cream

Candied Chestnuts:

8 ounces (227 g) peeled chestnuts, thawed if frozen

¾ cup (150 g) granulated sugar

3 tablespoons (45 ml) glucose syrup or light corn syrup

To Serve:

4 cups (1 L) Chocolate Sauce (page 285)

For the torrone: In the bowl of a stand mixer, whisk the powdered egg whites with 1 tablespoon (12 g) of the sugar to break up lumps. Add the egg white and whip on medium-low speed until combined, 1 minute. Let stand in the bowl.

Combine the remaining ¾ cup plus 2 tablespoons (175 g) of sugar with the glucose syrup, vanilla, and ¼ cup (60 ml) of water in a small saucepan, and cook over medium heat until the mixture reaches 302°F (150°C) on a candy thermometer. Meanwhile, heat the honey in a microwave until it is warm and pourable, 30 seconds to 1 minute. Add it to the 302°F (150°C) sugar mixture, and continue to cook until it reaches 311°F (155°C).

With the mixer running on low speed, pour in the hot sugar mixture; when incorporated, change to medium-high speed and whip until thickened, 1 to 2 minutes. Leaving the mixer running, quickly wave a kitchen torch all around the outside of the mixer bowl to heat the torrone mixture. The mixture should become thick and ribbony and start to pull away from the sides of the bowl. When it does, change to low speed, add the melted cocoa butter, and when incorporated, change back to high speed, and then wave the torch again around the outside of the bowl until the torrone thickens again and pulls back away from the sides of the bowl.

Quickly stir in the almonds and immediately transfer the torrone to a half-sheet-size silicone mat. Working quickly, top with another silicone mat and roll the torrone to an even ½-inch (1.25-cm) thickness before it hardens. Let cool and harden completely, about 30 minutes, and then chop into pieces the size of dimes.

For the semifreddo: Coat ten 4-ounce (120-ml) baking tins or ramekins with cooking spray.

In a large bowl, use a whisk to vigorously whip the egg yolks and sugar until pale yellow and thick, 2 to 3 minutes. In the bowl of a stand mixer, whip the egg whites on medium-high speed until they form medium-soft peaks when the beaters are lifted, 3 to 4 minutes. Fold the whites into the yolks in three additions. In a clean mixer bowl, whip the cream on medium-high speed until it holds medium-soft peaks when the beaters are lifted, 2 to 3 minutes. Fold the whipped cream into the eggs. Fold in the chopped torrone and spoon the semifreddo into the baking tins. Cover each tin and freeze until partially frozen, at least 2 hours or up to 1 week.

For the candied chestnuts: Put the peeled chestnuts in a saucepan and add enough water to just cover them. Simmer over medium heat until they are soft enough to eat and just start to fall apart, 5 to 8 minutes. Drain and reserve.

Combine the sugar, glucose syrup, and 2 cups (475 ml) of water in a large saucepan and boil over high heat until it reaches 224°F (107°C) on a candy thermometer, 12 to 15 minutes. Add the cooked chestnuts. This mixture can be refrigerated for up to 2 weeks before using.

To serve: Unmold the semifreddo onto plates (gently heat the outside of the molds, if necessary, to loosen the semifreddo; you can dip them in hot water or use a kitchen torch). Completely cover each semifreddo with chocolate sauce, and spoon some candied chestnuts on the side.

VENICE

LOSING MYSELF
IN THE CITY

IT'S LIKE A SURREALIST DREAM, WALKING DOWN STREETS THAT CIRCLE BACK TO WHERE THEY STARTED, OVER BRIDGES THAT LEAD TO NOWHERE, CONTEMPLATING UNFATHOMABLE BUILDINGS, AND GAZING AT MESMERIZING DISPLAYS OF ODD-LOOKING FISH AND VEGETABLES. HERE YOU STAND ON ONE OF ONE HUNDRED AND EIGHTEEN TINY ISLANDS BARELY HELD TOGETHER BY ONE HUNDRED AND FIFTY CANALS AND FOUR HUNDRED FOOT-WORN BRIDGES, ALL FLOATING ON A GIANT LAGOON. VENICE IS A CRAZY PLACE, AND IT'S MY FAVORITE CITY IN ITALY.

I first went there in the spring of 2005 and have gone back almost every year since. On that first visit, Claudia and I had been together for about twelve months, and her mother invited us to stay with her at her timeshare. Pina has an apartment right next to La Fenice, the opera house famous for hosting such great artists as Verdi and Donizetti since the late 1700s, despite burning down and being rebuilt several times. Just a few blocks away is Piazza San Marco (St. Mark's Square), the most happening piazza in Venice. Every time I visit, as a chef, I can't help admiring the architectural design of the Basilica di San Marco. I build little structures every time I send out a plate of food. It's part of my DNA. The buildings in Venice inspire me every time I visit.

But the food interests me most. I'm not talking about big-ticket restaurants. They're too touristy, catering to the ten million people who flock to the "City of Water" every year from all over the world. No, I'm talking about the markets and the pub food. Every time I come to Venice, we shop the markets in the morning, and before cooking our evening meal back at the apartment, we grab some bar snacks and a glass of wine in the afternoon. That afternoon meal is called *ombra e cicchetti* (wine and nibbles) and it gives you a better sense of Venetian food than you'll get at any of the touristy restaurants during dinnertime.

The big Rialto market is just a five-minute walk from Pina's apartment. Right near the city's oldest bridge, the fishmongers start selling at six in the morning. They sail in from the Adriatic Sea and the lagoon surrounding the city with some of the best-looking seafood I've ever seen. . . fresh whole turbot, sole, and sea bass; glistening steaks of tuna and swordfish; mountains of plump sardines; *moscardini* (baby octopus), calamari (squid), and *seppia* (cuttlefish); and unusual local shellfish, such as *lumache di mare* (sea snails), *arselle* (pinkie-tip-size clams), *vongole veraci* (2-inch/5-cm-diameter clams), *cape longhe* (razor clams), *granseole* (spider crabs), *schie* (small gray prawns), and *canoce* (mantis shrimp). You see fish brought in from farther away, too, such as *gambero rosso* (Mediterranean red shrimp), monkfish, grouper, and lobster. And twice a year in the spring and fall, you can buy *moleche*, tiny molting softshell crabs. They're barely bigger than silver dollars. Venetians like to soak them in beaten eggs until the crabs stuff themselves with egg. Then they deep-fry the softshells and eat them whole.

You have to get to the fish market before noon, or all the good stuff is gone. And don't be shy about haggling. They keep the best bits and pieces in back. Ask the fishmonger, "What else do you have back there?" One time I asked that question, and a guy came out with some of the biggest

monkfish cheeks I'd ever seen. Even if you don't cook fish in Venice, you owe it to yourself to check out the market, if only to know what you'll be eating when you order food later in the day.

Venetian cuisine is fish-based, but there are lots of vegetables, too. The vegetable market is right next door to the fish market, and it has everything you can think of. Depending on the season, you'll see purple artichokes, yellow and green zucchini, eggplant, *cuore di bue* (big beef-heart tomatoes), long Roma beans, mounds of porcini and chanterelle mushrooms, and all kinds of radicchio, such as early and late Treviso (tardivo), Castelfranco, and Chioggia. The fruit there is off the charts. Cherries, peaches, plums, figs. . . you name it. If it's in season, it's there. With the fish and vegetable markets, and a pretty good selection of meat and cheese, the Rialto market is a full city block of incredible ingredients waiting to become plates of delicious food.

On that first trip, we picked up squid, skate wing, baby mullet, *arborelle* (tiny fish you can eat whole), swordfish, shrimp, onions, zucchini, eggplant, and a few other things and made our way back to the apartment. By the time we got it all in the fridge it was around eleven thirty a.m., also known as *l'andar per ombre*, the time to "move into the shadows." It's when everyone in Venice walks through the city, stopping at local *bacari* (pubs) to nibble little bites of food and sip prosecco, negroni, or Campari and soda. *Ombre* literally means "shadows" but is local slang for "wine"; apparently, the local tradition started when wine vendors on the street would move from place to place to find shade, especially those in Piazza San Marco who followed the shade of the Basilica di San Marco's giant bell tower.

During the day, the pubs in every back alley of Venice display all manner of snacks, such as marinated octopus, fried calamari and anchovies, *baccalà mantecato* (creamed *baccalà* on bruschetta or polenta), and *sarde in saor* (sardines in sour onion and vinegar sauce). You'll find *polpettini* (little meatballs) of pork and beef, fried eggplant and zucchini, and miniature sandwiches. These bar snacks, called *cicchetti,* are sort of like Italian tapas, and they're some of the best eating in the city, if you ask me. Most places let you take the food

outside. Going from pub to pub, it's like having lunch in a citywide alfresco restaurant. The people-watching is unbeatable. And you really get a feel for the city. There are no cars. No scooters. Not even bicycles. Everyone is on foot, walking over bridges and down alleys to get where they're going. You stand outside a pub, holding a glass of chilled Prosecco in one hand, some freshly caught fried fish or polpettini in the other, lean against a wall built six centuries ago, and relax, taking in the incredible history of the city itself. You don't use maps. You don't bother with street names. You just wander around getting lost until you eventually find something overwhelming to look at or delicious to eat. That's the magic of Venice.

I found that magic when we got back to the apartment in the early evening. Claudia and I cleaned all the fish and shellfish and Pina heated up some oil in a big pot. She mixed together *tipo* 00 flour and semolina flour and we soaked the fish in milk until the fry oil was hot. We spread brown paper bags all over the table, dredged the fish, fried it, laid it on the paper, and then seasoned it with salt and pepper. A few squeezes of lemon later, the three of us had satisfaction written all over our faces. It was the best *fritto misto* I'd ever had. The seafood was unbelievably fresh. The preparation was simple. Plus, it was springtime, the windows were open, and the late-day sun lit up Claudia's high cheekbones, chestnut brown hair, and inviting smile in a way that I had never quite seen before.

Pinzimonio with Tarragon Vinaigrette
and Goat Cheese

•

Baccalà Cannelloni with Cauliflower
and Parmigiano

•

Tagliolini with Ragù di Seppia

•

Fried Stuffed Softshell Crabs
with Asparagus

•

Radicchio Ravioli with
Balsamic Brown Butter

•

Fritto Misto di Pesce

•

Coconut Latte Fritto with
Passion Fruit Curd

•

Heirloom Apple Upside-Down Cake
with Polenta Gelato

•

Rustic Peach Tart with
Goat Cheese Sorbet

PINZIMONIO with TARRAGON VINAIGRETTE and GOAT CHEESE

MAKES 8 SERVINGS

1 packed cup (50 g) fresh tarragon leaves, plus 5 to 6 leaves for garnish

1 to 2 tablespoons (15 to 30 ml) red wine vinegar

1 cup (235 ml) olive oil

Salt and freshly ground black pepper

2½ pounds (1.1 kg) assorted vegetables, thinly sliced (8 cups)

About 4 ounces (114 g) fresh, soft goat cheese

The Italian version of crudités is called *pinzimonio*. Use whatever vegetables look freshest at your market. Depending on the time of year, you could use baby zucchini, baby carrots, purple asparagus, white asparagus, blanched fava beans, peas, radishes. . . the sky's the limit. Just slice the vegetables thinly or cut them into manageable lengths or bite-size pieces. You could even shave them with a vegetable peeler or on a mandoline. In Venice, you'll find the best produce at the vegetable market near Ponte di Rialto, the oldest bridge over the Grand Canal. There's also a co-op nearby that sells a creamy goat cheese that I fell in love with. It's not crumbly like the goat cheese you find in logs. It's more like ricotta cheese. One spring, I was staying at Pina's timeshare a few blocks away from the market and put together this pinzimonio with that goat cheese and some market vegetables. When I got back to Philadelphia, I had a version of it on the Osteria menu all summer long.

Put the tarragon and vinegar in a blender and blend until the taragon is finely chopped, 1 to 2 minutes. With the motor running, slowly drizzle in the oil until thickened, 2 minutes. The mixture should be green and medium thick. Season with salt and pepper, then taste and adjust the vinegar and other seasonings as needed.

Toss the vegetables in the vinaigrette in a big bowl and season with salt and pepper. Arrange the vegetables on a wooden board or platter. I like to put them in a narrow line down a long board. Use two dinner spoons to scoop and shape the goat cheese into two football shapes (quenelles). Place them on opposite sides of the vegetables. Garnish with the remaining tarragon leaves and a drizzle of the remaining tarragon vinaigrette remaining in the bowl.

BACCALÀ CANNELLONI with CAULIFLOWER and PARMIGIANO

By now, *baccalà* is pretty well known in the United States, but in case you're not familiar with it, it is salted cod. Not salt cod. Salted cod. Salt cod is usually very thin and very dried out. That's not what you want here. You want baccalà that is at least half an inch (1.25 cm) thick and still somewhat pliable. It has to be soaked for two to three days to desalt it before using, so allow yourself some time when making this recipe. On the plus side, there's so much natural gelatin in baccalà that it whips up into a creamy mousse the Italians call *baccalà mantecato* (creamed codfish). I do a similar preparation here but stuff it into cannelloni and then blast the pasta in a hot oven. The filling has the look and creamy texture of a typical cheese-based cannelloni filling, but it tastes completely different and totally delicious. It makes a great casserole for a crowd, but you could cut the recipe in half to serve fewer people.

MAKES 8 TO 10 SERVINGS

Pasta and Filling:

1¾ pounds (795 g) boneless baccalà

4 ounces (1 stick/113 g) unsalted butter

¼ cup (60 ml) extra-virgin olive oil

1 medium-size yellow onion, finely chopped (1¼ cups/200 g)

3 anchovy fillets

½ teaspoon (1 g) red chili flakes

⅔ cup (83 g) *tipo* 00 flour (see page 277) or all-purpose flour

2½ cups (625 ml) whole milk

1 small garlic clove, smashed

1 bay leaf

Salt and freshly ground black pepper

8 ounces (227 g) Egg Pasta Dough (page 282), rolled into 2 sheets, each about ¹⁄₁₆ inch (1.5 mm) thick

4 tablespoons (57 g) unsalted butter, melted, plus a little more for greasing the pans

3½ ounces (100 g) Parmesan cheese, grated (1 cup)

Cauliflower:

½ head cauliflower, separated into florets

¼ cup (60 ml) extra-virgin olive oil, plus a little more for drizzling

Parmesan cheese for garnish

¼ cup (15 g) chopped fresh flat-leaf parsley for garnish

For the pasta and filling: Soak the baccalà in water to cover for 2 to 3 days, changing the soaking water two or three times a day.

Heat the butter and olive oil in a deep sauté pan over medium heat. Add the onion and sweat until soft but not browned, 4 to 5 minutes. Add the anchovies and chili flakes, and cook for 2 minutes. Add the baccalà, and cook until the fish flakes easily, 4 to 5 minutes, breaking it up with a spoon. Scatter in the flour, and cook out the floury taste for about 5 minutes. Gradually stir in the milk in a few additions, scraping the pan bottom between additions. Add the garlic and bay leaf, and cook over low heat until thick and creamy, 30 to 40 minutes, stirring frequently to prevent browning on the pan bottom. Taste, and season with salt and pepper as needed. Remove from the heat, let cool, and discard the garlic and bay leaf. Spoon the filling into a resealable plastic bag and refrigerate until ready to use or up to 1 day.

Lay a pasta sheet on a lightly floured work surface and cut it into 4-inch (10-cm) squares. You should get twelve to fourteen squares from the sheet. Repeat with the remaining pasta dough so you have a total of twenty-four to twenty-eight squares.

Bring a large pot of salted water to a boil and fill a large bowl with ice water. Drop in the pasta, quickly return the water to a boil, and cook for 15 to 20 seconds just to blanch it, stirring gently to prevent sticking. Immediately transfer the pasta to ice water to stop the cooking. Lay the pasta squares on kitchen towels or parchment paper and pat dry; they will be delicate and some may stick, but you should have plenty.

Preheat the oven to 500°F (260°C). Turn on convection if possible. Butter a 4-quart (4-L) baking dish, or use individual dishes if you like, allowing two to three cannelloni per dish.

Cut off a corner from the resealable plastic bag of filling, and pipe a ¾-inch (2-cm)-thick line of filling along one edge of each pasta square. Starting at the filled side, use the edge of the kitchen towel or parchment to lift and roll the pasta to the edge of the unfilled side to enclose the filling.

Place the cannelloni into the prepared baking dish, seam-side down. Brush the tops with the melted butter and sprinkle with the cheese. Bake until the cheese melts and browns on top, 8 to 10 minutes.

For the cauliflower: Thinly slice the cauliflower florets. Heat the oil in a large sauté pan over medium heat. Add the cauliflower in a single layer in batches and sweat until soft but not browned, 3 to 4 minutes per side.

To finish, place two to three cannelloni on each plate. Lay a few slices of cauliflower on top, drizzle with olive oil, and sprinkle with Parmesan and parsley.

TAGLIOLINI with RAGÙ DI SEPPIA

MAKES 4 TO 6 SERVINGS

1½ pounds (680 g) cuttlefish or squid, cleaned

¾ cup (175 ml) olive oil, divided, plus more as needed

1 medium-size yellow onion, julienned finely

⅛ teaspoon (0.25 g) red chili flakes

Salt and freshly ground black pepper

5 peeled canned tomatoes, preferably San Marzano, cored and crushed by hand

2 to 3 cups (500 to 750 ml) white wine

2 teaspoons (10 ml) squid ink

1 bay leaf

1 pound (450 g) fresh or frozen tagliolini pasta (page 282)

⅓ cup (20 g) chopped fresh flat-leaf parsley

Seppia (cuttlefish) is all over the fish market in Venice. It's similar to squid and octopus but tastes sweeter and more tender. It's my favorite cephalopod. You can eat it raw, stuffed, braised, baked, or even grilled. The best thing is the ink from the cuttlefish (often labeled as squid ink in stores). It turns everything black, like a busted ballpoint pen. Wear an apron when making this recipe! I use plenty of ink because if I'm going to eat a squid ink dish, I want it to be completely black, not gray. The sauce here should be so black that the pasta turns black. I use the ink from the cuttlefish plus some store-bought squid ink. You can buy jars of it from various gourmet retailers (see Sources on page 289). The cuttlefish itself you can get at most Asian fish markets. Or, if you can't find cuttlefish, use squid instead.

Reserve the cuttlefish or squid ink sacs. Finely julienne the bodies and tentacles (if using squid) and set aside. For directions on cleaning squid, see page 94.

Heat 1 tablespoon (15 ml) of the oil in a large, deep sauté pan over medium heat. Add the onion and sweat until soft but not browned, about 5 minutes. Stir in the chili flakes and salt and pepper to taste. Raise the heat to medium-high, add the cuttlefish and tomatoes, and cook for 5 minutes. Add enough wine to just cover the ingredients, and cook until the liquid reduces in volume by three-quarters, 10 to 12 minutes.

Meanwhile, carefully peel the skin off the ink sacs over a small bowl, which will release the ink. Cover the ink with just enough water so the ink can be poured out of the bowl. Add the inky water to the pan, and then rinse out the bowl with just enough water to capture all the ink, adding the inky liquid to the pan (you want maximum ink and minimum water). Add the 2 tablespoons (10 ml) of squid ink and the bay leaf and simmer over medium-low heat until the cuttlefish is tender, 15 to 20 minutes. Season to taste with salt and pepper and then remove from the heat. The *ragù* can be cooled and refrigerated for up to 2 days before using. Just reheat it gently in a sauté pan.

Meanwhile, bring a large pot of salted water to a boil. Drop in the pasta; quickly return the water to a boil, stirring the pasta gently, and cook until the pasta is tender yet firm, about 1 minute. Reserve 1 cup (235 ml) of pasta water, then drain the pasta.

Meanwhile, add the remaining ½ cup (120 ml) of oil to the *ragù*, stirring vigorously to blend it in. Add the pasta to the *ragù* (in batches if your pan is small), stirring immediately with a fork to prevent the pasta from clumping. Stir in the parsley, and cook over medium heat until most of the sauce coats the pasta; stir in additional oil and pasta water as necessary to create a creamy sauce.

Divide among warm plates, twirling the pasta into nests on each plate.

FRIED STUFFED SOFTSHELL CRABS with ASPARAGUS

MAKES 4 SERVINGS

Softshells and Vinaigrette:

1 to 1¼ pounds (450 to 570 g) softshell crabs (about 12 small or 4 large)

8 to 10 large eggs

1 tablespoon (15 ml) freshly squeezed lemon juice

3 tablespoons (45 ml) olive oil

Salt and freshly ground black pepper

4 ounces (113 g) white asparagus (3 to 5 spears)

4 ounces (113 g) green asparagus (3 to 5 spears)

Asparagus Mayonnaise:

8 ounces (227 g) green asparagus (6 to 10 spears)

½ packed cup (30 g) fresh flat-leaf parsley leaves and small stems

1 large egg yolk

About 1½ cups (375 g) olive oil

About 2 tablespoons (30 ml) freshly squeezed lemon juice

Salt and freshly ground black pepper

To Serve:

Oil, for frying

About 1 cup (125 g) *tipo* 00 flour (see page 277) or all-purpose flour, for dredging

Salt

1 teaspoon (1.5 g) chopped fresh chives for garnish

In the spring and fall in Venice, the fish market sells *moleche* (baby softshell crabs). They're a little bigger than a silver dollar but you could use larger, more mature softshells in this recipe. The classic Venetian preparation is to soak them in raw egg until they gorge themselves, and then bread and fry them until crispy. I serve them in the spring with asparagus vinaigrette and a loose asparagus mayonnaise. With the crispy crab, the creamy mayo, and the fresh asparagus, it's a great starter plate. You may have some leftover asparagus mayo. Save it for sandwiches, fries, or anywhere you'd use plain mayonnaise.

For the softshells and vinaigrette: Place the softshell crabs in a small saucepan or other high-sided container. Beat enough eggs to cover the crabs. Make sure the crabs are completely submerged in the eggs and keep them submerged in the refrigerator for 3 hours. Then clean the crabs by using scissors to cut off about ¼ inch behind the eyes; lift up the pointed sides of the crab to remove the gills underneath; then turn the crab over and snip off the flap or "apron" on the bottom. Return the cleaned softshells to the eggs until ready to use.

Put the lemon juice in a medium bowl and whisk in the oil. Season the vinaigrette with salt and pepper. Trim the tough ends of both the green and white asparagus. Using a mandoline or vegetable peeler, thinly shave the asparagus into the bowl of vinaigrette. Toss and let stand for 1 hour at room temperature. Taste and season with salt and pepper as necessary.

For the asparagus mayonnaise: Bring a medium pot of water to a boil and fill a large bowl with ice water. Trim the tough ends from the asparagus, add the asparagus to the boiling water, and blanch until crisp-tender, about 30 seconds. Transfer to the ice water to stop the cooking. When cool, coarsely chop the asparagus and puree in a blender. Add the parsley and egg yolk to form a smooth puree. With the blender running, slowly add the oil in a steady stream until the mixture emulsifies, about a minute. Season with the lemon juice, salt, and pepper.

To serve: Heat the oil in a deep fryer or deep saucepan to 350°F (175°C). Remove the crabs one by one from the egg, dredge in the flour, and deep-fry until golden brown, 4 to 5 minutes. Drain on paper towels and season immediately with salt.

While the crabs are frying, spoon a generous amount of asparagus mayo on each plate. Mound the asparagus salad near the mayo. Sprinkle with the chives and place the crab over the mayo.

RADICCHIO RAVIOLI with BALSAMIC BROWN BUTTER

The Veneto mainland grows incredible produce. It's all on display at the Rialto market in Venice. One of my favorites is radicchio. Not just the familiar round heads of red radicchio grown nearby in Chioggia, but also the longer heads of early and late radicchio from Treviso, the looser oval radicchio from Verona, and the red-speckled pale green radicchio from Castelfranco that's shaped like a huge rose blossom. They're all bitter and delicious, so use any type here. Mixed with ricotta, radicchio makes a great ravioli filling. For a sauce, I like to cut the bitterness with balsamic vinegar mixed into brown butter. When you taste it, it's almost like having a salad in pasta form.

Heat 1 tablespoon (14 g) of the butter with the oil and smashed garlic over medium heat in a large sauté pan until the garlic browns just a little, 3 to 4 minutes. Add the radicchio and sweat over low heat until tender but not browned, 5 to 6 minutes. Season to taste with salt and pepper, and then remove from the heat and let cool. Discard the garlic clove and drain off any excess liquid.

Mince the cooked radicchio and transfer to a large bowl. Add the egg, ricotta, and 2 tablespoons (12.5 g) of the Parmesan and season lightly with salt and pepper. Use immediately or transfer to a resealable plastic bag and refrigerate for up to 4 hours.

Lay a pasta sheet on a lightly floured work surface and dust with flour. Trim the ends to make them square, then fold the dough in half lengthwise and make a small notch at the center to mark it. Open the sheet so it lies flat again and spritz with water.

Beginning at the left-hand side, spoon two rows of ½-inch (1.25-cm)-diameter balls of filling along the length of the pasta, leaving a 1½-inch (3.75-cm) margin around each ball and stopping at the center of the sheet. Lift up the right-hand side of the pasta sheet and fold it over to cover the balls of filling. Gently press the pasta around each ball of filling to seal. Use a 2½-inch (6.25 cm) round fluted ravioli cutter or a similar size biscuit cutter to cut the ravioli. Repeat with the remaining pasta dough and filling. Use immediately, or freeze in a single layer, transfer the frozen ravioli to resealable plastic bags, and freeze for up to 1 week. You should have about forty-eight ravioli.

When ready to serve, bring a large pot of salted water to a boil. Drop in the ravioli, quickly return the water to a boil, and cook until tender yet firm, 2 to 3 minutes.

Meanwhile, melt the remaining 6 tablespoons (85 g) of butter in a large, deep sauté pan over medium heat. Add the thyme, and cook until the butter turns golden brown and the milk solids brown on the bottom of the pan, 8 to 10 minutes. Remove from the heat, stand back, and stir in the vinegar; it will sputter. Taste and season with salt and pepper.

Drain the ravioli, place twelve to fifteen on each plate, and sprinkle with the remaining 3 tablespoons (19 g) of Parmesan. Pour the balsamic brown butter over and around the ravioli.

MAKES 4 TO 6 SERVINGS

7 tablespoons (100 g) unsalted butter, divided

1 tablespoon (15 ml) olive oil

1 small garlic clove, smashed

½ round head red radicchio, julienned or shredded

Salt and freshly ground black pepper

1 small egg

4 ounces (120 ml) fresh whole-milk ricotta cheese (½ cup)

1 ounce (28 g) Parmesan cheese, grated (⅓ cup), divided

8 ounces (227 g) Egg Pasta Dough (page 282), rolled into 2 sheets, each about 1/32 inch (0.8 mm) thick

3 sprigs fresh thyme

3 tablespoons (45 ml) balsamic vinegar

FRITTO MISTO DI PESCE

MAKES 4 TO 6 SERVINGS

Oil, for frying

About 4 cups (1 L) whole milk, for soaking fish and vegetables

6 ounces (170 g) squid, cleaned and cut into 3-inch (7.5 cm)-wide strips (not rings)

6 ounces (170 g) skate wing, cut on the bone into 3-inch (7.5-cm) pieces

6 ounces (170 g) fresh whole anchovies, gutted and cleaned

6 ounces (170 g) baby cod, cut into 3-inch (7.5-cm) pieces

6 ounces (170 g) medium (U50 or 41/50) shrimp, left whole and unpeeled

1 medium-size white onion, thickly sliced and separated into rings

1 medium-size zucchini, cut into 3-inch (7.5-cm) sticks

¼ medium-size eggplant, cut into 3-inch (7.5-cm) sticks

2 cups (250 g) *tipo* 00 flour (see page 277) or all-purpose flour

1 cup (167 g) semolina flour

Salt and freshly ground black pepper

Lemon wedges, for squeezing

I make a fish fry every time I visit Venice. If you have an apartment with a small kitchen, fritto misto is the best thing to do with all that great fish in the market. I usually fry up some vegetables, too, such as eggplant and zucchini. But experiment with baby artichokes or whatever's fresh in the produce bins. A little semolina flour in the breading gives you great crunch. Just season everything with salt and pepper as it comes out of the fryer, squeeze on some lemon, and you're good to go!

Heat the oil in a deep fryer to 350°F (175°C). Divide the milk between two bowls.

Prepare all the fish and vegetables and place the fish in one bowl of milk to cover, and place the vegetables in the other bowl of milk.

Combine the flours in a medium bowl. Drain each piece of fish from the milk, dredge it in the flour mixture, and then fry it until golden brown, 4 to 5 minutes, adjusting the heat to maintain the 350°F (175°C) oil temperature at all times. Transfer the fish to paper towels and immediately season with salt and pepper. Repeat with the remaining fish and vegetables.

Serve on butcher paper with the lemon wedges.

COCONUT LATTE FRITTO with PASSION FRUIT CURD

You can find *latte fritto* anywhere in Venice. It's basically thickened pastry cream cut into little pieces, breaded and fried, and served as a sweet snack or dessert. The trick is to cook out the flour so the custard gets nice and thick. Then you can cut it easily when it cools. They don't use coconut milk in Venice but I wanted some more tropical flavors here. With passion fruit curd for dipping, it's a more aromatic twist on the traditional dish.

For the passion fruit curd: Set a fine-mesh sieve over the top of a double boiler or a medium heatproof bowl. Working over the sieve, cut the passion fruits in half and use a spoon to scrape the pulp, seeds and all, into the sieve. Use a rubber spatula to gently push the fruit pulp through the sieve. Discard the seeds. You should have 1 cup (235 ml) of passion fruit puree. Whisk in the eggs, egg yolks, sugar, vanilla, and salt and set the pan or bowl over a pan of gently simmering water. Whisk constantly until the mixture heats gently and thickens enough for the whisk to leave ribbons of curd when lifted from the pan, 10 to 15 minutes. Put the chopped butter in a medium bowl and pour the hot curd over the top. Whisk until the butter is completely melted and blended into the curd. Let cool and refrigerate until ready to serve or up to 5 days.

For the coconut latte fritto: Bring 2 cups (475 ml) of the coconut milk to a boil in a medium saucepan over medium-high heat. Meanwhile, whisk together the flour, sugar, remaining 1 cup (235 ml) of coconut milk, and egg yolks in a medium bowl. Temper the egg mixture by slowly adding and stirring in ½ cup (120 ml) of the hot coconut milk. Lower the heat to medium-low and pour the egg mixture into the saucepan of hot coconut milk. Cook until the mixture thickens, 15 to 20 minutes, whisking constantly to prevent scrambling the eggs on the bottom of the pan. The mixture should thicken enough to pull away from the sides of the pan, sort of like choux pastry when the liquid fat starts to separate out a tiny bit. Line a 2-quart (2-L) baking dish, such as an 8-inch (20 cm) square pan, with enough foil to overhang the edges as a sling. Pour in the fritto mixture, smooth the top, and let cool slightly. Press plastic onto the top, and then refrigerate until the mixture sets up enough to be cut into squares like soft fudge, at least 8 hours or up to 2 days.

Heat the oil in a deep fryer or deep pot to 325°F (160°C). Cut the cold coconut latte into 1-inch (2.5-cm) squares. Put the eggs, flour, and breadcrumbs in three separate bowls, and then carefully dip each square of coconut latte in the flour, then the egg, then the breadcrumbs, making sure the cubes are thoroughly coated. Fry in the hot oil until golden brown, 3 to 4 minutes. Fry in batches, if necessary, to prevent overcrowding. Drain on paper towels, and then toss in granulated sugar to coat.

To serve: Place a few pieces of hot coconut latte fritto on each plate with a generous spoonful of passion fruit curd for dipping.

MAKES 4 TO 6 SERVINGS

Passion Fruit Curd:

15 passion fruits, or 1 cup (235 ml) passion fruit puree

2 large eggs

12 large egg yolks

1 cup plus 1 tablespoon (213 g) granulated sugar

1 vanilla bean, split and scraped

Pinch of salt

8 ounces (2 sticks/227 g) unsalted butter, chopped

Coconut Latte Fritto:

3 cups (750 ml) unsweetened fresh or canned coconut milk, divided

¾ cup (94 g) *tipo* 00 flour (see page 277) or all-purpose flour, plus 1 cup (125 g), for dredging

⅔ cup (133 g) granulated sugar, plus some for coating

3 large egg yolks

Oil, for frying

3 large eggs

1 cup (108 g) plain, dry breadcrumbs

HEIRLOOM APPLE UPSIDE-DOWN CAKE
with POLENTA GELATO

MAKES 8 SERVINGS

Apple Cake:

6 ounces (1½ sticks/170 g) unsalted butter, softened, plus some for greasing the pan

7 Granny Smith apples

3¾ cups (750 g) granulated sugar, divided

3 large eggs

6 large egg yolks, divided

¾ cup (120 g) finely ground cornmeal, sifted

¾ teaspoon (3.5 g) baking powder

½ teaspoon (3 g) salt

Apple Coulis:

1 pound (450 g) heirloom apples (about 3)

1 cup (200 g) granulated sugar

1 small cinnamon stick

To Serve:

½ cup (80 g) coarse yellow cornmeal (polenta)

4 cups (1 L) Polenta Gelato (page 287)

This recipe has little to do with Italy, except for the polenta gelato. I started making it a few years ago at Osteria in Philadelphia. Some guys from Agusta, an Italian helicopter company in northeast Philly, came into the restaurant and couldn't believe I had polenta gelato on the menu. They were from Bergamo! They started coming in regularly and one guy, Giovanni, from the south of Italy, refused to eat the gelato because polenta is only found in northern Italy. It was like moving mountains to get him to try it. He finally tried it and all the northerners made fun of him, calling him a *polentone* (slang for a polenta eater from the north). We eventually became friends with the Bergamascans in their group and now celebrate Easter with them. It makes Claudia feel more at home.

For the cakes: Butter a 9-inch (23-cm) round cake pan. Peel, core, and slice the apples about ¼ inch (6.25 mm) thick. Pour 2¾ cups (550 g) of the sugar into a deep sauté pan and add just enough water to moisten the sugar into a thick paste, about ½ cup (120 ml). Bring to a simmer over medium-high heat and cook until the sugar dissolves and turns medium amber, 6 to 8 minutes. Stand back and add 2 tablespoons (30 ml) of water, stirring to soften the caramel. Stir in the apples, and cook over high heat until the apples begin to soften and the caramel thickens, 3 to 5 minutes. Pour the apples into the prepared pan and let cool.

Preheat the oven to 325°F (160°C). In the bowl of a stand mixer, cream the butter and remaining 1 cup (200 g) of sugar on medium speed until light and fluffy, 2 to 3 minutes. Add the eggs and half of the egg yolks, one at a time, scraping down the sides of the bowl a few times. Mix together the cornmeal, baking powder, and salt and alternately add the mixture to the bowl with the remaining yolks. Pour the batter over the apples and bake until a toothpick inserted into the center of the cake comes out clean, about 40 minutes. Remove and let cool in the pan on a rack for 15 minutes. When almost cooled, invert onto a large plate or platter.

For the apple coulis: Peel, core, and coarsely chop the apples. Transfer to a large deep sauté pan and add the sugar, cinnamon stick, and 1 cup (235 ml) of water. Bring to a simmer over medium-high heat, then lower the heat to medium and simmer until the apples become very soft, about 20 minutes, stirring a few times. Remove the cinnamon stick and puree the mixture in a blender until smooth. Refrigerate until ready to use or up to 5 days.

To serve: Toast the coarse polenta in a dry pan over medium-high heat until fragrant, 3 to 4 minutes, shaking the pan often. To plate, draw an X on each plate with the apple coulis and put a slice of apple cake over the coulis a little off center. Sprinkle some toasted polenta in the open area and place a scoop of polenta gelato on top.

RUSTIC PEACH TART
with GOAT CHEESE SORBET

I don't know how to describe the peaches in Italy. They're just amazing. Small, soft, and dense with liquid sugar. In summertime, you have no trouble finding mounds and mounds of perfect ones in the produce markets. Here's something simple to do with them. Nothing fancy. At Osteria, we serve these as individual tarts (as shown on page 192), but I wrote the recipe here for a single tart because it's easier to make and serve that way at home. If you want to make individual tarts, just roll out several smaller rounds of tart dough instead of one large one. This recipe reminds me of the rustic pies and tarts my grandmother Jacqueline Michaud used to make when I was growing up in New Hampshire. I grew up right next door to her. She was the chef in the family and one of my earliest culinary inspirations. I had ice cream with my peach pie as a kid, but as an adult I crave sharper flavors. Goat Cheese Sorbet adds just the right amount. You could also serve this with Raspberry Sorbet (page 288) if you like.

MAKES 10 TO 12 SERVINGS

Tart Dough and Peaches:

3⅔ cups (460 g) *tipo* 00 flour (see page 277) or all-purpose flour

1 teaspoon (6 g) salt

1⅓ cups (300 g) cold unsalted butter, cut into small cubes

⅔ cup (150 ml) cold water

6 ripe peaches

Almond Frangipane:

2 cups (190 g) finely ground almonds

1 tablespoon (8 g) *tipo* 00 flour (see page 277) or all-purpose flour

1¾ cups (210 g) confectioners' sugar, divided

9 tablespoons (213 g) unsalted butter, at room temperature

2 large eggs

1 large egg yolk

To Serve:

2 tablespoons (25 g) granulated sugar

1 large egg

2 tablespoons (25 g) turbinado or raw sugar

5 cups (1.25 L) Goat Cheese Sorbet (page 288)

(continued on next page)

For the tart dough and peaches: Combine the flour and salt in a stand mixer fitted with the paddle attachment on low speed, or whisk together in a mixing bowl. Add the butter and mix on medium-low speed until the butter is cut into very small pieces throughout the flour, or use a pastry cutter to cut the butter into the flour in the bowl. Slowly pour in the water and mix just until the dough comes together. Turn out onto a sheet of plastic wrap and quickly gather the dough into a ball. Press it into a disk and wrap in the plastic. Refrigerate for at least 1 hour or up to 1 day.

Meanwhile, bring a large pot of water to a boil and fill a large bowl with ice water. Score an X on the bottom of each peach. Working in two batches, drop the peaches in the boiling water for 1 minute, and then transfer them to the ice water to cool. Remove the peels with a paring knife, cut in half around the pits, and remove the pits. Slice the peaches about ¼ inch (6 mm) thick and set aside.

For the frangipane: Combine the ground almonds, flour, and ¼ cup (30 g) of the confectioners' sugar in a food processor and process to a very fine meal. In a stand mixer, cream the butter and remaining 1½ cups (180 g) confectioners' sugar on medium speed until light and fluffy, 3 to 4 minutes. Add the eggs, one at a time, and then the yolk, beating until each is incorporated before adding the next. Add the almond mixture on low speed just until blended. The frangipane can be refrigerated for up to 1 day before using. Let stand until spreadable before using.

Preheat the oven to 350°F (175°C).

Transfer the pie dough to a large sheet of lightly floured parchment paper. Top with overlapping sheets of plastic and roll the dough from the center outward to a 14-inch (35.5-cm) circle. Remove the plastic from the dough, then spread the frangipane over the pie dough, leaving a 2-inch (5-cm) border of dough around the perimeter. Use the parchment to slide the dough and frangipane to a large baking sheet (you can use the back of a rimmed baking sheet, if necessary).

Fan the sliced peaches over the frangipane, sprinkling them with sugar as you go and leaving a 2-inch (5-cm) border of dough at the edges. Lift the border of dough over the edge of the fruit, making a few small folds of dough as you go around the circle. Whisk the egg with 1 teaspoon (5 ml) of water and brush all over the exposed dough. Sprinkle generously with turbinado sugar.

Bake until the crust is browned and the fruit is tender, 40 to 50 minutes. Let cool slightly, then cut into wedges. Serve each wedge with a large scoop of gelato.

LEFFE

BECOMING A CHEF

"HOW DID YOU GET TO ITALY?" A SHORT, TWITCHY OLD MAN NEAR THE COUNTER ASKED ME IN ITALIAN. I GUESS HE COULD TELL I WAS AMERICAN WHEN I ORDERED MY CAPPUC-CINO AND CROISSANT. "I'M A CHEF IN BERGAMO," I SAID. "MY GIRLFRIEND IS FROM THERE, TOO." IT WAS ONLY TEN IN THE MORNING, BUT THE GUY ALREADY LOOKED AND SMELLED HALF IN THE BAG. "DOES SHE HAVE A BIG LAWN?" HE ASKED. "EXCUSE ME?" I REPLIED. "THEY HAVE BIG LAWNS IN BERGAMO," HE WENT ON, "WITH LOTS OF ROOM FOR SEX!" THEN HE SMILED, LAUGHING.

Turning away, I figured this dirty old man must work in one of the local textile factories, weaving fancy napkins, tablecloths, and drapes for famous companies, such as Frette. As I drove out of downtown Leffe, up Via Monte Beio, the scene changed completely. Beautiful red, blue, and yellow homes poked through trees on the hillsides above Val Seriana (Seriana Valley). Near the top of the area called San Rocco, I pulled into Locanda del Biancospino and took in the incredible views from the inn's covered dining terrace. You could see all of "*le cinque terre della valgandino*," the five lands of the Gandino valley, and, in the distance, the snow-capped peaks of the Italian Alps. This would be my first executive chef position in Italy. It was an utterly stunning location, but, so far out of town and up the hills, would the restaurant be successful? One glance at the gleaming new kitchen equip-ment and induction burners replaced all doubt with excitement. The Servalli family who hired me spent more than 100,000 euros ($135,000) on the kitchen alone. I sali-vated at the opportunity to show off my cooking chops and honor the cuisine that had given me so much.

That winter, I developed the menu, opened the restau-rant, and ran the kitchen. Through the spring, I cooked for dozens of big parties and banquets and hundreds of guests.

Locanda del Biancospino celebrated the mountain cuisine of the alpine foothills, and my go-to ingredients were wild game, such as pheasant and guinea hen, and forest vegetables and herbs, such as porcini mushrooms and spring onions. The seasons dictated every dish. I bought my vegetables at the local farmers' market in Cene, shopped for meats at the Camotti butcher shop in Nembro, and purchased fish from Pescheria Orobica, one of the best fishmongers in northern Italy. Every ingredient was pristine; each piece of fruit, cra-dled in its own nest; each slice of prosciutto, neatly layered between sheets of butcher paper. Even the quality of the cured sausage I bought showed that in food, as in fashion, Italians excel at craftsmanship.

Biancospino was relatively small and we changed the menu often, so I could flex my muscles as a chef there. I cre-ated elaborate, composed dishes. The local guinea hens were huge, about four pounds (1.75 kg) each, so I made guinea hen four ways with multiple components, marinating and poaching the breast, searing off the livers like foie gras, and making rillettes with the legs. I crisped up the skin and served the cracklings over guinea hen salad made from the rest of the bird.

It was 2005 and molecular gastronomy was exploding in

Italy. I experimented with alginates, sous vide, and xanthan gum. I deconstructed familiar dishes and presented them in new ways. I pureed fruits and vegetables and foamed them up with nitrous oxide. I plated everything to be as spectacular as the alpine view from the inn's terrace, arranging a few slices of hen here, a julienne of fennel there, some decorative drops of sauce and a well-placed herb near the edge. I served such dishes as baby horse rib eye with squash gratin, rabbit roasted in black olives with apple and celery root *involtini,* pork ribs with Brussels sprout and walnut fricassee, licorice savarin with coffee sorbetto, and warm bitter chocolate mousse with peperoncino. For a spring party, I made rabbit *casoncelli* with crushed amaretti cookies and chopped raisins in the pasta filling. The locals were used to traditional casoncelli filled with beef and pork, and they loved the subtle twist using rabbit, stunned that an American could put this kind of spin on their local pasta. And do it well.

After a few months, I learned to create successful menus and to manage food costs. First thing in the morning, I would check the walk-in, take ingredient inventory, read the guest list, and put together my food order. I learned how to control everything from my kitchen staff and inventory to my purchasing and budget.

But now that I was executive chef, my most important lessons came from within. Months of flaunting my talents and pushing culinary limits taught me that you can't just cook from your head. You have to cook from your heart. I started seeing parallels between Pina's and Claudia's home cooking and the Michelin-star cooking done at such restaurants as Frosio, La Brughiera, and Loro. They all had heart and soul. I found that even something as simple as an unadorned, spit-roasted goat could be incredibly satisfying when cooked with care. If tended and nurtured, a dead-easy pot of Bolognese sauce can be the most delicious thing you have ever eaten.

Toward the end of that spring, instead of preparing guinea hen four ways, I just stuffed it and roasted it with spring onions. Instead of pureeing and foaming zucchini, I simply grilled it and served it with lemon dressing and local herbs. I still cooked with skill but also with passion—minus the bells and whistles on which I had been relying. I discovered that, as a chef, I wanted to cook less precious food. More rustic. Bold. And beautiful. It was a huge lesson. I'd lost my appetite for such ingredients as methycellulose and tapioca maltodextrin. I wanted to cook with truffles, Taleggio, porcini, and pork. I wanted pheasant and duck hunted from the woods, snails and wild berries harvested from the hills, and local cheeses aged in caves for months until they were perfectly ripe. I wanted to cook with the amazing food that was growing around me.

Locanda del Biancospino was like a petri dish for my professional development. But by the end of that spring, I had to leave. The restaurant was doing well, except that Anna Servalli had hired me on the condition that I get a work visa. My uncle was helping me secure one. But work visas are almost impossible for Americans to get in Italy. It was taking forever, and by the late spring, I still didn't have it. Anna said she would have to pay me less. I was already deep in debt and couldn't afford a pay cut. My only option was to leave. But where to go? Without a work visa, I couldn't make much money in Italy. Yet, moving back to the States meant leaving Claudia here.

Sweet Onion Flan with Morels

•

Snail Spiedini with Celery Root Puree
and Truffle Butter

•

Sweetbread Saltimbocca with Squash Puree

•

Duck Casoncelli with Quince,
Brown Butter, and Sage

•

Pheasant Lasagna

•

Milk-Braised Pork Cheeks
with Porcini Polenta

•

Porcini Ravioli with Taleggio
and Burro Fuso

•

Chinotto Affogato

•

Fried Huckleberry Ravioli
with Mascarpone Crema

SWEET ONION FLAN with MORELS

The forests behind Locanda del Biancospino are full of amazing spring ingredients, such as morel mushrooms, wild herbs, and young green onions. I tried to capture the forager's spirit in this dish by pureeing green onion tops to make an emerald-colored flan as an appetizer. The morels are simply sautéed with garlic and served on the side. I like to leave morels whole, but if they're big, you can cut them in half or quarters lengthwise. Whatever you do, make sure you dunk them in water several times to get the dirt out of the crevices. I spin the mushrooms in a salad spinner to dry them.

MAKES 6 TO 8 SERVINGS

Spring Onion Flan:

1½ pounds (680 g) spring onions or scallions

2 tablespoons (30 ml) olive oil

4 tablespoons (57 g) unsalted butter

6 tablespoons (47 g) *tipo* 00 flour (see page 277) or all-purpose flour

2½ cups (625 ml) whole milk

Pinch of grated nutmeg

3 large eggs, lightly beaten

5¼ ounces (150 g) Parmesan cheese, grated (1½ cups)

Salt

Morels:

1 pound (450 g) morel mushrooms

2 tablespoons (30 ml) olive oil

2 tablespoons (28 g) unsalted butter

1 garlic clove, smashed

½ cup (50 g) sliced spring onions or scallions, including tops

1½ teaspoons (7 ml) sherry vinegar

Salt and freshly ground black pepper

For the spring onion flan: Cut the spring onions into 1-inch (2.5-cm) lengths, keeping the green tops and white bottoms separate.

Heat the oil in a large sauté pan over medium heat. Add the onion bottoms and sweat until soft but not browned, 3 to 5 minutes, adding a little water, if necessary, to soften them and keep them from browning. When soft, add the green tops, and cook until tender, 2 to 3 minutes. Transfer to a food processor and puree until super-smooth, 4 to 5 minutes, scraping down the sides a few times.

Meanwhile, melt the butter in a medium saucepan over medium heat. Whisk in the flour to make a roux, and then cook for 3 to 4 minutes, whisking to prevent burning. Gradually whisk in the milk, stirring constantly with a wooden spoon until the mixture is free of lumps. Continue cooking, stirring occasionally, until the sauce is thick enough to coat the back of a spoon, about 5 minutes. Stir in the nutmeg, pour into a medium bowl, and let cool. Add the pureed onions, eggs, and Parmesan, and stir until combined. Strain through a fine-mesh sieve into a bowl, and then season with salt.

Preheat the oven to 375°F (190°C). Set a kettle of water to boil.

Butter six to eight 4-ounce (120-ml) ramekins and fill each with the flan mixture. Place the tins in a large, deep pan, such as a roasting pan, and pour enough hot water into the pan to come halfway up the sides of the tins. Bake in the water bath until set on the sides but still slightly jiggly in the center, 20 to 25 minutes.

Transfer the flans from the water bath to a baking sheet and let cool. When cool, cover and refrigerate until cold, at least 2 hours or up to 2 days.

For the morels: Fill a large bowl with cold water and dunk the morels up and down in the water half a dozen times to rinse any dirt from their crevices. Pat dry or spin dry in a salad spinner. Leave any small morels whole but cut the large ones lengthwise into halves or quarters.

Heat the oil, butter, and garlic in a large sauté pan over medium heat. When the butter melts, add the spring onions and morels, and cook until tender, 3 to 4 minutes. Season with the vinegar, and salt and pepper to taste and let cool. Remove the garlic.

To plate, dip the bottom and sides of the ramekins in hot water to loosen the flans, then invert and unmold the flans onto plates. Serve with a spoonful of morels.

SNAIL SPIEDINI with CELERY ROOT PUREE and TRUFFLE BUTTER

MAKES 4 SERVINGS

Every year, Claudia's aunt Irene and her mother, Pina, hike the Italian Alps, foraging for snails. One year, they came back with fifty kilos (110 pounds) of live snails. It took three days to get them ready to eat. Day one was soaking them in polenta for twenty-four hours. Day two was boiling them. Day three was picking out the meat and freezing it. What a pain! Thank God we can get snails already prepared (see Sources on page 289). I like to wrap them in pancetta to keep them moist and grill them quick before they get rubbery. You'll need twelve small bamboo skewers to make the *spiedini* (kebabs). Soak the skewers in water for twenty minutes to help keep them from burning.

For the snails: Melt the butter in a large sauté pan over medium-low heat. Add the onion, garlic, and bay leaf, and sweat until the onion is soft but not browned, 10 to 12 minutes. Add the snails, toss to coat, and cook for 8 to 10 minutes more. Remove from the heat, season with salt and pepper, and let cool in the pan. When cool, wrap each snail with a piece of pancetta and thread onto short, presoaked skewers, allowing three snails per skewer.

For the celery root puree: Melt 2 tablespoons (28 g) of the butter in a medium saucepan over medium-low heat. Add the onion and sweat until the onion is soft but not browned, 8 to 10 minutes. Add the celery root, potato, and enough water to cover the ingredients by ½ inch (1.25 cm). Cover and bring to a boil over high heat, and then lower the heat and gently simmer uncovered until the celery root is tender, 20 to 25 minutes. Drain and pass the solids through a food mill or potato ricer, along with the remaining ½ cup (113 g) of butter, until creamy, or puree until smooth in a small food processor. Season with salt and pepper and keep warm.

For the truffle butter: Mix the butter, lemon zest and juice, parsley, truffle paste, and salt and pepper to taste together in a small bowl. Taste and adjust the seasoning as necessary.

Heat a grill for direct, medium heat. When hot, coat the grill grate with oil. Grill the snails until nicely grill-marked on all sides, 2 to 3 minutes per side.

Melt the truffle butter in a small saucepan or microwave. Spoon a pool of warm celery root puree on each plate, top with three skewers, and drizzle with melted truffle butter.

Snails:

4 tablespoons (57 g) unsalted butter

½ medium-size yellow onion, minced (½ cup/80 g)

2 garlic cloves, minced

1 bay leaf

36 large cooked snails

Salt and freshly ground black pepper

36 thin slices of pancetta or bacon (about 1½ pounds/680 g)

Vegetable oil, as needed

Celery Root Puree:

2 tablespoons plus ½ cup (141 g) unsalted butter, divided

¼ cup (40 g) minced yellow onion

6 ounces (170 g) celery root, peeled and diced (1 cup)

½ small potato, peeled and diced (¼ cup/40 g)

Salt and freshly ground black pepper

Truffle Butter:

4 tablespoons (57 g) unsalted butter, melted

Zest of 1 lemon

1 tablespoon (15 ml) freshly squeezed lemon juice

1 tablespoon (4 g) chopped fresh flat-leaf parsley

2 tablespoons (30 ml) white or black truffle paste

Salt and freshly ground black pepper

SWEETBREAD SALTIMBOCCA with SQUASH PUREE

MAKES 4 SERVINGS

Squash Puree and Sautéed Squash:

6 tablespoons (90 ml) olive oil, divided

1 garlic clove, smashed

1 bay leaf

½ medium-size yellow onion, chopped (⅔ cup/107 g)

1 pound (450 g) Hubbard squash, peeled and cut into ¼-inch (6-mm) cubes (3 cups), divided

1½ teaspoons (7 ml) honey

1 tablespoon (15 ml) sherry vinegar

Salt and freshly ground black pepper

Sweetbread Saltimbocca:

8 ounces (227 g) veal sweetbreads

4 leaves fresh sage

4 thin slices prosciutto (2 ounces/57 g)

2 tablespoons (30 ml) grapeseed oil

2 tablespoons (28 g) unsalted butter

Salt and freshly ground black pepper

About 1 cup (125 g) *tipo* 00 flour (see page 277) or all-purpose flour, for dredging

To Serve:

2 tablespoons (28 g) unsalted butter

16 leaves fresh sage

Italian cuisine encourages you to experiment and make dishes your own. I took classic saltimbocca—pounded veal rolled up with prosciutto and sage—and substituted sweetbreads. The sweetbreads' soft texture is similar to that of pounded veal, but they get even crispier in the pan. To add something creamy, I made a simple squash puree and served some diced, sautéed squash on the side. I like Hubbard squash here, but if you can't find that, use Jarrahdale or butternut squash.

For the squash: Heat 1 tablespoon (15 ml) of the oil with the garlic and bay leaf in a medium saucepan over medium heat. Add the onion and sweat until soft but not browned, 4 to 6 minutes. Add 2 cups (11 ounces/310 g) of the squash, season with salt and pepper, and add enough water to cover the ingredients by 1 inch (2.5 cm). Cover and bring to a simmer over high heat, then lower the heat to medium-low and gently simmer uncovered until the squash is soft, 20 to 25 minutes. Drain off most of the water and discard the garlic and bay leaf. Puree the squash in a blender until smooth. With the blender running, add the honey, vinegar, and ¼ cup (60 ml) of the remaining olive oil, blending until you get a smooth, pourable, medium-thick puree. Season with salt and pepper and keep warm over low heat or refrigerate for up to 2 days.

Heat the remaining 1 tablespoon (15 ml) of oil in a medium sauté pan over medium heat. Add the remaining 1 cup (5 ounces/140 g) of squash and sauté until tender, 8 to 10 minutes. Season with salt and pepper and keep warm over low heat or refrigerate for up to 2 days.

For the sweetbread saltimbocca: Rinse the sweetbreads in cold water, then soak in a bowl of ice water for 10 minutes. Pat dry, then remove some of the outer membrane from the sweetbreads, keeping each portion whole. Cut the sweetbreads into equal 2-ounce (57-g) portions, about the size of three fingers. Place each portion between sheets of plastic and gently pound from the center outward to an even ⅛- to ¼-inch (3- to 6-mm) thickness. Layer the sage and prosciutto over each sweetbread portion and then fold in half to cover the sage and prosciutto. Wrap each portion in plastic, cover, and refrigerate until ready to use or up to 8 hours. It's important to keep the sweetbreads cold right up until you cook them.

Heat the grapeseed oil and butter in a large sauté pan over medium-high heat. Season the saltimbocca with salt and pepper and dredge in the flour, keeping the portions whole. Add to the pan and sauté until golden brown on both sides, 3 to 4 minutes per side.

To serve: Add the butter and sage to the pan with the squash cubes, and cook over medium heat until hot, 2 to 3 minutes.

Spoon a pool of warm squash puree in the middle of each plate and top with a portion of sweetbreads, a spoonful of sautéed squash cubes, and the fried sage.

DUCK CASONCELLI with QUINCE, BROWN BUTTER, and SAGE

Casoncelli is the local stuffed pasta of Bergamo. It's made a little differently from town to town but the backbone is the same: a thick ravioli dough filled with whatever scraps of food are hanging around—odds and ends of meat, stale cookies, breadcrumbs. . . you name it. The sauce is usually just crispy bits of pancetta, brown butter, and sage, and it brings the whole dish together. At Locanda del Biancospino, I sometimes made casoncelli with rabbit and prunes; other times, with duck and persimmons. Here's one of my favorite versions with duck and quince.

MAKES 8 SERVINGS

About 2 tablespoons (30 ml) blended oil (see page 276)

1½ pounds (680 g) bone-in duck legs

Salt and freshly ground black pepper

½ medium-size yellow onion, chopped (⅔ cup/107 g)

1 large rib celery, chopped (⅔ cup/68 g)

1 medium-size carrot, chopped (⅔ cup/82 g)

1 sachet of 2 sprigs each parsley, rosemary, and thyme (see page 277)

2 to 3 cups (500 to 750 ml) red wine

4¼ ounces (120 g) Parmesan cheese, grated (1¼ cups), divided

3 tablespoons (22 g) finely ground amaretti cookies

2 tablespoons (20 g) raisins, chopped

1 large egg

8 ounces (227 g) Egg Pasta Dough (page 282), rolled into 2 sheets, each about 1/32 inch (0.8 mm) thick

1 quince, peeled

3 sprigs fresh thyme

1 sprig fresh rosemary

8 ounces (2 sticks/227 g) unsalted butter

20 small leaves fresh sage

Put enough oil into a Dutch oven to coat the bottom and heat over medium-high heat. Pat the duck dry and season with salt and pepper. Sear the duck in the hot oil until nicely browned all over, 4 to 5 minutes per side. Transfer to a platter and add the onion, celery, and carrot, sweating the vegetables until soft but not browned, 4 to 5 minutes. Add the duck back to the pot, along with the sachet and wine. Bring to a simmer, and then cover and simmer over medium-low heat until the duck is almost tender enough to fall off the bone, 30 to 40 minutes.

Transfer the duck to a platter, and when cool enough to handle, pick the meat and skin from the bones, discarding the bones. Meanwhile, strain the braising liquid, reserving the liquid and vegetables separately. Grind the vegetables and picked meat and skin on the small ($\frac{1}{8}$-inch/3-mm) die of a meat grinder or pulse in a food processor until finely chopped but not pureed. Transfer to a mixing bowl and stir in $\frac{1}{4}$ cup of the Parmesan, ground cookies, raisins, and egg. Season with salt and pepper, and then use immediately or spoon the filling into a resealable plastic bag and refrigerate for up to 1 day.

Lay a pasta sheet on a lightly floured surface and trim the short edges square. Cut the pasta in half lengthwise to make two long sheets, each about 3 inches (7.5 cm) wide. Pipe the filling in $\frac{3}{4}$-inch (2-cm)-diameter balls in a row down the length of each sheet, placing each ball near one edge of each sheet and leaving a $1\frac{1}{2}$-inch (3.75-cm) margin around each ball. Spritz the dough lightly with water and fold it over the filling, long edge to long edge. Gently press around each ball of filling to eliminate air pockets. Using a $2\frac{1}{2}$-inch (6-cm) round pasta or cookie cutter, cut out a series of half-moons, placing the cutter off center so the folded edge of the pasta bisects the equator of the cutter. Roll each half-moon from the folded edge to the cut edge to prop up the filling, and then pinch the pasta on each side of the filling to make "wings." The finished pasta should resemble a piece of wrapped candy. Repeat with the remaining pasta dough and filling. Transfer the casoncelli to parchment-lined baking sheets and refrigerate for up to 1 hour or freeze until solid; transfer to resealable plastic bags and freeze for up to 1 week. You should have about one hundred casoncelli.

Put the whole peeled quince in a small saucepan with the reserved duck braising liquid, thyme, and rosemary. Bring to a boil over high heat, then lower the heat to medium-low and simmer until a fork slides easily in and out of the quince, 20 to 25 minutes. Remove from the liquid, and when cool enough to handle, cut lengthwise into quarters and remove the core. Cut the quince into small cubes.

Bring a large pot of salted water to a boil. Drop in the casoncelli in batches if necessary to prevent crowding, and cook until tender yet firm, 5 to 6 minutes. Using a slotted spoon, transfer the casoncelli to warm pasta plates, arranging ten to twelve upright in a tight circular pattern in the center of each plate.

Meanwhile, heat the butter and sage in a sauté pan over medium heat, and cook until the sage is lightly browned, the butter turns golden, and the milk solids lightly brown on the bottom of the pan, 8 to 10 minutes. Add the quince and remove from the heat.

Sprinkle 2 tablespoons of the remaining Parmesan over each plate of casoncelli and spoon the quince and brown butter mixture over and around the pasta. Garnish with one or two fried sage leaves.

PHEASANT LASAGNA

In Leffe, the trees are jam-packed with birds. Travelers stay in the area to go birding and to hunt small game like pheasant, partridge, quail, dove, and guinea hen. In this lasagna, I like pheasant best. It's such a rich-tasting dark-meat bird. But almost any bird will work, even chicken. The best part is the pasta dough that hangs over the edge of the dish and gets crispy in the oven. How often do you get to enjoy crispy pasta? With creamy porcini béchamel and hearty pheasant ragù, this lasagna makes a great fall dish.

MAKES 8 SERVINGS

1 pheasant (2 to 3 pounds/1 to 1.3 kg)

Salt and freshly ground black pepper

1 tablespoon (15 ml) grapeseed oil

1 medium-size carrot, chopped (½ cup/61 g)

1 medium-size rib celery, chopped (½ cup/51 g)

½ medium-size yellow onion, chopped (½ cup/80 g)

1 cup (240 g) canned plum tomatoes, preferably San Marzano, cored and crushed by hand

2 to 3 cups (500 to 750 ml) white wine, or as needed

8 ounces (227 g) Egg Pasta Dough (page 282), rolled into 2 sheets, each about ¹⁄₁₆ -inch (1.5 mm) thick

Unsalted butter, for greasing the pan

1 quart (1 L) Porcini Béchamel (page 281)

8¾ ounces (250 g) Parmesan cheese, grated (2 ½ cups)

Remove the pheasant innards, rinse inside and out, and pat dry. Cut the legs from the body and then season all the pieces with salt and pepper. Heat the oil in a Dutch oven over medium-high heat. When hot, add the pheasant legs and body in batches if necessary to prevent crowding, and sear until browned on all sides, 10 to 15 minutes total. Transfer to a plate. Add the carrot, celery, and onion to the pan, and cook until tender, 6 to 8 minutes. Add the tomatoes, along with the browned pheasant legs and enough wine to barely cover the ingredients (you won't use all of the wine here). Bring to a boil, then lower the heat to medium-low and simmer for 30 minutes. Add the pheasant body and enough wine to come about three-quarters of the way up the body. Cook until all the meat is fall-apart tender, another 30 to 40 minutes. Transfer the meat to a platter and, when cool enough to handle, pick the meat from the bones, discarding the bones and skin. Shred the meat. Strain the vegetables, and return the braising liquid to the pan. Boil the liquid over high heat until reduced in volume by about half, 10 to 15 minutes. Meanwhile, pass the vegetables through a food mill or potato ricer or coarsely puree them in a food processor. When the braising liquid is reduced, stir in the shredded meat and pureed vegetables. Season with salt and pepper and keep warm over low heat or cool and refrigerate for up to 2 days.

Lay a pasta sheet on a lightly floured work surface, trim the edges so they are square, and cut the sheet into two 17-inch (43-cm) lengths and one 13-inch (33-cm) length. Repeat with the remaining pasta, but cut that sheet into three 13-inch (33-cm) lengths.

Bring a large pot of salted water to a boil, and fill a large bowl with ice water. Drop in the pasta in batches to prevent overcrowding, quickly return to a boil, and blanch for 20 seconds. Transfer the pasta to the ice water to stop the cooking. Lay the pieces of pasta flat on kitchen towels and pat dry.

Preheat the oven to 450°F (230°C). Coat a 13 x 9-inch (33 x 23-cm) baking dish with butter. Arrange the two 17-inch (43-cm) lengths of pasta in the buttered dish, leaving a little hanging over the top of the dish. Spread about 1⅓ cups (360 ml) of porcini béchamel over the pasta and then about the same amount of pheasant *ragù*. Sprinkle with ¾ cup (75 g) Parmesan. Lay down another layer of pasta, a layer of béchamel, a layer of ragù, and a layer of Parmesan. Top with a final layer of pasta, the remaining béchamel, and the remaining Parmesan. Bake until golden and crispy on the edges, 8 to 10 minutes. Serve hot.

MILK-BRAISED PORK CHEEKS
with PORCINI POLENTA

Pork cheeks are a seriously under-utilized part of the pig. The jowls are cured for guanciale, but you don't see much else done with the cheeks. This recipe fixes that. I braise the cheeks in my favorite braising liquid: milk. It's a classic Italian technique. The protein and fat in the milk add incredible richness to the meat and keeps it moist. When the meat is tender, the caramelized milk and juices become the sauce. Don't worry if the liquid looks curdled when you open the pot. A quick puree transforms the hot mess into a silky sauce you can ladle over the pork cheeks and porcini polenta.

MAKES 4 TO 6 SERVINGS

2½ pounds (1.1 kg) pork cheeks

Salt and freshly ground black pepper

1 tablespoon (15 ml) grapeseed or olive oil

2 cups (475 ml) whole milk

1 orange

1 small sprig rosemary

1 small garlic clove

3 peppercorns

About ¼ cup (60 ml) extra-virgin olive oil

4 cups (1 L) Porcini Polenta (page 281)

1 tablespoon (4 g) chopped mixed herbs
(parsley, rosemary, thyme) for garnish

Preheat the oven to 350°F (175°C).

Remove the silverskin and any large fat deposits from the pork cheeks so you're left with mostly meat. Pat the cleaned cheeks dry and season all over with salt and pepper.

Heat the oil in a large, deep ovenproof sauté pan or Dutch oven over high heat. When hot, add the cheeks and sear until nicely browned, 3 to 4 minutes per side, working in batches and transferring the cheeks to a plate as they are seared. The pork will leave a dark film (fond) on the bottom of the pan, which is exactly what you want. After all the cheeks have a nice dark brown sear and have been removed from the pan, add the milk to the pan and scrape up the brown bits. Simmer for a minute, then lower the heat to low.

Using a vegetable peeler, peel the zest from half of the orange in strips, removing as little of the bitter white pith as possible. Finely julienne the orange zest and set aside. Cut the orange in half and squeeze the juice from the un-zested half over a strainer into the pan. Drop the juiced orange half into the pan. (Eat the other orange half or save for another use.) Tie up the rosemary, garlic, and peppercorns in cheesecloth or a clean coffee filter and drop that into the pan. Return the seared cheeks to the pan and bring to a simmer, then cover and transfer to the oven. Cook until the meat is tender to the touch but not falling apart, 2 to 2½ hours.

Remove the cheeks from the pan, cover, and let cool. At this point, the cheeks can be refrigerated for up to 3 days. Remove the orange rind and sachet from the braising liquid and transfer the liquid to a blender, scraping in as much of the clumpy milk solids as possible. Buzz until the mixture is blended and light brown in color. Taste and season with salt and black pepper. The sauce can be cooled and refrigerated for up to 3 days (makes about 3 cups/750 ml sauce).

Meanwhile, put the julienned orange zest in a small saucepan and cover with cold water. Bring to a boil over high heat (this is the first blanching). As soon as the water boils, drain the hot water and cover the peels again with fresh cold water. Repeat the process so the peels are blanched three times, then pat them dry and slice into very thin strips. Put the strips in an airtight container and add olive oil to cover. The orange strips can be kept covered at room temperature for 3 days.

Preheat a grill or griddle to medium-high heat. Rub a little oil on the grill or griddle, then grill or sear the pork cheeks just until heated through, 1 to 2 minutes per side. Bring the braising liquid to a gentle simmer over low heat.

Spoon about 1 cup (235 ml) polenta on each plate. Top with four to five pork cheeks and a spoonful of sauce. Garnish with the orange zest and mixed herbs.

PORCINI RAVIOLI with TALEGGIO and BURRO FUSO

Twice a year, mushroom foragers flock to the hills around "*le cinque terre della valgandino.*" Porcinis are everywhere! You'll need a mushroom hunting license, just as you would get a license for hunting animals. Be careful if you go out foraging. It's shocking how many people die from foraging on steep hillsides and falling over the cliffs in the dark, early morning hours. This straightforward ravioli is my homage to a local passion for mushrooms. The twist is putting pieces of Taleggio cheese right over the mushroom filling. When you cook the ravioli, the Taleggio melts into the mushrooms, creating a beautiful creamy filling. Melted butter infused with fresh thyme is all the sauce you need.

MAKES 4 TO 6 SERVINGS

2 teaspoons (10 ml) olive oil

4 ounces (1 stick/113 g) plus 2 teaspoons (9.5 g) unsalted butter, divided

1 small garlic clove, smashed

10 ounces (283 g) fresh or frozen porcini mushrooms, thawed if frozen, sliced

Salt and freshly ground black pepper

2 teaspoons (2.5 g) chopped fresh flat-leaf parsley

1¼ ounces (35 g) Parmesan cheese, grated (6 tablespoons), divided

1 small egg

Pinch of grated nutmeg

4 ounces (113 g) Egg Pasta Dough (page 282), rolled into 1 sheet, about ¹⁄₃₂ inch (0.8 mm) thick

4 ounces (113 g) Taleggio cheese

4 sprigs fresh thyme

Put the oil, the 2 teaspoons (9.5 g) of butter, and the garlic in a large deep sauté pan over medium-high heat. When hot and bubbly, add the mushrooms, season with salt and pepper, and shake the pan so the mushrooms are in a single layer. Cook without stirring until the bottoms of the mushrooms brown in the hot fat, 4 to 6 minutes. Shake the pan and flip the mushrooms to brown them evenly, another 4 to 6 minutes. Add the parsley and transfer the mushrooms to a colander or mesh strainer to drain and cool. Discard the garlic.

Transfer the mushrooms to a food processor and pulse until finely minced but not pureed, about a minute. Transfer to a bowl and stir in 2 tablespoons (12.5 g) of the Parmesan, along with the egg and nutmeg. Season with salt and pepper and use immediately or spoon into a resealable plastic bag and refrigerate for up to 1 day.

Lay the pasta sheet on a lightly floured surface and trim the short edges square. Cut the sheet in half lengthwise to make two long sheets, each about 3 inches (7.5 cm) wide. Pipe the filling in ½-inch (1.25-cm)-diameter balls down the length of each sheet, right in the center, leaving 2 inches (5 cm) between each ball. Pinch off ½-inch (1.25-cm) pieces of Taleggio and place each piece on the porcini filling. Spritz the dough lightly with water and fold it over the filling, long edge to long edge. Gently press around each ball of filling to eliminate air pockets, minimizing folds in the dough. Using a 2½-inch (6-cm) round pasta or cookie cutter, cut out a series of half-moons, placing the cutter off center so the folded edge of the pasta bisects the equator of the cutter. Transfer the ravioli to parchment-lined baking sheets and refrigerate for up to 1 hour, or freeze until solid, transfer to resealable plastic bags, and freeze for up to 1 week. You should have fifty to sixty ravioli.

Bring a large pot of salted water to a boil. Drop in the ravioli in batches if necessary to prevent crowding, and cook until tender yet firm, 5 to 6 minutes. Using a slotted spoon, transfer the ravioli to warm pasta plates, arranging 10 to 12 on each plate in a single layer.

Meanwhile, heat the thyme and the remaining 4 ounces (113 g) of butter in a large deep sauté pan over medium heat until melted but not browned, 4 to 5 minutes. Sprinkle the ravioli with the remaining ¼ cup (25 g) of Parmesan and drizzle on the herbed butter.

CHINOTTO AFFOGATO

MAKES 8 SERVINGS

4 cups plus 2 tablespoons (390 g) almond flour

2 cups plus 2 tablespoons (255 g) confectioners' sugar, plus some for dusting

1 teaspoon (4.5 g) baking powder

2 lemons

4 large egg whites

4 cups (1 L) Chinotto Gelato (page 286)

4 cups (1 L) chilled chinotto

Affogato is an Italian float, but it's usually espresso poured over a scoop of gelato in a cappuccino cup. Here's my version made with *chinotto*, the Italian soft drink flavored with the same bittersweet orange used in Campari. From my first sip, I loved chinotto. It reminded me of Moxie, a soda I drank as a kid. Both sodas have a bitter, molasses, savory, only slightly sweet taste. I boiled the chinotto to a thick syrup and made gelato with it, and then poured some fresh chinotto over the gelato and served the float with a couple of lemon cookies. People went nuts for it.

Preheat the oven to 300°F (150°C). Stir together the almond flour, confectioners' sugar, and baking powder in a medium bowl. Zest both lemons into the mixture, then cut one of the lemons in half and squeeze its juice through a strainer into the bowl. Stir in the egg whites just until the ingredients are combined and crumbly.

Fill a shallow dish with confectioners' sugar for dusting. Roll the dough into 1-inch (2.5-cm)-diameter balls between your palms. Roll the balls in confectioners' sugar and place on a baking sheet. Flatten slightly and bake until set but not browned, 8 to 10 minutes. Let cool on the sheet for 10 minutes, and then cool completely on wire racks.

Freeze eight cappuccino cups. Place a scoop of Chinotto Gelato in each frozen cup and top with some chilled chinotto. Serve three lemon cookies on the saucer of each cup.

FRIED HUCKLEBERRY RAVIOLI
with MASCARPONE CREMA

On the Leffe mountainsides, there grew these intense purple blueberries that reminded me of the huckleberries I grew up with on the hills of Nashua, New Hampshire. It was like coming home! I made a jam with the wild berries, stuffed them into sweet pastry dough, and fried them for dessert at Locanda del Biancospino. All the dessert needed was a creamy sauce, and mascarpone goes perfectly with berries. I just mixed it with whipped egg yolks and sugar. Boom! If you can't find huckleberries for the ravioli, blueberries work just as well.

MAKES 8 SERVINGS

Huckleberry Filling:

2¼ pounds (1 kg) fresh huckleberries or blueberries (6¾ cups)

1½ cups (300 g) granulated sugar

1 tablespoon (14 g) unsalted butter

Zest of 1 lemon

2 tablespoons (30 ml) freshly squeezed lemon juice

Sweet Pastry Dough:

3½ cups (440 g) *tipo* 00 flour (see page 277) or all-purpose flour

⅔ cup (133 g) granulated sugar

Pinch of salt

2 large eggs

½ vanilla bean, split and scraped

4 tablespoons (57 g) melted unsalted butter

1⅓ cups plus 1 tablespoon (335 g) white wine

Mascarpone Crema:

3 large egg yolks

½ cup (100 g) granulated sugar

¾ cup plus 2 tablespoons (200 g) mascarpone

To Serve:

Oil, for frying

1 tablespoon (6 g) grated lemon zest

Confectioners' sugar, for dusting

(continued on next page)

For the filling: Combine the huckleberries, sugar, butter, lemon zest, and lemon juice in a medium saucepan. Bring to a simmer over medium heat and simmer until the mixture thickens and reaches 224°F (107°C) on a candy thermometer. Let cool, then spoon the mixture into a resealable plastic bag and refrigerate for up to 3 days.

For the dough: Combine the flour, sugar, salt, eggs, vanilla, butter, and wine in a stand mixer fitted with the dough hook. Mix on medium speed until the dough is smooth, 3 to 4 minutes. Gather the dough into a ball, wrap in plastic, and refrigerate for at least 1 hour or up to 2 days.

Position a pasta roller at the widest setting. Cut the dough into three equal pieces and shape each piece into a thick rectangle the width of your pasta machine. Return two pieces to the refrigerator and roll one piece of dough through the pasta roller, lightly dusting the dough with flour to prevent sticking. Reset the rollers to the next-narrowest setting and pass the dough through the rollers. Pass the dough once through each progressively narrower setting, concluding with the second to last setting. Between rollings, continue to dust the dough lightly with flour, if needed, always brushing off the excess. You should end up with a sheet 4 to 5 feet (1.25 to 1.5 m) long and about $\frac{1}{16}$ inch (1.5 mm) thick. Lay the sheet on a floured work surface and trim the edges so they are square. Notch the center of the sheet on the edge to mark it. Spritz the dough with a little water to keep it from drying out.

Pipe $\frac{3}{4}$-inch (2-cm)-diameter balls of filling at 1-inch (2.5-cm) intervals in two rows down the length of the dough just to the center. Leave a 1-inch (2.5-cm) margin all the way around each ball of filling. Lift the opposite end of the sheet and fold it over the filling so the edges meet. Gently press the dough around each ball of filling to seal. Use a 3-inch (7.5-cm) round fluted cutter to cut round ravioli, or use a knife to cut squares. Repeat with the remaining dough and filling. Dust the ravioli with flour, cover loosely, and refrigerate until ready to use, up to 8 hours. If you have any leftover filling, keep it refrigerated for up to a week and spread it on toast or use it like any other jam.

For the mascarpone crema: Combine the egg yolks and sugar in a stand mixer fitted with the whisk attachment. Whip on high speed until the mixture forms stiff peaks when the whisk is lifted, 4 to 5 minutes. Use a rubber spatula to fold in the mascarpone until smooth.

To serve: Heat the oil in a deep-fryer to 350°F (175°C). Add the ravioli in batches to prevent overcrowding and fry until golden brown, 3 to 4 minutes. Transfer to paper towels to drain and keep warm while you fry the rest of the ravioli.

Spread the mascarpone cream in a circle on each plate. Top with four or five ravioli, a scattering of lemon zest, and a dusting of confectioners' sugar.tttttttt

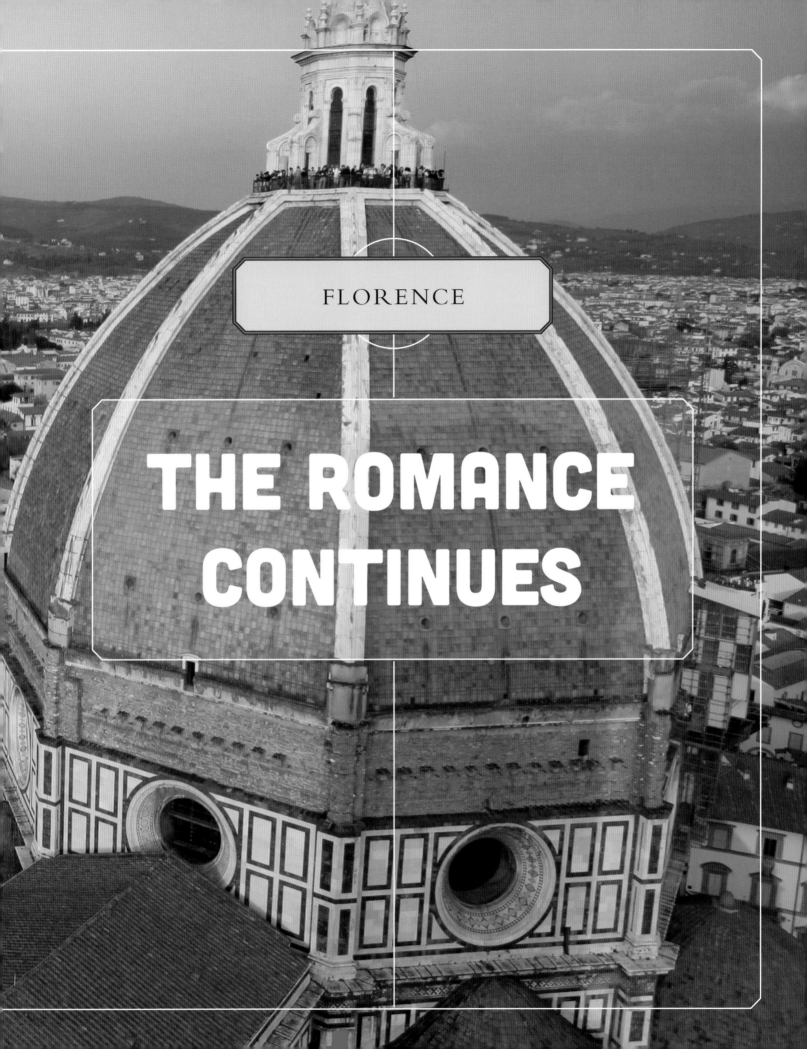

FLORENCE

THE ROMANCE CONTINUES

I PARKED CLAUDIA'S RED MINI COOPER ON A SIDE STREET. IT WAS MY FIRST TRIP TO FLORENCE AND THERE WERE NO PARKING SPOTS AT OUR BED-AND-BREAKFAST, B&B NOVECENTO ON VIA RICASOLI. THREE MONTHS LATER, CLAUDIA GOT A 350-EURO PARKING TICKET. INSTEAD OF "NO PARKING" SIGNS IN FLORENCE, THEY JUST USE STREET CAMERAS AND SEND YOU A BILL!

That's what happens when you can't wait to spend your last weekend together in one of the world's most romantic cities. Plus, after months of tasting incredible Tuscan food at La Brughiera in Bergamo, we couldn't wait to taste the cuisine in Tuscany itself. We checked into the B&B and hit the streets of Santa Maria Novella, the most happening quarter in Florence. Near the Florence cathedral, we stumbled across a little wine bar called Fiaschetteria Nuvoli just in time for lunch. The greeter walked us down the stone steps into what seemed like a cave filled with long wooden tables. Wine bottles lined every wall. Service was family style as in most Tuscan trattorias. We sat next to strangers and started passing plates of artisan salumi, grilled crostini, and chicken liver pâté, chatting and nibbling. Then came the ribollita and hand-rolled pici with wild boar Bolognese. The pasta, chewy and delicate, blew away every other pici I'd ever had. And the boar ragù tasted completely different than what I was used to in the north. The meat was ground with pork fat and simmered with Chianti into a chunky Bolognese rather than being braised in beer and shredded. Uncomplicated and absolutely delicious. We didn't order wine. It just showed up at the table in old-school bottles with wicker baskets, all of it made from Sangiovese grapes grown a few kilometers south of the city. I especially love the family-style dining in Tuscany. For Florentines, it's the most natural thing in the world to meet new people over a casual meal at one big table.

After lunch, we dipped cantucci cookies in tiny glasses of vin santo—the classic meal closer in the region. That taste of sweetness set us up for an afternoon of wandering through Florence, "the cradle of the Italian Renaissance." Claudia loves sculpture, so we headed to Galleria dell'Accademia to see the marble statue of *David* by Michelangelo. How he managed to make that Carrara marble come alive is beyond me. But it reminded me that chefs do the same thing when they cook. You can always tell when a dish is dead on the plate. It just sits there. No charm, no aroma, no life! It's usually because the chef failed to put life into the food. This

element of cooking is impossible to quantify, but it's the most important one, if you ask me.

From the Galleria, we walked to Ponte Vecchio, the old bridge first built over the Arno River in the year 996. They built shops right into the side of the bridge over the arches. Jewelers occupy most of the shops now, but as we walked the bridge I imagined myself as one of the original butchers housed there hundreds of years ago, tossing meat scraps into the Arno.

That night we lined up for dinner at Il Latini on Via dei Palchetti. The restaurant doesn't let anyone in until seven-thirty or eight and the line stretches around the block. It looks like something out of a movie. Just before opening, the owners hand out glasses of prosecco to everyone outside. They start slicing prosciutto and mortadella and giving you little slivers to whet your appetite. Then they call out names. If you don't have a reservation, you don't get in. Luckily, Claudia' mom's boyfriend got us two seats. Alluring aromas of wood smoke and salted meat greet you as you walk in. Whole legs of Tuscan prosciutto hang from the arched white ceilings. We sat down, and they handed us menus, saying, "We have this tonight; you should try that; you definitely need to order this. . . " By the time you order, they've done the ordering for you. I love that. The steak here comes by the kilo—a generous two pounds of porterhouse grilled over oak with just a sprinkle of rock salt. It was my first true taste of *bistecca alla Fiorentina*. The meat is cut from Chianina, a giant white cattle breed indigenous to the valley near Arezzo. They cook it rare and the beef is super-tender, the fat content perfect. It needs no adornment, but you can order sides of potatoes or beans stewed in tomatoes. As with other Tuscan food, the magic of bistecca alla Fiorentina lies in the high-quality ingredients and focused, unhurried techniques used to prepare them. There's no special sauce or spicing. No showy garnishes. Tuscans don't even put salt in

their bread. Instead, they grill slices of bruschetta over wood and only then sprinkle on some salt, maybe some olive oil. Seasoning at the end gives Tuscan food a huge flavor impact. That simplicity and boldness is something I've tried to capture in my cooking ever since.

The next day was pure relaxation. Claudia and I spent hours mesmerized by the paintings of Leonardo da Vinci, Botticelli, Michelangelo, and Raphael at the Uffizi Gallery. On the street, we traded bites of *lampredotto* (tripe panini), licked cones of licorice gelato, watched street performers, and stared over the shoulders of aspiring portraitists. As the sun began to sink on the horizon, we made our way back to B&B Novecento and the domed Santa Maria del Fiore cathedral. Built in the 1400s by one of Italy's most famous architects, Filippo Brunelleschi, the Duomo is probably the best-known spot in Florence. Dozens of stained glass windows glow within its 75-foot (23-m)-tall arches, shining sunlight on sculptures, paintings, and even the tomb of Brunelleschi himself. You have to walk four hundred and sixty-three steps to the top of the dome. There is no elevator. Claudia said she'd meet me outside.

When I got to the top, the view of the city and the late-day sun over the rolling Tuscan hills was utterly breathtaking. I looked down and saw Claudia sitting in the Piazza del Duomo. Her face was turned so I could see the profile of her confident nose and forehead. I grabbed my camera, zoomed in, and snapped a picture. When I checked the image on the screen, my thoughts slowed and my stomach tightened. What if this was it? My last image of Claudia: what I would stare at when I returned to the States next week, alone.

Duck Liver alla Fiorentina
with Egg Yolk and Bruschetta

•

Warm Beef Carpaccio
with Roasted Mushrooms

•

Guinea Hen Tortellini
with Farro Crema

•

Candele Pasta with
Wild Boar Bolognese

•

Wild Hare Pappardelle

•

Bistecca alla Fiorentina
with Braised Corona Beans

•

Cantucci Sundae

•

Strawberry Zuppa Inglese
with Mascarpone Cake

•

Blood Orange Crostata
with Bitter Chocolate

DUCK LIVER ALLA FIORENTINA
with EGG YOLK and BRUSCHETTA

Almost all of the Tuscan trattorias and *fiaschetterie* (wine bars) start you off with *crostini Toscani*, warm chicken liver pâté on toast. I can house about a half-dozen in 3 minutes. It's just chicken livers sautéed with onions and pureed with some chicken stock, but it's so good. I love the creaminess of it. Sometimes they add a little pancetta for richness. The pate reminds me of warm tartare served with egg yolk, so I decided to put a raw yolk on my duck liver version.

Rinse, clean, and pat dry the livers. Heat the butter and 1 tablespoon of the oil in a large, deep sauté pan over medium heat. Add the onion and pancetta, and cook until lightly browned, 5 to 7 minutes. Add the liver, sage, and rosemary, and cook until the liver is lightly browned all over, 6 to 8 minutes. Pour in the brandy, and cook until most of the liquid evaporates and the livers are cooked through, 4 to 5 minutes. Transfer the mixture to a food processor and pulse to a coarse but not completely smooth puree. Transfer to a saucepan and add just enough stock to make a spreadable pâté. Stir in the vinegar and 2 tablespoons (7 g) of the parsley. Taste and season with salt, pepper, and vinegar, as needed. Heat gently just until warmed through, 1 to 2 minutes.

Light a grill or broiler to medium heat. Brush the ciabatta slices with olive oil and season with salt and pepper. Grill or broil until nicely browned on both sides, 1 to 2 minutes per side, taking care not to burn the bread. Cut each slice in half on the diagonal and sprinkle with the remaining parsley.

Spoon the warm liver pâté into small bowls. Place an egg yolk on each portion of pâté. Serve with the bruschetta. (You can refrigerate the leftover whites for 3 to 4 days and use them to make meringue.)

MAKES 4 TO 6 SERVINGS

1¼ pounds (570 g) duck livers

1 tablespoon (14 g) unsalted butter

1 tablespoon (15 ml) olive oil, plus some for the bruschetta

1 small yellow onion, chopped (⅔ cup/107 g)

2 ounces (57 g) pancetta, chopped

3 sage leaves

Leaves from 1 sprig rosemary

2 tablespoons (30 ml) brandy

About ½ cup (120 ml) Chicken Stock (page 279), as needed

1½ teaspoons (7 ml) sherry vinegar

3 tablespoons (12 g) chopped fresh flat-leaf parsley, divided

Salt and freshly ground black pepper

8 ounces (227 g) ciabatta, sliced ¼ inch (6 mm) thick

4 to 6 large egg yolks

WARM BEEF CARPACCIO with ROASTED MUSHROOMS

Eating in and around Florence, you notice food is often served raw, at room temperature, or just barely warm. I tried warming up some raw beef carpaccio one day and it came out awesome. The fat softens, barely starting to melt, and the meat gets just a little warmer than body temperature. With dry-aged beef it tastes better than plain old carpaccio. I usually use 100 percent Black Angus rib-eye steaks aged for seven weeks. The Angus are grass-fed in Arkansas at Creekstone Farms, one of the best producers of natural beef in the United States. It's the closest I've found to Chianina beef from Tuscany. Sliced paper-thin, warmed in a wood oven, and topped with roasted mushrooms and red wine vinaigrette, it's the perfect appetizer for a fall meal.

MAKES 4 SERVINGS

8 ounces (227 g) maitake mushrooms, left in whole clusters

16 garlic cloves, crushed

8 sprigs rosemary, divided

6 tablespoons (90 ml) extra-virgin olive oil, divided

Salt and freshly ground black pepper

½ cup (120 ml) Chianti Vinaigrette (page 277)

8 ounces (227 g) very thinly sliced aged beef rib eye, preferably from Creekstone Farms

Maldon sea salt

Parmesan cheese, for shaving

Preheat a wood oven, charcoal grill, or conventional oven to 300°F (150°C). If using a charcoal grill, pile all the coals to one side.

Toss the mushrooms, garlic, four of the rosemary sprigs, and 4 tablespoons (60 ml) of the oil in a bowl. Season with salt and pepper, then spread on a baking sheet. Roast in the oven or on the unheated side of the charcoal grill until tender but not crisped, 6 to 8 minutes. Tear the mushrooms into small pieces and toss in a bowl with the vinaigrette.

Meanwhile, arrange the sliced beef in a single layer on a rimmed baking sheet, then season with salt and pepper and drizzle with the remaining 2 tablespoons (30 ml) of oil. Roast in the oven or on the unheated side of the grill until just warm but not cooked through, about 2 minutes. Transfer to warmed plates and season conservatively with Maldon sea salt. Arrange the mushrooms over the beef and scatter on the rosemary leaves picked from the remaining sprigs. Shave Parmesan over the top. Drizzle the remaining vinaigrette from the bowl over the mushrooms and beef. Serve warm.

Note

If you can't find aged beef in your market, age it yourself. You'll need an extra refrigerator or empty wine refrigerator. Put a thermometer and hygrometer in the fridge to monitor the temperature and humidity. These are the most important factors to regulate. Set the fridge temperature to between 34° and 38°F (1° and 3°C). Put a small cool-mist humidifier inside the fridge (Crane makes a compact 1-gallon/4-L model) and adjust the humidifier for 65 to 75 percent humidity. Buy the highest-quality whole rib-eye roast that you can. You want a thick cap of fat to protect the meat and you'll need about 20 percent extra because the meat will lose 20 percent of its weight during the aging process. Rinse and pat the rib-eye roast dry, then wrap it loosely in a triple layer of cheesecloth. Put it on a wire rack set in a rimmed baking sheet, then put it in the fridge uncovered for three to seven weeks. The longer it ages, the more flavor it will develop. Enzymes will work their magic and create deep, beefy flavors in the meat. Moisture will also evaporate, concentrating the flavors, and mold will grow on the surface. Change the cheesecloth every day or so and replenish the water in the humidifier as necessary. But avoid opening the fridge any more than that, because you want a constant temperature and humidity. After three to seven weeks, cut off the mold and the beef is ready to cook. Thinly slice it for this recipe, cut it into steaks, or roast the rib eye whole.

GUINEA HEN TORTELLINI with FARRO CREMA

Valeria Piccini is one of Tuscany's most famous chefs. Her family has a beautiful Michelin 2-star restaurant in Manciano called Da Caino. Reading her cookbooks inspired me. She does amazing things with traditional Tuscan ingredients, such as farro. I usually make farro into a salad or side dish, such as risotto. But she pureed it into a sauce. Genius! I was working on a fall menu and guinea hen sprang to mind as a complement to the farro. The hen is richer than chicken and stands up better to the hearty grain.

MAKES 8 TO 10 SERVINGS

Pasta and Filling:

1 guinea hen (about 3 pounds/1.3 kg)

Salt and freshly ground black pepper

2 tablespoons (30 ml) olive oil

1 small yellow onion, chopped (½ cup/80 g)

1 small carrot, chopped (¼ cup/31 g)

1 small rib celery, chopped (¼ cup/25 g)

1 sachet of 1 sprig rosemary, 2 sprigs thyme, 1 bay leaf, 1 small garlic clove, and ½ teaspoon peppercorns (see page 277)

3½ ounces (100 g) chopped prosciutto (scraps are fine)

1 ounce (28 g) Parmesan cheese, grated (⅓ cup), plus some for garnish

1 large egg

1 pound (450 g) Egg Pasta Dough (page 282), rolled into 4 sheets, each about 1/16 inch (1.5 mm) thick

Farro Crema:

⅔ cup (150 ml) olive oil, divided, plus some for garnish

1 small yellow onion, chopped (¾ cup/120 g)

2 medium-size ribs celery, chopped (1 cup/100 g)

1 garlic clove, smashed

⅓ cup (90 ml) white wine

1 cup (180 g) farro

4 sprigs fresh thyme

1 bay leaf

Salt and freshly ground black pepper

To Serve:

1 tablespoon (15 ml) white truffle paste

½ cup (68 g) hazelnuts, toasted and chopped, for garnish

For the pasta and filling: Preheat the oven to 325°F (160°C). Remove the guinea hen innards, rinse inside and out, and pat dry. Discard excess fat deposits and flaps of skin. Cut the legs and wings from the hen and season all over with salt and pepper. Heat the oil in a Dutch oven or braising pan over medium-high heat. When hot, add all the hen pieces and body in batches if necessary to prevent overcrowding; sear until browned on all sides, 10 to 15 minutes total. Transfer to a plate. Add the onion, carrot, and celery, and cook over medium heat until tender, 4 to 6 minutes. Return the meat to the pan and add the sachet and enough water to come about two-thirds of the way up the meat. Bring to a simmer, and then cover the pan and braise in the oven until the meat is fall-apart tender, 40 to 50 minutes. Let cool slightly in the liquid, and then discard the sachet. Transfer the meat to a cutting board, and when cool enough to handle, pick all the meat from the bones, discarding the skin and bones. You should get about 1 pound (450 g) of meat from the hen.

Strain the vegetables and reserve the braising liquid. Discard the vegetables. Grind the meat and prosciutto in a meat grinder fitted with the small die, or grind in a food processor to a coarse puree. If using a food processor, grind the prosciutto first. Add a little of the reserved braising liquid, if necessary, to create a moist, coarse puree somewhat like pâté. Transfer to a bowl and stir in the Parmesan and egg. Season with salt and pepper and use immediately or spoon into a resealable plastic bag and refrigerate for up to 1 day.

Lay a pasta sheet on a lightly floured work surface and cut it in half lengthwise and then crosswise every 2½ inches (6.3 cm) to make 2½-inch (6.3-cm) squares. You should get twenty to twenty-four squares from each sheet. Snip a corner from the bag, and pipe a ¾-inch (2-cm)-diameter ball of filling in the center of each square. Spritz the pasta with water and fold the pasta corner to corner over the filling to make a triangle. Dampen your fingertips and bring the two outer corners together up over the filling and then pinch and hold to seal. Repeat with the remaining pasta dough and filling. You should have eighty to ninety tortellini. Transfer to parchment-lined baking sheets and refrigerate for up to 2 hours or freeze until solid; transfer to resealable plastic bags and freeze for up to 1 week.

For the farro crema: Heat 2 teaspoons (10 ml) of the oil in a medium saucepan over medium heat. Add the onion, celery, and garlic and sweat until the vegetables are soft but not browned, 4 to 6 minutes. Pour in the wine and simmer until most of the liquid evaporates, 2 to 3 minutes. Remove and discard the garlic. Stir in the farro, thyme, bay leaf, and 2 cups (475 ml) of water. Season the water with salt as you would pasta water (about ½ teaspoon/ 3 g). Bring to a boil and then lower the heat to medium-low, cover, and simmer until the farro is very soft, 25 to 30 minutes. Drain off any excess water and remove and discard the herbs. Transfer the mixture to a blender, along with the remaining ½ cup plus 2 tablespoons (140 ml) of oil. Puree until smooth, 3 to 4 minutes, and then taste and season with salt and pepper as needed. You'll have about 2 cups (475 ml) of farro crema.

Bring a large pot of salted water to a boil. Drop in the tortellini in batches if necessary to prevent crowding, and quickly return the water to a boil. Cook until the tortellini are tender yet firm, 2 to 3 minutes.

To serve: Heat the farro crema in a large, deep sauté pan over medium heat. Add the truffle paste to the pan, along with 4 cups (1 L) of pasta water, and simmer until creamy, 4 to 5 minutes, stirring now and then. Add the tortellini, in batches, if necessary, and toss gently to coat with sauce. Divide among plates and garnish with Parmesan, the chopped hazelnuts, and a drizzle of olive oil.

CANDELE PASTA with WILD BOAR BOLOGNESE

By the time Claudia and I spent our last long weekend together, I had tried all sorts of Italian ragù. Every region makes it differently. In the north, they make it with pork; in Bologna, they make it with beef (Bolognese); and in Florence, they make it with wild boar. To cut the gaminess of boar, they add cocoa powder, which has just enough bitterness to even out the flavors. If you have an old rind of Parmesan lying around, bury the rind in the sauce as it simmers. It adds great flavor.

For the Bolognese: Spread the meat and fatback in a single layer on a sheet pan or other shallow pan that will fit in your freezer. Freeze until firm but not solid, about an hour. Freeze all the parts of a meat grinder, too. Grind the cold meat and fat with the meat grinder, using the fine die of the grinder. If you don't have a meat grinder, you can chop the meat in small batches in a food processor, using brief pulses. Try not to chop it too finely; you don't want meat puree.

Preheat the oven to 350°F (175°C).

Heat the oil in a large deep sauté pan or Dutch oven over medium-low heat. Add the ground meat mixture, and cook until the fat melts and the meat browns, stirring often, 6 to 8 minutes. Add the onion and carrot, and cook until very soft, about 20 minutes. Add the wine and bring to a boil over medium-high heat, scraping up any brown bits from the pan bottom. Boil for 2 minutes.

Bury the sachet in the sauce. If necessary, add enough water so that most of the meat is resting in liquid. Cover the pan, transfer to the oven, and cook until the flavors blend, 2 to 2½ hours. Remove and discard the sachet.

Stir in the butter, 2 teaspoons (10 ml) of the vinegar, 2 tablespoons (11 g) of the cocoa powder, and salt and pepper to taste. Season with additional vinegar, cocoa, salt, and pepper as needed. Use immediately, refrigerate for up to 2 days, or freeze for up to 3 months.

For the pasta: Bring a large pot of salted water to a boil. Drop in the pasta, quickly return the water to a boil, and cook until tender yet firm, about 4 minutes (9 minutes for boxed pasta).

Heat the Bolognese in a large deep sauté pan until boiling.

Drain the pasta, reserving a little pasta water, and add the pasta to the sauce. Stir in a ladle of pasta water, the butter, and ½ cup (55 g) of the Parmesan, and toss until the sauce is creamy. If the sauce gets too thick, add more pasta water.

Divide among warm pasta bowls and garnish with the remaining ¼ cup (30 g) of Parmesan.

MAKES 4 TO 6 SERVINGS

Wild Boar Bolognese:

2½ pounds (1.1 kg) wild boar shoulder, cut into 1-inch (2.5-cm) cubes

8 ounces (227 g) pork fatback, cut into 1-inch (2.5-cm) cubes

1 tablespoon (15 ml) olive oil

1 small yellow onion, finely chopped (½ cup/80 g)

1 medium-size carrot, finely chopped (½ cup/61 g)

1 cup (235 ml) red wine

1 sachet of 1 bay leaf, 3 sprigs thyme, 5 parsley stems, 5 peppercorns, and 1 Parmesan cheese rind (see page 277)

1 tablespoon (14 g) unsalted butter

2 to 3 teaspoons (10 to 15 ml) sherry vinegar

2 to 3 tablespoons (11 to 16 g) unsweetened dark cocoa powder

Salt and freshly ground black pepper

Pasta:

1 pound (450 g) fresh extruded Candele (page 283), or 14 ounces (400 g) dried long ziti

4 tablespoons (57 g) unsalted butter

3 ounces (85 g) Parmesan cheese, grated (¾ cup), divided

WILD HARE PAPPARDELLE

Rabbits and hares are related, but hares are bigger, longer, and quicker, which makes them taste leaner, richer, and gamier. The meat is deep red and usually covered in blood when you get it. Don't be grossed out. Just rinse the hare well and marinate it for a day or two in red wine and strong spices, such as cinnamon, clove, and black pepper. The wine draws out the gamey funk, and the spices add great aroma. Discard the marinade and you're good to go. Ragù is the easiest thing to make, and it's perfect with strips of tender pappardelle pasta. Look for wild hare at D'Artagnan (see Sources on page 289).

MAKES 6 TO 8 SERVINGS

1 wild hare (about 4 pounds/1.75 kg)

1 large yellow onion, chopped (2 cups/320 g), divided

4 medium-size carrots, chopped (2 cups/244 g), divided

4 medium-size ribs celery, chopped (2 cups/202 g), divided

2 sachets, each with ½ teaspoon peppercorns, 1 small cinnamon stick, 3 whole cloves, 3 whole juniper berries, 2 sprigs thyme, 2 sprigs rosemary, and 1 small bay leaf (see page 277)

8 to 9 cups (2 to 2.25 L) red wine

Salt and freshly ground black pepper

½ cup (62 g) *tipo* 00 flour (see page 277) or all-purpose flour

3 tablespoons (45 ml) plus ½ cup (120 ml) olive oil, divided

1 pound (450 g) Egg Pasta Dough (page 282), rolled into 4 sheets, each about ¹⁄₁₆ inch (1.5 mm) thick

4 ounces (1 stick/113 g) unsalted butter

2½ ounces (71 g) Parmesan cheese, grated (¾ cup), divided

Dutch-process cocoa powder, as needed (optional)

Rinse the hare and then remove and discard the innards and excess fat deposits. Remove the hind legs and forelegs by driving your knife straight through the hip and shoulder joints. Snip through the breast bone with kitchen shears, and snip through one side of the ribs near the backbone to remove that side, then cut the hare crosswise into two pieces. You should have seven pieces total. Place the pieces in a large resealable plastic bag or a bowl, along with 1 cup (160 g) of the onion, 1 cup (122 g) of the carrots, 1 cup (101 g) of the celery, and one of the sachets. Add enough wine to cover the pieces, 4 to 5 cups (1 to 1.25 L). Seal or cover and refrigerate for 24 hours.

Preheat the oven to 325°F (160°C). Drain the hare, discarding the wine, vegetables, and sachet. Pat the hare pieces dry, season all over with salt and pepper, and then dredge in flour, shaking off the excess. Heat 3 tablespoons (45 ml) of the oil in a Dutch oven over medium-high heat. Add the hare in batches if necessary to prevent overcrowding, and sear until golden brown on all sides, about 5 minutes per side. Transfer to a platter. Add the remaining 1 cup (160 g) of onion, 1 cup (122 g) of carrots, and 1 cup (101 g) of celery to the pan, and cook until deeply browned, 5 to 6 minutes. Add the remaining 4 cups (1 L) of wine and simmer for 2 minutes. Return the hare to the pan, and if necessary, add enough water for the liquid to almost cover the hare. Add the remaining sachet and bring to a boil. Cover and braise in the oven until the meat is fall-apart tender, about 2 hours.

Transfer the meat to a cutting board, and when cool enough to handle, pick the meat from the bones, shredding the meat and discarding the skin and bones. Discard the sachet and strain the vegetables, reserving the braising liquid. Pass the vegetables through a food mill or pulse in a food processor to a coarse puree, adding a little braising liquid, if necessary, to get the vegetables to puree. Combine the braising liquid, pureed vegetables, and shredded meat and season with salt and pepper. Use immediately or refrigerate for up to 1 week. You will have 5 to 6 cups (1.25 to 1.5 L) of ragù.

Lay a pasta sheet on a lightly floured work surface and trim the edges square. Cut crosswise into strips a little less than 1 inch (2.5 cm) wide, preferably with a fluted cutter. Repeat with the remaining pasta dough.

Bring a large pot of salted water to a boil. Add the pasta in batches, if necessary, to prevent crowding, and cook until tender yet firm, about a minute.

Meanwhile, heat the butter and remaining $\frac{1}{2}$ cup (120 ml) of oil in a large deep sauté pan over medium heat. Stir in the ragù and 1$\frac{1}{2}$ cups (375 ml) of pasta water, and simmer until creamy, 3 to 4 minutes. Drain the pasta and add to the ragù in batches along with $\frac{1}{2}$ cup (50 g) of the Parmesan, stirring gently until the mixture is creamy. Taste and season with salt and pepper as needed. Divide among plates and garnish with the remaining Parmesan. If you like, you could dust the pasta with a little Dutch-process cocoa powder before garnishing with the Parmesan.

BISTECCA ALLA FIORENTINA
with BRAISED CORONA BEANS

MAKES 4 SERVINGS

1 cup (185 g) dried corona beans, soaked in water to cover overnight

½ medium-size yellow onion, finely chopped (½ cup/80 g)

1 medium-size rib celery, finely chopped (½ cup/51 g)

1 medium-size carrot, finely chopped (½ cup/61 g)

2 ounces (57 g) pancetta, finely chopped

1 sachet of 1 sprig parsley, 1 sprig rosemary, 2 sprigs thyme, 1 bay leaf and 5 black peppercorns (see page 277)

Coarse salt and cracked black pepper

1 bone-in porterhouse steak, 2 pounds (1 kg) and 2 inches (5 cm) thick

¼ cup (60 ml) olive oil, plus more as needed

4 garlic cloves, minced

1 pound (450 g) mustard greens, washed, trimmed, and coarsely chopped

1 cup (240 g) canned plum tomatoes, preferably San Marzano, cored and crushed by hand

½ cup (120 ml) Veal Stock (page 279)

3 tablespoons (42 g) unsalted butter

When my family came to Italy from the United States to visit, I took them to Florence to taste the steak. You order *bistecca alla fiorentina* by the kilo and we ordered six kilos (13 pounds). It came to the table like a giant Brontosaurus steak right out of *The Flintstones.* My family had never seen anything like it—not even my eighty-six-year-old grandmother, who was a butcher during World War II! You can order different sides, such as gigante beans stewed with tomatoes. Here's my twist using big white corona beans. You could also use sweet white runner beans or even fresh lima beans, if they're in season.

Drain the soaked beans and combine with the onion, celery, carrot, pancetta, and sachet in a medium saucepan. Add enough water to cover the ingredients by 1 inch (2.5 cm). Bring to a boil over high heat and then lower the heat to medium-low and simmer gently until the beans are tender, about 1 hour. Season generously with salt and pepper, then let the beans cool down in the liquid. Use immediately or refrigerate for up to 3 days.

Heat a grill, preferably with wood, to high heat. Let the steak stand at room temperature for 20 minutes to take the chill off. Brush the grill grate with a little oil. Grill the steak until deeply grill-marked, 5 to 6 minutes. Rotate it 90 degrees to create crosshatch marks, grilling another 5 to 6 minutes. Flip and grill the other side for 5 minutes, then rotate it 90 degrees and move it to a cooler part of the grill or lower the heat to medium and cook until the steak is rare to medium-rare (115° to 125°F/46 to 52°C internal temperature), another 6 to 8 minutes. Transfer to a cutting board and season with coarse salt and cracked black pepper. Let the steak rest for 5 to 10 minutes before slicing.

Meanwhile, heat the oil in a large sauté pan over medium-high heat. Add the garlic, and cook until golden but not burned, 1 to 2 minutes. Add the mustard greens, season with salt and pepper, and cook until the greens release their liquid, 3 to 4 minutes. Add the tomatoes and veal stock, cover, and cook until the greens are tender, 4 to 5 minutes, stirring occasionally.

Use a slotted spoon to remove the beans and solids from their cooking liquid to the pan of greens (remove and discard the sachet). Add the butter, and cook until the beans and greens are hot and the sauce is a little creamy. Serve with the sliced steak.

CANTUCCI SUNDAE

Claudia and I are suckers for gelato, and when you walk through Florence, gelaterie are everywhere. Here's my secret for spotting the best ones: look for the pistachio flavor. If it looks neon green in the case, go to the next gelateria because they probably use artificial colorings and flavorings in their gelato. But if the pistachio gelato looks pale green in color, you know they're using the highest-quality pistachios or pistachio puree instead of artificial flavoring and coloring. One day, I had the idea of crushing up some of Tuscany's famous cantucci cookies and adding them to gelato. It's something I'd never seen in any gelateria but it made perfect sense. I served the sundae in a cup with almonds in vin santo syrup and more cookies on the side. It's a twist on the classic Tuscan dessert of cantucci served with vin santo for dipping.

For the vin santo almonds: Combine the glucose syrup, sugar, ½ cup (120 ml) of the vin santo, and ½ cup (120 ml) of water in a medium saucepan. Boil over high heat until the mixture reaches 220°F (104°C) on a candy thermometer, 10 to 15 minutes. Put the almonds in a heatproof bowl and pour the sugar mixture over the top. Let cool slightly and then pour on the remaining 1 tablespoon (15 ml) of vin santo. Cover and let soak in the refrigerator overnight or up to 3 days.

For the cantucci: Sift together the flour, baking powder, polenta, and salt into a medium bowl. Set aside. Cream the butter and sugar together in a stand mixer fitted with the paddle attachment on medium speed until light and fluffy, 2 to 3 minutes. Add the eggs one at a time, mixing between additions until completely incorporated. Mix in the grappa. Slowly add the sifted dry ingredients on low speed until a moist batter forms, and then stir in the cooled toasted almonds.

Roll the dough on a lightly floured work surface into logs about 2 inches (5 cm) in diameter and 12 inches (30 cm) long. Wrap in plastic and refrigerate until cold and firm, at least 1 hour or up to 2 days.

Preheat the oven to 350°F (175°C). Bake the logs on baking sheets until lightly browned on the edges and firm to the touch, 10 to 12 minutes. Remove from the oven and let the logs cool until barely warm. Slice the logs crosswise on a steep diagonal into ½-inch (1.25-cm)-thick cookies and lay the cookies flat on the baking sheets. Lower the oven temperature to 300°F (150°C) and return the cookies to the oven to bake until they are dry, 15 to 20 minutes. Remove from the oven and let cool completely.

To serve: Put a scoop of gelato in each of six to eight ice-cream or coffee cups. Spoon on a generous amount of vin santo almonds and their syrup. Serve one or two whole cantucci with each cup.

MAKES 6 TO 8 SERVINGS

Vin Santo Almonds:

2½ tablespoons (37 ml) glucose syrup or light corn syrup

½ cup (100 g) granulated sugar

½ cup plus 1 tablespoon (140 ml) vin santo, divided

¾ cup (107 g) whole skinless almonds, toasted

Cantucci:

2¾ cups (345 g) *tipo* 00 flour (see page 277) or all-purpose flour

¾ teaspoon (3.5 g) baking powder

2½ tablespoons (25 g) coarse yellow cornmeal (polenta)

1¼ teaspoons (7.5 g) sea salt

4 ounces (1 stick/113 g) unsalted butter, softened

1 cup plus 2 tablespoons (225 g) granulated sugar

2 large eggs

1 tablespoon (15 ml) grappa or brandy

¾ cup (107 g) whole skinless almonds, toasted

To Serve:

6 cups (1.5 L) Cantucci Gelato (page 286)

STRAWBERRY ZUPPA INGLESE
with MASCARPONE CAKE

MAKES ABOUT 8 SERVINGS

Zuppa:

4¼ cups (1060 ml) whole milk

1 vanilla bean, split and scraped

10 large egg yolks

1¼ cups (250 g) granulated sugar

½ cup (62 g) *tipo* 00 flour (see page 277) or all-purpose flour

2½ cups (625 ml) heavy cream

Mascarpone Cake:

6 ounces (1½ sticks/170 g) unsalted butter, softened, plus some for greasing pans

1½ cups (300 g) granulated sugar

12 ounces (350 g) mascarpone

3 large eggs

1½ cups (205 g) pastry flour

2½ teaspoons (11.5 g) baking powder

1 teaspoon (6 g) salt

Strawberry Marmalade:

2 pounds (1 kg) strawberries

½ cup (120 ml) glucose syrup or light corn syrup

1⅓ cups plus ½ cup (370 g) granulated sugar, divided

1 tablespoon (14 g) powdered pectin

Although its name translates to "English soup," *zuppa inglese* is a classic Italian dessert. It's like an English trifle, with layers of cake, jam, and sweet custard. You can use almost any combination of flavors you like. My favorite is a mascarpone cake layered with strawberry jam and vanilla custard. It's the first thing I think of when fresh strawberries start popping up in May. You could layer the dessert in a big glass bowl, but I like to do it in individual half-pint mason jars.

For the zuppa: Bring the milk and vanilla to a boil in a medium saucepan. Meanwhile, whip the egg yolks, sugar, and flour in a stand mixer on medium-high speed until fluffy and pale, 2 to 3 minutes. Temper the eggs by gradually stirring in ½ cup (120 ml) of the milk mixture, then another ½ cup (120 ml). Scrape the egg mixture into the saucepan, and cook over medium heat until thickened, 6 to 8 minutes, stirring frequently. Remove from the heat and let cool. Whip the cream on medium-high speed until the beaters leave soft peaks when they are lifted, 2 to 3 minutes. When the zuppa is completely cool, fold in the whipped cream. Use immediately or cover and refrigerate for up to 2 days.

For the mascarpone cake: Preheat the oven to 350°F (175°C). Line a half-sheet pan (an 18 x 13-inch/46 x 33-cm rimmed baking sheet) or two smaller rimmed baking sheets with parchment. Butter the parchment. Cream the butter and sugar in a stand mixer on medium speed until light and fluffy, 2 to 3 minutes. Mix in the mascarpone, and with the machine running, add the eggs, one at a time. Sift together the flour, baking powder and salt and add to the mascarpone mixture on low speed until incorporated. Spread the batter in the perpared pan and bake until a toothpick inserted into the center comes out clean, 18 to 20 minutes. Let cool and use immediately or cover and refrigerate for up to 1 day.

For the strawberry marmalade: Hull and quarter the strawberries. Bring the glucose syrup, 1⅓ cups (270 g) of the sugar, and 1 cup of water to a boil in a large saucepan. Add the strawberries, and cook over medium-high heat until they soften and begin to fall apart, 10 to 12 minutes, mashing the strawberries a little with a spoon. Whisk together the pectin and remaining ½ cup (100 g) of sugar, and then whisk into the marmalade. Cook until the mixture thickens, 3 to 5 minutes. Remove from the heat and let cool. Use immediately or refrigerate for up to 1 week.

To finish: Use a cookie cutter to cut out rounds of cake that will fit into your containers. I like to use a total of eight 8-ounce (235-ml) mason jars or glass mugs. For those you'll need sixteen 2-inch (5-cm) rounds of cake. Lay a cake round on the bottom of a mason jar or mug. Spoon on a layer of about 2 tablespoons (30 ml) marmalade, and then a layer of about ¼ cup (60 ml) zuppa and repeat with additional layers of cake, marmalade, and zuppa until the jar or mug is filled (about two layers each for 8-ounce/235-ml jars or mugs).

BLOOD ORANGE CROSTATA
with BITTER CHOCOLATE

Crostatas aren't just for dessert. Italians will wake up and have some with a cup of morning coffee. The crust is the most important part; hence the name. It has to be somewhat thicker than a normal tart shell and stay on the softer side. I use cake flour because it stays tender, and I add a little baking powder for puff. Toasted and ground hazelnuts add incredible richness and flavor. I usually fit the dough into a 9-inch (23-cm) square tart pan with a removable bottom, but you could use a ten- or 11-inch (25 or 28-cm) round tart pan. My favorite filling is blood oranges. In the winter, I make a reddish-orange marmalade with them, and then I use the marmalade all spring long. Serve the crostata warm or at room temperature. A little chocolate sauce makes it irresistible for dessert or for breakfast.

MAKES 12 SERVINGS

Blood Orange Marmalade:

6 pounds (2.75 kg) blood oranges (about 16)

¼ cup (60 ml) freshly squeezed lemon juice

1 teaspoon (4.5 g) unsalted butter

5 cups (1 kg) granulated sugar

2½ teaspoons (11.75 g) powdered pectin

Linzer Dough:

1 pound (4 sticks/450 g) unsalted butter, at room temperature

1½ cups (300 g) granulated sugar

1 vanilla bean, split and scraped

2 large eggs, divided

4¼ cups (582 g) cake flour

2½ ounces (½ cup/71 g) finely crushed vanilla wafer cookie crumbs

1 tablespoon (8 g) ground cinnamon

2 teaspoons (9 g) baking powder

8 ounces (227 g) hazelnuts, toasted and ground (about 2 cups)

To Serve:

2 cups (475 ml) Chocolate Sauce (page 285)

Confectioners' sugar for garnish

(continued on next page)

For the marmalade: Cut the rind from each orange, following the contour of the fruit and trying to cut as little of the flesh as possible. Working over a large saucepan, make V-shaped cuts around each segment, releasing the segments from the surrounding membranes and dropping the segments into the pan (this is called supreming the fruit); squeeze the membranes to release the juice. You should have about 6 cups (1.5 L) of orange segments and juice. Add the lemon juice and butter and bring to a simmer over medium-high heat. Whisk together the sugar and pectin and stir the mixture into the pan. Bring to a boil and cook until the mixture reaches 217°F (103°C) on a candy thermometer, 20 to 25 minutes, stirring occasionally. Let cool in the pan until ready to use or refrigerate for up to 1 week. You should have about 3½ cups (875 ml) of marmalade.

For the Linzer dough: Cream the butter, sugar, and vanilla in a stand mixer on medium speed until light and fluffy, 3 to 4 minutes. Switch to low speed and add one of the eggs. Sift together the cake flour, cookie crumbs, cinnamon, and baking powder and add to the dough. Mix until incorporated, then add the ground hazelnuts and mix just until incorporated. Divide the dough in half and scrape each half onto a sheet of plastic wrap. Seal the dough in the plastic wrap and refrigerate for at least 1 hour, or up to 2 days.

Let the dough sit at room temperature for a few minutes so it is soft enough to roll. Roll half of the dough on a lightly floured surface to a circle about 12 inches (30 cm) in diameter and ¼ inch (6 mm) thick. Carefully fold the dough over the rolling pin and transfer it to a 9-inch (23-cm) square or 10-inch (25-cm) round tart pan with a removable bottom. Unfold the dough and fit it into the pan without stretching the dough. The dough will be delicate and crumbly; patch any tears or holes with pieces of dough from the edge. Trim the dough so that it sits flush with the top of the tart pan.

Preheat the oven to 350°F (175°C). Fill the tart shell three-quarters full with the marmalade; save any remaining marmalade for another use. Roll the remaining half of the dough on lightly floured parchment to about ¼ inch (6 mm) thick and 3 inches (7.5 cm) larger than the dimensions of your pan. Cut twelve to fourteen strips of dough, each ½ to ¾ inch (13 to 19 mm) wide, preferably with a fluted cutter. Slide half of the strips to a floured cookie sheet, arranging them in parallel bars on the sheet with ½ to ¾ inch (12 to 19 mm) between each strip. Carefully fold back every other strip half way. Insert a new strip at the center perpendicular to the parallel strips. Reposition the folded strips back over the new strip. Next, fold back the alternate parallel strips and insert another perpendicular strip next to the first one. Then reposition the folded strips back over the new strip. Continue until they reach the outer edge of the strips. Then, turn the crust and repeat the process on the other half, working from the center toward the edge. Carefully slide the lattice over the filling. The dough will be crumbly; if any of the strips break, seal them back together with your fingers. Trim the excess dough from the tart and pinch together the edges of dough around the perimeter of the tart to seal. Beat the remaining egg with 1 teaspoon (5 ml) of water and brush all over the dough, sealing any cracks. Bake until golden brown, 20 to 25 minutes. Let cool before slicing into wedges.

To serve: Gently heat the chocolate sauce just until pourable and spoon a pool of sauce off center on each plate. Top with a slice of crostata, positioning the front corner over the sauce. Garnish with confectioners' sugar.

OUR BIG ITALIAN WEDDING

THAT SUMMER I MOVED BACK INTO MY PARENTS' HOUSE IN NASHUA, NEW HAMPSHIRE. I RAN THE KITCHEN AT THE BEDFORD VILLAGE INN, A LUXURY B&B AND RESTAURANT. CLAUDIA WAS STILL IN ITALY, RUNNING HER VIDEO RENTAL BUSINESS IN ALBINO. EVERYONE KNOWS LONG-DISTANCE RELATIONSHIPS DON'T WORK. BUT WE TOOK A CHANCE AND SPENT THE SUMMER TALKING VIA WEBCAM. WHEN SHE DECIDED TO VISIT ME IN THE STATES, I TOOK IT AS A STRONG STATEMENT.

I arranged a weekend getaway for us in Ogunquit, Maine. We stayed at Parson's Post House on Shore Road, with a gorgeous ocean view. We strolled through the white-washed shops of Ogunquit and lunched on lobster rolls piled high in buttered split-top buns. At the end of Shore Road, we wandered onto the Marginal Way, a beautiful mile-long walking path along Maine's rugged coastline. The clean smell of seawater reminded me of all the fresh fish and salty cured meats I'd fallen in love with over the past three years in Italy. I thought about the places that Claudia and I had been together like Alba, Barolo, Venice, and Florence, and when we reached a little inlet called Devil's Kitchen, we rested on a boulder overlooking the Atlantic. Almost directly east of us across the ocean sat the rocky cliffs of le Cinque Terre, where we held hands and kissed along the Via dell'Amore. My heart raced and my mind cycled through decades of images from my childhood to Italy to the present to the future. I turned to face Claudia, the tide receded, the squawk of the seagulls softened, and I opened my other hand, which had been clamped around a tiny object. "Will you marry me?" I asked, showing Claudia the ring and placing it in her palm. She started crying and shaking. I thought she was going to drop the ring in the ocean! Claudia clenched her palm, looked at me through teary eyes, and exclaimed, "*Si!*"

It took me a few minutes to pry open her hand, but I retrieved the ring and slid it onto her finger.

With the ring on her finger, Claudia returned to Italy and we spent the next five months apart, just like the last five. Finally, her fiancée visa came through, and we had ninety days to get married in the United States. Her brother Alex bought her business in Italy to help Claudia make the move. I flew to Italy to pick her up and, at the airport, Pina cried because she had just lost her mother, Nonna Anna, and now her daughter was leaving.

For the next several months, we lived with my parents in New Hampshire. Claudia's English was still shaky, and communicating with my mother and father wasn't easy. She tried to form a bond with them over food. But my dad likes what he likes. Teriyaki, for instance. He makes it every few days. Claudia ate it, but eventually wanted to taste something different. Every other day it was steak teriyaki, chicken teriyaki. . . teriyaki, teriyaki, teriyaki! And my parents weren't warming up to Claudia's favorite foods. She would make risottos, pastas, and salads, and my dad would say, "No thanks, I already had dinner." But he was secretly sneaking bites at night. Once Claudia found out that my dad was eating her food, she felt more at home.

That year, we had two weddings: one in Nashua, New Hampshire, at Alpine Grove with a justice of the peace; and another in Trescore Balneario, Italy, which was an all-day extravaganza. Trescore Balneario is where I had my first cooking job at Loro, so my life in Italy had come full circle. We were married in Italian by Claudia's childhood priest, Don Camillo at Santuario della Madonna dello Zuccarello, a tiny mountainside church in Nembro. Twelve of my family members came from America, including my eighty-five-year-old grandmother. Around noon, the reception began at Locanda Armonia, a drop-dead gorgeous inn and restaurant nestled among the olive groves and vineyards above Trescore

Balneario. We started with *stuzzichini* (hors d'oeuvres), such as house-cured prosciutto sliced to order, oysters with caviar zabaione, grilled veal sausage with spring onion mostarda, eggplant cannoli with burrata and oregano, and mortadella pigs in a blanket. We took pictures among the vineyards, danced, and dined on beef tartare with fried egg yolk and Tropea onions, grilled seppia with sweet peas and mâche, fava bean and robiola agnolotti with culatello, and whole roasted quail stuffed with foie gras and fig agrodolce. Lunch lasted until five p.m. After cutting the cake and sipping lemon sgroppino, a kind of alcoholic slushy, the party moved downstairs to the tavern with a DJ, more dancing, and a dessert buffet full of citrus rum babas, olive oil panna cotta, and other sweets. It was an orgy of food. The party went from noon to midnight and brought together two big, boisterous families from the United States and Italy. Neither family spoke the other's language, so the only way we could communicate was through food. As Claudia and I danced, we looked over and her Uncle Bruno was shoving little cotechino panini, grilled to order, into my Uncle Al's mouth. It was a daylong celebration of everything I loved about Italy.

Corn Tortelli with Ricotta Salata

•

Schisola (Polenta Stuffed
with Gorgonzola Dolce)

•

Prosciutto Cotto with Stone Fruits

•

Ciareghi

•

Pizzoccheri with Chard, Potato,
and Bitto Cheese

•

Wild Branzino with Fennel
and Artichokes

•

Citrus Rum Babas alla Crema

•

Olive Oil Panna Cotta with
Summer Berries

•

Chiacchiere with Coffee and
Chocolate Budino

CORN TORTELLI with RICOTTA SALATA

When it was my birthday in Italy, I threw myself a party. That's what you do there! I planned an all-American barbecue with smoked meat and boiled corn. I went to every *supermercato* for the corn and all I could find was preshucked three-packs of corn that had probably been sitting in the case for the whole month of July. Let me tell you, it wasn't Jersey corn! In the land of polenta, I couldn't find any sweet corn! But it was a great birthday anyway. When I got back to the States, I made this dish thinking that this is what I would have made if sweet corn had been available in Italy. When pureed and mixed with a little cheese and egg to bind it, fresh corn makes an incredibly creamy pasta filling. Turn to this recipe in the height of summer when corn is sweetest.

Shuck the corn, stand each ear upright on a cutting board, and cut the kernels from the cobs. Heat the oil in a large, deep sauté pan over medium heat, add the onion, and sweat until soft but not browned, 4 to 5 minutes. Add the corn, and cook until tender, 3 to 4 minutes. Transfer to a blender and puree until very smooth and thick, 2 to 3 minutes. If the mixture is thin and easily pourable, stir it in a fine-mesh sieve to drain some of the liquid. The corn mixture should be thick enough to stand on a spoon. Let cool slightly, then quickly blend in the egg and season with salt and pepper. Transfer to a resealable plastic bag, seal, and refrigerate for up to 1 day.

Lay a pasta sheet on a lightly floured work surface and trim the edges square. Cut the pasta into 3-inch (7.5-cm) squares. Spritz the dough lightly with water to keep it from drying out. Put teaspoon-size spoonfuls of filling on each square, then bring the opposite corners together over the filling to make a triangle. Press gently on the edges to seal. Bring the two opposite points of the triangle up over the pasta and pinch them together to seal: you should have a large tortellini shape. Repeat with the remaining pasta dough and filling. The filled pasta can be refrigerated for up to 8 hours on a sheet pan or frozen for up to 3 days before cooking. You should have about fifty tortelli.

Bring a large pot of salted water to a boil. Drop in the tortelli in batches if necessary to prevent overcrowding; quickly return the water to a boil and cook until tender yet firm, 2 to 3 minutes. Drain the pasta, reserving about 1 cup (235 ml) of the pasta water.

Just before the pasta is done, melt the butter and truffle paste in a large deep sauté pan over medium heat. Spoon in about $\frac{1}{2}$ cup (120 ml) of pasta water, and cook until the sauce is creamy, 1 to 2 minutes. Add the pasta in batches if necessary, and toss gently to coat. Transfer to a large serving bowl and shave or grate the ricotta salata over the top.

MAKES ABOUT 4 SERVINGS

5 ears fresh corn

1 tablespoon (15 ml) olive oil

$\frac{1}{2}$ medium-size yellow onion, chopped ($\frac{2}{3}$ cup/80 g)

1 small egg

Salt and freshly ground black pepper

8 ounces (227 g) Egg Pasta Dough (page 282), rolled into 2 sheets, each about $\frac{1}{16}$ inch (1.5 mm) thick

4 ounces (1 stick/113 g) unsalted butter

$\frac{1}{2}$ cup (120 ml) black truffle paste

4 ounces (113 g) ricotta salata

SCHISOLA (POLENTA STUFFED with GORGONZOLA DOLCE)

Claudia's grandfather kept cows and made butter and cheese. He would put some formagella cheese and leftover polenta in his pocket to eat as a snack in the fields. The two would get smooshed in his pocket and they called it *schisola*, which means "squished" in the Bergamascan dialect. I like to roll the polenta into balls, squish pieces of Gorgonzola inside, and then broil them. Just be sure to blast them at high heat so the polenta browns before the cheese oozes out.

Using a 2-ounce (60-ml) ice-cream scoop or your fingers, scoop out twelve balls of polenta, each 1 to 1½ inches (2.5 to 3.75 cm) in diameter. Wet your hands, make a dimple in each polenta ball, and press a piece of Gorgonzola into the dimple. Form the polenta around the Gorgonzola, rolling it between your wet palms into a neat ball. Use immediately or place on a parchment-lined tray, cover, and refrigerate for 2 hours.

Preheat the oven to 500°F (260°C). Turn on convection if possible. You want to blast these at a pretty high temperature. Grease a baking sheet with some of the butter. Melt 3 tablespoons (42 g) of the butter, arrange the polenta balls on the sheet, and brush each one with butter. Bake until the polenta lightly browns and the cheese just starts to melt inside, 5 to 7 minutes.

Meanwhile, melt 5 tablespoons (71 g) of the butter over medium heat in a small skillet and add the sage leaves. Cook until the sage lightly browns, the butter turns golden, and the milk solids fall to the bottom of the pan and turn light brown, 6 to 7 minutes.

Divide the schisola among plates, sprinkle on the Parmesan, drizzle with brown butter, and garnish with the sage leaves.

MAKES 4 SERVINGS

2 cups (475 ml) cooked Polenta (page 281)

4 ounces (113 g) Gorgonzola cheese, divided into 12 pieces

4 ounces (1 stick/113 g) unsalted butter, divided, plus some for greasing the pan

1 ounce (28 g) Parmesan cheese, grated (¼ cup) for garnish

8 sage leaves for garnish

PROSCIUTTO COTTO with STONE FRUITS

Ham, or prosciutto, is the hind leg of the pig. Italians make two different kinds: *prosciutto crudo,* the raw dry-cured type that's sliced paper-thin; and *prosciutto cotto,* which is similar to American wet-cured, cooked ham. The difference is that Italians leave the bone, fat, and skin on the cooked ham during the entire curing and cooking process, which keeps the meat moist and makes it taste richer. At our wedding, we served slices of prosciutto cotto wrapped around melon as an appetizer. I also like to serve it with a salad of late-summer fruits, such as plums, apricots, and peaches. You'll need a large marinade injector for this recipe (see Sources, page 289). Or you could soak the raw, bone-in ham in brine for thirty days. If using boneless ham, soak it for twenty-five days. Either way, you will have leftover ham from this recipe. It keeps for several weeks in the refrigerator.

Ham:

1 uncooked bone-in ham (pork hind leg), 20 pounds (9 kg)

3 gallons (12 L) 3-2-1 Brine (page 280)

4 teaspoons (24 g) curing salt #1 (see page 277)

4 teaspoons (9. 5 g) ground mace

4 teaspoons (8.5 g) ground coriander

4 teaspoons (8.5 g) freshly ground black pepper

2 teaspoons (8 g) ground juniper berries

Stone Fruits:

2 tablespoons (30 ml) sherry vinegar

6 tablespoons (90 ml) extra-virgin olive oil

2 tablespoons (7 g) chopped mixed fresh herbs (parsley, rosemary, and thyme), divided

Salt and freshly ground black pepper

2 ripe plums

2 ripe apricots

2 ripe peaches

For the ham: Rinse the ham and leave it wet. Combine the brine, curing salt, ground mace, coriander, pepper, and juniper, and stir to dissolve the salt. Set the ham on a rimmed baking sheet. Using a marinade injector, inject one-quarter of the brine (3 quarts/3 L) into the ham. Try to hit all of the areas around the bone. If you can find the central vein near the bone, inject the brine in there and it should go throughout the meat. If not, find about ten different spots near the bone and inject the brine into the meat. The ham should swell a bit and brine should leak out of it. Place the injected ham in a large tub or plastic-lined bucket that will fit in your refrigerator. Cover the ham and refrigerate for 14 days. Refrigerate the remaining brine. If you're low on refrigerator space, chill the ham, the brine, or both in an ice-filled cooler in a cool, dark spot, replenishing the ice as necessary.

Transfer the brined ham to a large, heavyweight roasting pan or stockpot and add about 1½ gallons (6 L) of the remaining brine. Add enough water so that the liquid covers the meat completely. Cover and bring to a boil over high heat, and then lower the heat so that the liquid is just under a simmer and reads about 155°F (68°C) on an instant-read thermometer. Cover and braise at 155°F

(68°C) until the ham reaches the same internal temperature of 155°F (68°C), 9 to 10 hours. Turn off the heat and let the ham cool overnight in the liquid. Remove from the liquid and carve out the bone by making one cut along the length of the ham, cutting down to the bone; cut around the bone to remove it, leaving as much meat as possible on the ham. Cover the ham and refrigerate until ready to use or up to 3 weeks.

For the stone fruit salad: Pour the vinegar in a medium bowl. Whisk in the oil in a slow, steady trickle until blended and thickened, 1 to 2 minutes. Whisk in 1 tablespoon (4 g) of the herbs and salt and pepper to taste. Cut the plums, apricots, and peaches in half from top to bottom, twist the halves apart and remove and discard the pits. Slice the fruit into thin half-moon slices and add to the bowl, tossing to coat.

When ready to serve, use a large sharp knife to slice the ham crosswise into very thin slices, removing the skin as you go. Lay a few slices of ham on a plate and top with the stone fruit salad. Garnish with the remaining 1 tablespoon (4 g) of the herbs.

CIAREGHI

My first job in Italy was at Michelin-starred Loro in Trescore Balneario. For staff meal, we would eat *ciareghi*, which is Bergamascan dialect for an egg over easy with browned butter. At the restaurant, we added wood-grilled cotechino sausage and soft polenta to bulk up the dish. *Cotechino* is classic fresh sausage from Bergamo, ground a bit coarse with some warm and peppery spices. It's easy to make, but if you don't want to make it you could use another Italian black pepper or fennel sausage.

MAKES 4 SERVINGS (PLUS LEFTOVER SAUSAGES)

Cotechino:

4 pounds (1.75 kg) boneless pork shoulder

5 ounces (141 g) pork fatback

3 tablespoons (25 g) kosher salt

4 teaspoons (9.5 g) powdered dextrose, or 3 teaspoons (7.75 g) superfine sugar

¾ teaspoon (2 g) ground cinnamon

½ teaspoon (1 g) freshly ground black pepper

½ teaspoon (1 g) ground allspice

¼ teaspoon (0.5 g) freshly grated nutmeg

¼ teaspoon (0.5 g) ground cloves

¼ cup (60 ml) white wine

About 12 feet (3.5 m) hog casings, soaked in cold water for 1 hour, then rinsed inside and out

To Serve:

2 cups (475 ml) hot cooked Polenta (page 281)

Olive oil, as needed

4 teaspoons (19 g) unsalted butter

4 large eggs

2 teaspoons (2.5 g) chopped mixed herbs (parsley, rosemary, and thyme) for garnish

Rock salt for garnish

For the cotechino: Cut the pork shoulder and fatback into 1 to 1½-inch (2.5 to 3.75-cm) cubes. Lay the cubed meat on a sheet tray and freeze until firm but not solid, about 1 hour. At the same time, freeze all parts of a meat grinder.

Fit the meat grinder with the large (¼-inch/6-mm) die, then put on plastic gloves and stick your hands in a large bowl of ice until very cold. Place the bowl of a stand mixer in the bowl of ice, and set the grinder on high speed. Scatter the kosher salt, dextrose, cinnamon, pepper, allspice, nutmeg, and cloves over the semi-frozen meat. Grind the meat through the large die twice, catching it in the cold mixing bowl. Add the white wine and mix with a stand mixer or electric mixer on low speed until the meat feels sticky, like wet bread dough, 2 to 3 minutes.

Attach a large sausage stuffer tube to the meat grinder and lubricate the tube with some water. The next step of stuffing the sausage is much easier with two people: if you can, have one person feed in the meat mixture and the other person handle the casing as it fills up. Feed some of the meat mixture into the feed tube on high speed until it just starts to poke out the end of the sausage stuffer. Turn off the machine. Use butcher's string to tie a double knot into the end of a hog casing, then slip the open end of the casing onto the stuffer all the way to the tied end, like putting a sock on your foot. Put pressure on the end of the casing so it's gently pressed against the stuffer. Turn the machine to high speed and feed in the meat mixture. Keep gentle pressure on the casing so the mixture packs into the middle of the casing as tightly as possible. You do not want any air bubbles in there because air can allow bacteria to breed and spoil the sausage. As the meat gets stuffed into the casing, it should pack around the end of the stuffer tube by at least 1 inch (2.5 cm) to prevent air

from getting into the sausage. Constantly check the sausage for air bubbles, working them out the open end of the casing as necessary. Continue stuffing the mixture into the casing until it is full and evenly stuffed and all of the meat mixture is used, using additional casings as necessary. Remove the stuffed casing from the stuffer, grab the open end, and squeeze it down tightly against the meat to pack it firm. Twist the open end several times against the meat until the sausage is firm and sealed. Tie off the twisted end with butcher's string and poke any air pockets with a needle to eliminate air. Pinch the sausage every 4 to 5 inches (10 to 13 cm), twisting in opposite directions and tying knots to make 4- to 5-inch (10- to 13-cm) sausage links. Cover and refrigerate overnight or up to 1 week. You should have twenty to twenty-five 4-inch (10-cm) sausage links. Any leftover sausage will keep frozen for 1 month.

To serve: Make the polenta. When it is done, slice four sausages lengthwise almost in half, and open like a book. Heat a grill or skillet on high heat and brush the grates with a little oil. Grill the sausages face-down until browned and firm on that side, 3 to 4 minutes. Flip, and cook until the other side is lightly browned, 1 to 2 minutes. Remove from the heat and set aside. Melt the butter in a large sauté pan and crack all four eggs directly into the pan. Cook over medium heat until the whites are firm but the yolks are still runny, 2 to 3 minutes. Do not flip the eggs.

Spoon ½ cup (120 ml) hot cooked polenta into each bowl and top with a grilled sausage face up. Lay a sunny-side up egg on top of each sausage, Return the sauté pan to high heat and cook the butter until it turns golden brown. Spoon the browned butter over the egg and garnish with the remaining herbs and rock salt.

PIZZOCCHERI with CHARD, POTATO, and BITTO CHEESE

MAKES 6 SERVINGS

1 pound (450 g) Swiss chard

6 ounces (1½ sticks/170 g) unsalted butter

12 leaves fresh sage

8 ounces (227 g) Buckwheat Pasta Dough (page 282), rolled into 2 sheets, each about 1/16 inch (1.5 mm) thick

1 pound (450 g) gold potatoes, peeled and cut into ½-inch (1.25-cm) cubes

4 ounces (113 g) Bitto cheese, shredded (1½ cups)

4 ounces (113 g) fontina cheese, shredded (1½ cups)

Salt and freshly ground black pepper

Claudia's friend Laura has a mountain house in Valtellina, about an hour from the Swiss border. There's a little river in the backyard, cattle come ambling down the mountain, and there's a pig farm next door. It's idyllic, to say the least. The first time Claudia took me there, we picked up some formagella, fontina, and pizzoccheri at a local cheese shop. Pizzoccheri are short pasta strips like tagliatelle but made with 80 percent buckwheat flour. Claudia, Laura, and their friend Consuela made the pasta and tossed it with both cheeses, some boiled potatoes, and a leafy green called *bieta* that's similar to Swiss chard. They finished the dish with brown butter and sage. It was awesome, and one of the most traditional dishes from Valtellina. I like to serve it family style on a big platter, but you could serve it on individual plates if you like.

Strip the leaves from the stems of the chard and coarsely chop the leaves. Set aside.

Put the butter and sage in a large deep sauté pan over medium heat, and cook until the sage lightly browns, the butter turns golden, and the milk solids lightly brown on the bottom of the pan, 6 to 8 minutes.

Meanwhile, lay a pasta sheet on a lightly floured work surface and trim the edges square. Cut crosswise into strips a little less than 1 inch (2.5 cm) wide, preferably with a fluted cutter. Repeat with the remaining pasta dough.

Bring a large pot of salted water to a boil. Add the potatoes and blanch until barely tender, 3 to 4 minutes. Using a slotted spoon, transfer the potatoes to the browned butter (reserving the pot of boiling water for the pasta), and cook over medium heat until the potatoes are tender, 3 to 4 minutes. Add the chard and 1½ cups (375 ml) of pasta water, and cook until the chard wilts and the sauce is creamy, 3 to 4 minutes.

Add the pasta to the boiling water, and cook until tender yet firm, about a minute. Drain the pasta and add to the pan, along with the Bitto and fontina, tossing until the cheese melts and looks stringy. Season generously with salt and pepper and serve on a large platter or divide among warm pasta plates.

WILD BRANZINO with FENNEL and ARTICHOKES

At Ristorante Loro, the chef Antonio Rochetti was very particular about his fish. He only ordered from Pesceria Orobica in Bergamo because it had the freshest fish. This fishmonger also ships to the United States for a pretty penny! Antonio would only order wild fish, never farm-raised. To show me the difference, he ordered both wild and farmed branzino one day. The wild fish looked plump and clear in color, and the meat tasted extra-flavorful. The farmed fish looked smaller and duller, and it tasted that way. Don't worry; if you can't find wild branzino, you can use another wild white fish, such as bass, snapper, or sea bream. For the artichokes, I use what restaurants term the "24-count" size, meaning twenty-four to a carton; each is about three inches in diameter. If you use bigger artichokes, reduce the total number of them here.

MAKES 4 SERVINGS

2 bulbs fennel

13 sprigs fresh thyme, divided

3 garlic cloves, sliced, divided

⅔ cup (150 ml) olive oil, divided, plus some for oiling the fish

4 tablespoons (60 ml) melted unsalted butter, divided

½ cup (120 ml) freshly squeezed lemon juice, divided

Salt and freshly ground black pepper

6 artichokes, each about 3 inches (7.5 cm) in diameter

½ cup (120 ml) white wine

4 wild European branzino fillets, (5 to 6 ounces/142 to 170 g each), skin on

1 cup (235 ml) Fish Stock (page 279)

1 tablespoon (15 ml) truffle paste

2 tablespoons (7 g) chopped fresh flat-leaf parsley

(continued on next page)

Preheat the oven to 400°F (205°C). Trim the fennel bulbs and then cut them in half lengthwise, keeping the cores intact. Slice the fennel lengthwise into strips so the cores keep the slices whole. Toss the fennel with ten sprigs of the thyme, two of the sliced garlic cloves, 1 tablespoon (15 ml) of the oil, 1 tablespoon (15 ml) of the melted butter, and 3 tablespoons (45 ml) of the lemon juice on a rimmed baking sheet. Season with salt and pepper and then lay the pieces in a single layer. Roast until tender, about 1 hour, turning once halfway through.

Combine 3 tablespoons (45 ml) of the remaining lemon juice with 3 cups (750 ml) of water in a medium bowl. Cut one of the artichokes in half through the equator to remove most of the leaves and expose the choke (the fuzzy part). Scoop out and discard the choke. Use a paring knife to pare down the artichoke to just the tender white part (the heart) with some of the tender white stem attached. Cut the artichoke heart into eight equal-size wedges. Toss in the acidulated water to prevent discoloration, then repeat the process with the remaining artichokes. Using a slotted spoon, transfer the artichokes to a roasting pan and add the wine, ½ cup (120 ml) of the remaining oil, 1 tablespoon (15 ml) of the remaining melted butter, the remaining garlic clove, and the remaining three sprigs of thyme, tossing to coat. Cover with foil and roast until the artichokes are tender, about 45 minutes.

Heat a grill to medium-high heat. Coat the fish lightly with oil and season with salt and pepper. Scrape the grill rack and coat it with oil. Grill the fish, skin-side down, until the skin is crispy, 3 to 4 minutes. Flip, and grill until the fish is still a little filmy and moist in the center, 3 to 4 minutes more.

Meanwhile, transfer the roasted fennel and roasted artichokes to a large deep sauté pan, discarding the thyme sprigs. Add the fish stock, remaining 2 tablespoons (30 ml) of melted butter, remaining 2 tablespoons plus 1 teaspoon (35 ml) of oil, remaining 2 tablespoons (30 ml) of lemon juice, and the truffle paste, and cook over medium heat until the sauce gets a little creamy and coats the vegetables, 3 to 4 minutes. Stir in the parsley and season with salt and pepper.

Lay the branzino on plates, skin-side up. Spoon the fennel and artichokes over the fish, spooning the sauce over the vegetables and around the plate.

CITRUS RUM BABAS ALLA CREMA

MAKES 16 TO 18 SMALL BABAS

Starter:

4 packed teaspoons (25 g) fresh yeast, or 2 teaspoons (8 g) active dry yeast

1 tablespoon (15 ml) warm water (110°F/43°C)

3 tablespoons (25 g) bread flour

4 teaspoons (16 g) granulated sugar

Babas:

1½ cups (205 g) bread flour

1 cup plus 4 teaspoons (216 g) granulated sugar, divided

3 large eggs

5 tablespoons (71 g) unsalted butter, softened

1 vanilla bean, split and scraped

Pinch of salt

7 ounces (200 g) candied orange peel, finely chopped (about 1 cup) (see page 288)

½ cup (120 ml) dark spiced rum, such as Myers's

2 cups (475 ml) Pastry Cream (page 285)

The greatest thing about rum cake is that it's saturated with rum syrup. When you bite into the cake, it's like taking a shot of rum with syrup running over your lips and down your chin. It's a classic Neapolitan dessert. We served miniature rum babas at our wedding, but make these any size you like. I serve them with a squeeze of pastry cream and some diced strawberries marinated in sugar and lemon juice.

For the starter: Stir together the yeast, water, flour, and sugar in the bowl of a mixer. Let stand in a warm spot until the surface looks foamy, 20 to 30 minutes.

For the babas: Add the flour, 4 teaspoons (16 g) of the sugar, and the eggs, butter, vanilla, and salt to the starter and mix with the paddle attachment on medium speed until the dough is so sticky that it wraps around itself, 20 to 30 minutes, scraping down the sides several times. Mix the candied orange peel into the dough. Coat sixteen to eighteen 1- to 2-ounce (30- to 60-ml) silicone baking cups with cooking spray (I use a single tray of 1.5-ounce/45-ml cone-shaped silicone cups; you could also use larger baking cups or muffin cups). Divide the dough into sixteen to eighteen pieces, each about 1 ounce (28 g), and place each piece in a prepared cup (if using larger baking cups, use larger pieces to fill them). Cover loosely and let rise in a warm spot until doubled in size, about 1 hour.

Preheat the oven to 325°F (160°C). Bake the babas until a toothpick inserted in the center comes out clean, about 15 minutes.

Meanwhile, combine the remaining 1 cup (200 g) of sugar with 1 cup (235 ml) of water in a small saucepan. Bring to a simmer over medium heat, then remove from the heat and stir in the rum. When the babas come out of the oven, remove them from their molds, let cool slightly, then immerse each one completely in the rum syrup for 10 to 15 seconds until completely saturated. Transfer to a wire rack to cool. The babas can be covered and refrigerated for up to 2 days.

When ready to serve, spoon the cooled pastry cream into a pastry bag or resealable plastic bag. Cut a deep slit in the babas from top to bottom, leaving the babas intact at the back, and pipe the pastry cream into the slit. Serve immediately or refrigerate for up to 1 hour before serving.

OLIVE OIL PANNA COTTA with SUMMER BERRIES

Claudia and I got married in Italy in the summertime, and this dish was the star of the dessert buffet. It was served with wild blackberries, raspberries, gooseberries, and red and white currants. But you can use whatever berries are freshest when and where you make it. The important thing is to use a good, strong olive oil, preferably a peppery one from southern Italy. That's what makes this panna cotta different from others. The peppery olive oil jumps out at you and marries perfectly with the sweet berries.

For the panna cotta: Coat six 4-ounce (125-ml) ramekins with olive oil and fill a large bowl with ice water. Bring the cream, milk, and sugar to a boil in a small saucepan. Lower the heat so that the mixture simmers gently, and sprinkle the gelatin over the top, whisking to disperse it evenly. Use a stick blender to buzz in the ⅔ cup (150 ml) of olive oil in a thin steam until the mixture is blended and emulsified.

Briefly dip the bottom of the pan into the ice water to cool down the mixture slightly, whisking gently as it cools. Before it gets too firm to pour, divide the mixture among the prepared ramekins. Refrigerate overnight or up to 2 days.

For the berries: Stir together the berries, sugar, honey, and lemon juice in a small bowl, cover, and let marinate at room temperature for 24 hours.

Unmold the panna cotta onto plates and spoon on the marinated berries and their syrup.

MAKES 6 SERVINGS

Panna Cotta:

⅔ cup (150 ml) olive oil, plus some for greasing ramekins

1½ cups (375) heavy cream

1 cup (235 ml) whole milk

⅔ cup (133 g) granulated sugar

2¼ teaspoons (5.25 g) powdered gelatin

Berries:

2 cups (300 g) mixed fresh berries (blueberries, huckleberries, strawberries, blackberries, and raspberries)

¼ cup (50 g) granulated sugar

2 tablespoons (30 ml) farmers' honey (any variety)

3 tablespoons (45 ml) freshly squeezed lemon juice

CHIACCHIERE with COFFEE and CHOCOLATE BUDINO

During *carnevale* in Italy, you see *chiacchiere* everywhere. They're crispy little strips of fried dough. The dough usually includes a little grappa. It is a celebration, after all. I like to shape them into little knots so you can dip them like edible spoons into creamy coffee and chocolate pudding. Serve the pudding in coffee cups, if you like. That hints at the meaning of *chiacchiere,* which translates literally to "chatter" or "small talk," the sort of thing that happens over a cup of coffee.

MAKES 4 TO 6 SERVINGS

Budino:

3½ teaspoons (6.5 g) very finely ground espresso

1¾ cups plus 2 tablespoons (455 ml) heavy cream

6 tablespoons (75 g) granulated sugar, divided

Pinch of salt

½ vanilla bean, split and scraped

4 large egg yolks

3 ounces (85 g) bittersweet chocolate, finely chopped (about ½ cup)

Chiacchiere:

¾ cup (94 g) *tipo* 00 flour (see page 277) or all-purpose flour, plus some for dusting

2½ teaspoons (10.5 g) granulated sugar

Pinch of salt

2 teaspoons (9 g) unsalted butter, softened

1 small egg

1½ teaspoons (7 ml) grappa

Zest of ½ orange

½ vanilla bean, split and scraped

5 teaspoons (25 ml) whole milk

Oil for frying

Confectioners' sugar, for dusting

For the budino: Preheat the oven to 325°F (160°C). Whisk together the espresso, cream, 3 tablespoons (38 g) of the sugar, and the salt and vanilla in a saucepan and bring to a simmer over medium heat.

Combine the egg yolks and remaining 3 tablespoons (38 g) of sugar in the bowl of a mixer and whip on high speed until light and fluffy, 3 to 4 minutes. Very gradually whisk the cream mixture into the egg mixture to prevent scrambling the eggs. When combined, pour the hot mixture over the chocolate in a medium bowl. Let stand until melted enough to be stirred smooth. Strain the mixture and pour into four to six 4-ounce (175-ml) ramekins. Set the ramekins in a roasting pan and pour enough hot water into the pan to come halfway up the sides of the ramekins. Bake until the sides are set but the center is still a little jiggly, 25 to 35 minutes. Remove the ramekins from the water bath and let cool completely on a rack. Cover and refrigerate until cold, at least 2 hours or up to 2 days.

For the chiacchiere: Combine the flour, sugar, salt, butter, egg, grappa, orange zest, vanilla, and milk in the bowl of a mixer. Mix on medium speed with the paddle attachment until the dough comes together and gathers around the paddle, 2 to 3 minutes. Scrape the dough onto a sheet of plastic and wrap tightly. Refrigerate for 1 hour or up to 1 day.

Shape the dough into an oblong disk the width of your pasta machine. Lightly flour a work surface and position a pasta roller at the widest setting. Roll the dough through the rollers, lightly dusting the dough with flour and brushing off the excess with your hands. Reset the rollers to the next narrowest setting and again pass the dough through the rollers, dusting again with flour. Pass the dough once or twice through each progressively narrower setting. Roll the dough to about $\frac{1}{16}$ inch (1.5 mm) thick, about setting #4 or 5 on the KitchenAid pasta attachment. Trim the edges square and then cut the dough crosswise into $\frac{1}{2}$-inch (1.25-cm)-wide strips. Tie each strip into a knot like a pretzel. You should have thirty-five to forty knots, which can be covered and refrigerated for up to 1 day or frozen for up to 1 month.

Heat the oil in a deep fryer or deep pot to 350°F (175°C). Drop in the chiacchiere a few at a time and fry until golden brown, 3 to 4 minutes, flipping once and adjusting the heat to maintain a 350°F (175°C) oil temperature at all times. Immediately transfer to paper towels to drain. Dust with confectioners' sugar and serve with the budino.

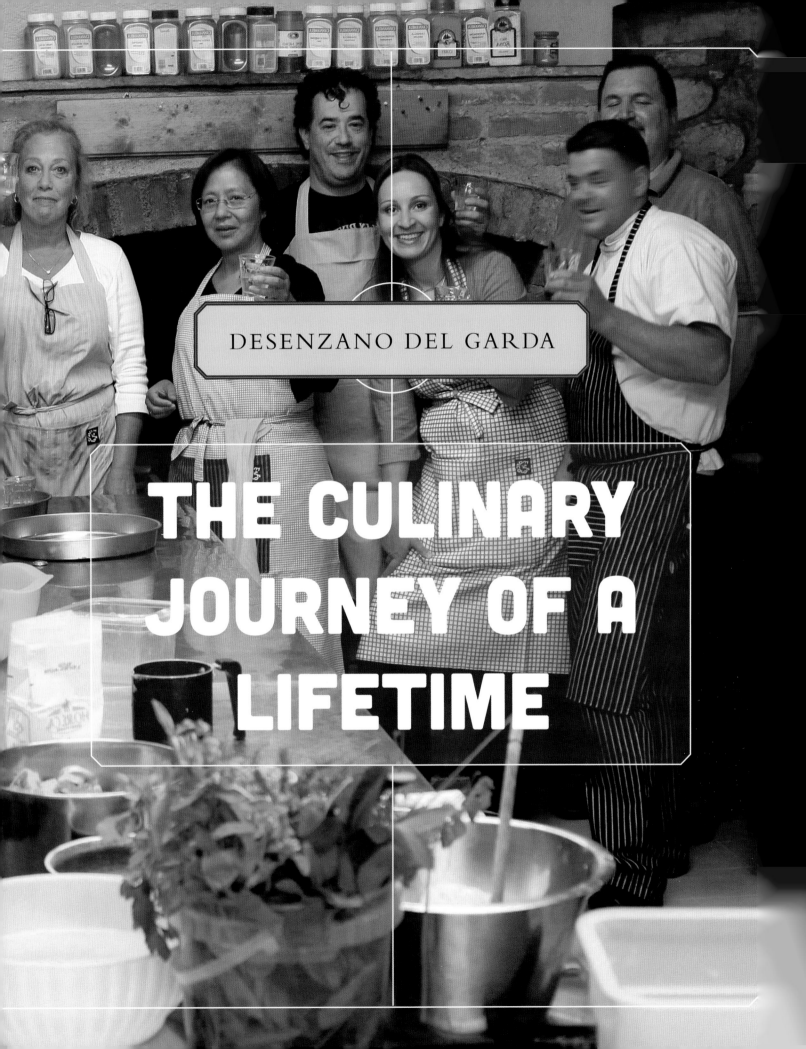

DESENZANO DEL GARDA

THE CULINARY JOURNEY OF A LIFETIME

I GOT THE CALL IN EARLY 2006. MY HANDS WERE DEEP IN BREAD DOUGH AT THE BEDFORD VILLAGE INN. IT WAS MARC VETRI AND JEFF BENJAMIN CALLING FROM THE CA' MARCANDA VINEYARDS OF GAJA WINERY IN TUSCANY. THEY HAD AN IDEA AND A LOCATION FOR A PHILADELPHIA RESTAURANT: A TRADITIONAL ITALIAN *OSTERIA* WITH A WOOD-BURNING STOVE, SERVING RUSTIC YET REFINED FOOD IN A CASUAL, UPSCALE ATMOSPHERE. THEY OFFERED ME A PARTNERSHIP IN THE RESTAURANT. I STARED AT THE KITCHEN WALL FOR HALF A MILLISECOND AND SAID YES! EVERY CHEF DREAMS OF OWNING HIS OR HER OWN RESTAURANT.

The real eye-opener came over the next six months. I spent every spare moment before and after work helping to design the restaurant space, draft blueprints for the kitchen, frame out and lay concrete for the building itself with the construction crew, develop the menu, test the dishes, and interview and hire everyone from line cooks to dishwashers. We spent months staining the concrete floors red, filling the restaurant with antique country tables, seeking out a vintage Faema espresso machine, and finding a decent price on three antique Berkel meat slicers for slicing our house-cured prosciutto paper-thin right in front of our guests.

For six months, I dreamed in menus. The dishes for this restaurant had to capture the bold flavors and rustic simplicity of all the food I cooked in Italy. The wood-burning grill and oven took center stage in our collective visions, and we put more than half a dozen wood-fired pizzas on the menu, including the Lombarda, topped with house-made cotechino sausage, Bitto and mozzarella cheeses, and a baked egg. Roasted vegetable antipasto, spit-roasted suckling pig, bistecca alla Fiorentina, and rustic copper-pot polenta all underscored the importance of a live wood fire in Italian

cooking. I also included some traditional dishes from Bergamo, such as ciareghi, and a few I learned from my mother-in-law, Pina, such as Nonna's rabbit and candele with wild boar Bolognese. Pastas and desserts are among my specialties, so I featured plenty on the menu, including robiola and fava francobolli, chicken liver rigatoni, bonet, chocolate flan with pistachio gelato, polenta budino with gianduia mousse and candied hazelnuts, and torrone semifreddo with candied chestnuts and chocolate sauce.

From working in Italy in such Michelin-star restaurants as Frosio and Loro to running the kitchen at Locanda del Biancospino, I can honestly say that building, opening, and running Osteria in Philadelphia has been, by far, the greatest learning experience of my career. More than any other, this restaurant has taught me that being a chef isn't always about cooking. An executive chef spends roughly 30 percent of his or her time preparing food—and it's the easiest 30 percent. The rest of the time is consumed with organizing schedules, writing checklists, taking inventory, placing orders, doing payroll, acting as mentor and psychiatrist to the staff, and dealing with countless little crises that arise on any given

day. If all a chef had to do was cook, the job would be easy!

But I love every minute of it. I love Italian food and cooking so much that Osteria eventually wasn't enough. I soon wanted to give people a more immersive experience by taking them directly to Italy. In 2010, Claudia and I led our first culinary tour of northern Italy, anchored in Desenzano, a popular vacation city on the largest lake in Italy, Lake Garda. We hosted ten guests at Agriturismo Armea, a beautiful inn near the southern shores of Lake Garda with an outdoor pool and a stone-walled dining room. From Desenzano, you get a stunning lakeside view of the Italian Alps. Shops and cafés buzz with tourists by day and restaurants and clubs come alive at night. Formed by glaciers, Lake Garda enjoys a climate that's unusually mild this far north but perfect for growing both olives and citrus. The deep waters teem with fresh fish like lake salmon, trout, perch, eel, and fresh sardines. It's a cook's dream region. On Mondays, the nearby town of Peschiera hosts an incredible open-air market where you can stock up on local foods, and there's a great butcher shop in Rivoltella that specializes in horse, a meat that's more popular in Italy than in any other country in the European Union.

On that first tour, Claudia and I showed Americans the food and wine of Italy in a way that only a native Italian could reveal it. As expected, guests dined in Michelin-star restaurants, such as La Brughiera in Villa d'Almè, Loro in Trescore Balneario, and Frosio in Almè. And they enjoyed wine tastings at famous Franciacorta wineries, such as Bellavista and Ca' del Bosco. But Claudia and I also escorted them to our favorite gelateria, Gelateria Peccati de Gola in Albino, so they could taste the incredible licorice gelato. We gave them personal tours of Venice, Verona, and the historic Città Alta in Bergamo. And we enjoyed an intimate, home-cooked lunch under Pina's pergola in Cene, overlooking the foothills of the Alps, digging into her classic stuffed zucchini

blossoms and polenta with wild boar ragù and her amazing crespelle. Best of all, we taught three cooking classes so guests could continue to enjoy the taste of Italy after returning home to the States. We showed them preparations that could be easily adapted, such as stuffed focaccia, mixed-meat grill, and fresh stone-fruit tart.

The culinary tour has become an annual event, and we recently expanded the experience by traveling south. In 2012, we chartered a private forty-two-foot (13-m) yacht in Sicily and cruised among the volcanic Aeolian Islands. We toured the entire eastern coast of Sicily, stopping in Taormina, Catania, Ragusa, Siracusa, Noto, Modica, and Giardini Naxos. Guests stayed at the Donna Franca villa in Trappitello and we held cooking classes that made use of all the incredible local products, such as fresh swordfish, tuna, sea urchin, tomatoes, lemons, mozzarella, and ricotta. Of all the restaurants we visited on that trip, Locanda Don Serafino was by far the best. It's built from stone right in the side of a hill in Ragusa, and when you enter the huge stone archways, you feel as if you're dining in a beautifully restored cave of kings.

Both Osteria and my culinary tours make me feel incredibly lucky. Through the restaurant, the cooking classes, and the food trips, I get to share the best of Italy with anyone who wants to enjoy it. Bringing guests into our restaurant and back to Italy offers a unique opportunity for me to say thanks and to honor the cuisine and culture that has given me so much.

Focaccia Stuffed
with Taleggio and Pancetta

•

Pecorino Flan with Fava Beans
and Artichokes

•

Fazzoletti with Lamb Breast
and Pea Ragù

•

Squash and Fontina Lasagnetta

•

Tomato Tortellini
with Burrata and Basil

•

Meat Grigliata
with Mixed Bean Salad

•

Fresh Prune
and Almond Tart

•

Braised Blueberries
with Sbrisoluna

•

Grappa Torta

FOCACCIA STUFFED with TALEGGIO and PANCETTA

MAKES TWELVE TO SIXTEEN
3-INCH (7.5-CM) SQUARES

1½ packed tablespoons (28.5 g) fresh yeast, or 2¼ teaspoons (9 g) active dry yeast

3¾ cups (514 g) bread flour

1½ teaspoons (9 g) salt

1 tablespoon (15 ml) extra-virgin olive oil, plus more for drizzling

8 ounces (227 g) Taleggio cheese, shredded (2 cups)

4 ounces (113 g) pancetta, julienned

1 teaspoon (6 g) flake sea salt

1 teaspoon (2 g) freshly ground black pepper

On our first trip to Liguria, Claudia and I stopped in Bergeggi, a tiny beach town near Genoa. Claudia stuck her head out the window, took one whiff, and said, "Stop the car." She didn't know where the focaccia was, but she could smell it. We found a line of people, pulled over, and got in line. The store sold twenty different kinds of stuffed focaccia—Speck and blue cheese, tomatoes and arugula, Nutella. . . you name it. You order whatever you like in hundred-gram increments, and they slice off your order and warm it in a wood oven. We got Speck and *crescenza*, cipolline and Gorgonzola, artichoke and Parmigiano, and Nutella. That was our lunch. Here's my northern Italian twist with pancetta and Taleggio. Try it warm out of the oven or at room temperature alongside a soup or pasta dish.

If using fresh yeast, put the yeast, flour, and 1⅓ cups (330 ml) of cold water in the bowl of a stand mixer. If using active dry yeast, put 1⅓ cups (330 ml) warm tap water (about 110°F/43°C) in the bowl of a stand mixer, mix in the yeast, and let stand for 5 minutes until foamy; then add the flour. Using the dough hook, mix on low speed for 2 to 3 minutes. Switch to medium speed, add the salt, and stream in the olive oil. Mix until the dough is smooth and silky, about 10 minutes. Transfer the dough to an oiled bowl and let rise in a warm spot until doubled in bulk, about 1 hour.

Oil a half-sheet pan (an 11 x 14-inch/28 x 35-cm rimmed baking sheet), and then punch down the dough and turn it out onto the oiled pan. Fold the dough over itself in thirds, and let rise in a warm spot for 30 minutes. Punch down the dough, fold it over itself in thirds again, and let rise in a warm spot for another 30 minutes.

Cut the dough in half and press half of the dough into the baking sheet so it is about ¼ inch (6 mm) thick. Roll up the pressed out dough and set aside. Re-oil the pan and press the other half of the dough into the pan so it is about ¼ inch (6 mm) thick. Scatter the cheese and pancetta over the dough in the pan, leaving a ¼-inch (6-mm) border around the edge. Unroll the other half of the dough over the cheese and pancetta and pinch the edges to seal. Dimple the surface all over with your fingertips and let rise in a warm spot for 30 minutes.

Preheat the oven to 500°F (260°C). Turn on convection if possible. Drizzle the top of the focaccia with olive oil and sprinkle on the flaked salt and freshly ground black pepper. Bake until golden brown, 20 to 25 minutes. Let cool in the pan on a wire rack and cut into 3-inch (7.5-cm) squares. Serve warm or at room temperature.

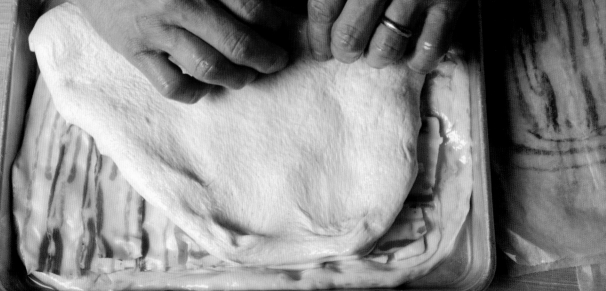

PECORINO FLAN with FAVA BEANS and ARTICHOKES

When I started doing culinary tours of Italy, I wanted to teach people how to make traditional Italian molded and unmolded dishes, such as flan, sformato, and tortino. This recipe became the blueprint. It's as basic as can be: a straightforward custard of eggs, milk, and cheese that you can customize however you like. Cook some onions or leeks into it. Puree some carrots, peas, or fava beans and replace a little of the milk with the vegetable puree. Change the cheese from pecorino to Taleggio, Gorgonzola, or fontina. I use fava beans and pecorino because it's a classic flavor combination that works. After looking through some old Italian cookbooks, I got the idea to toss in some shaved raw artichokes.

For the pecorino flan: Preheat the oven to 250°F (120°C). Butter eight 4-ounce (125-ml) ramekins and place in a roasting pan or deep baking dish. Set aside.

Bring the milk to a boil in a medium saucepan over medium heat. Remove from the heat and stir in the cheese until melted. Use a stick blender or pour the mixture into a blender and blend until smooth, 1 to 2 minutes. With the blender running, add the eggs and egg yolk, and season with salt and pepper. Turn the blender to low speed, and with the machine running, blend in the cream just until incorporated. Strain the mixture through a fine-mesh strainer into a bowl. Crack some black pepper over the mixture and stir slowly. Remove any skin that forms on the surface of the mixture, then carefully pour it into the ramekins to come up just under the lip. Pour hot water into the bottom of the pan to come at least halfway up the sides of the ramekins. Cover the pan tightly with aluminum foil and bake until set around the sides and still a little jiggly in the center, 25 to 30 minutes. Remove the pan from the oven and let cool, covered, in the water.

For the fava beans and artichokes: Bring a large pot of water to a boil and fill a large bowl with ice water. Add the whole fava pods and blanch for 1 minute. Transfer to the ice water to stop the cooking. When cool, pluck the favas from the pods, then pinch open the pale green skin on each bean and pop out the bright green favas into a bowl. You should have about ½ cup (90 g).

Add the oil and lemon juice to the bowl.

Trim off or peel any tough stems from the artichokes and snap off any dark green leaves so you are left with only tender green-yellow leaves and tender stems. Shave the artichokes on a mandoline, even an inexpensive handheld one, adding them to the fava beans as they are shaved. Stir to coat them in lemon juice. Add the mint, season with salt and pepper, and stir to combine.

For each plate, turn out a flan into the center of the plate. Spoon the fava bean mixture around each flan. Use a vegetable peeler to shave a few curls of pecorino cheese around each plate. Finish with a few grindings of fresh black pepper.

MAKES 8 SERVINGS

Pecorino Flan:

Unsalted butter, for greasing ramekins

⅔ cup (150 ml) whole milk

3¼ ounces (92 g) pecorino cheese, grated (⅞ cup), plus a few ounces for shaving over top

2 large eggs

1 large egg yolk

Salt and freshly ground black pepper

⅔ cup (150 ml) heavy cream

Fava Beans and Artichokes:

8 ounces (227 g) fava beans in the pods

¼ cup (60 ml) olive oil

1 cup (235 ml) freshly squeezed lemon juice

8 baby artichokes

¼ cup (15 g) chopped or chiffonade of fresh mint

Salt and freshly ground black pepper

FAZZOLETTI with LAMB BREAST and PEA RAGÙ

MAKES 6 SERVINGS

1 bone-in lamb breast, 2 to 3 pounds (1 to 1.3 kg)

Salt and freshly ground black pepper

2 tablespoons plus ¼ cup (90 ml) olive oil, divided

½ medium-size yellow onion, finely chopped (⅔ cup/107 g)

1 medium-size carrot, finely chopped (⅔ cup/81 g)

1 large rib celery, finely chopped (⅔ cup/67 g)

1 garlic clove, smashed

4 sprigs fresh rosemary

1 bay leaf

2 cups (480 g) canned plum tomatoes, preferably San Marzano, cored and crushed by hand

1 cup (235 ml) white wine

8 ounces (227 g) Egg Pasta Dough (page 282), rolled into 2 sheets, each about ¹⁄₁₆ inch (1.5 mm) thick

1 cup (145 g) freshly shelled spring peas, from about 1 pound (450 g) pea pods

1 ounce (28 g) pecorino cheese, grated (⅓ cup) for garnish

In my cooking classes, I like to demonstrate techniques that apply to dozens of dishes. Braising is something that applies to every northern Italian ragù. You braise a big piece of meat, shred it, season it, and then serve it with polenta or pasta. When it comes to lamb, most people think of chops and loin, but lamb breast makes a fantastic ragù. It's inexpensive and full of rich flavor. Spring peas add a shot of freshness to brighten up the ragù. *Fazzoletti* means "handkerchiefs;" you just toss the ragù and simple pasta squares together until the dish looks like little handkerchiefs folded over one another.

Preheat the oven to 300°F (150°C). Season the lamb all over with salt and pepper. Heat 2 tablespoons (30 ml) of the oil in a Dutch oven over medium-high heat. When hot, add the seasoned lamb, and cook until seared and well browned, 5 to 6 minutes. Flip the breast, and sear the other side, 5 to 6 minutes.

Transfer the meat to a plate and add the onion, carrot, celery, garlic, rosemary, and bay leaf to the pan. Sweat the vegetables until they are tender but not browned, 4 to 6 minutes. Add the tomatoes, and cook until they start to break down, 5 to 6 minutes. Pour in the wine and simmer until the liquid in the pan reduces in volume by about half, 10 to 15 minutes. Return the meat to the pan, cover, and braise in the oven until the meat is fall-apart tender, 2 to 2½ hours. Remove the pan from the oven and let the meat cool in the liquid until cool enough to handle. Transfer the meat to a cutting board and use tongs and a fork to shred the meat from the bones, silverskin, and fat, saving only the meat.

Remove and discard the rosemary stems, garlic, bay leaf, and any stray bones. Skim off any excess fat from the braising liquid and then pour the vegetables and braising liquid into a food processor. Puree briefly with short pulses to make a chunky, rustic puree. Return the puree and shredded meat to the pan and season with salt and pepper. Use immediately or refrigerate for up to 1 week.

Bring a large pot of salted water to a boil. Lay a pasta sheet on a lightly floured work surface and trim the edges square. Cut the pasta into 3-inch (7.5-cm) squares. Repeat with the remaining pasta dough. You should get about forty squares total. Drop the pasta squares into the boiling water in batches if necessary to prevent overcrowding; quickly return the water to a boil, and cook until tender, 1 to 2 minutes.

Meanwhile, heat the ragù in a large, deep sauté pan over medium heat. Add about 1 cup (235 ml) of pasta water, along with the fresh peas and remaining ¼ cup (60 ml) of olive oil, and cook until creamy, 3 to 4 minutes. Drain the pasta and add to the ragù, tossing for 1 to 2 minutes. Divide among plates and sprinkle with the pecorino.

SQUASH and FONTINA LASAGNETTA

Claudia's grandmother, Nonna Anna, used to make lasagne without pasta. She roasted slices of squash, layered them with béchamel and blue cheese, and then baked the whole thing. I just ran with the idea, adding some pasta sheets to bulk up the dish, making a truffle béchamel, and using creamy fontina cheese. It's a great fall dish that I serve in individual baking dishes as lasagnetta.

Preheat the oven to 375°F (190°C). Prick the squash all over with the tip of a knife, and then microwave on high to make it easier to peel, 2 to 3 minutes. Peel and seed the squash and then slice it into rounds about ¼ inch (6 mm) thick. Toss the slices with the oil and season with salt and pepper. Spread flat on rimmed baking sheets and roast until tender, 10 to 12 minutes. Let cool in the pan.

Lay the pasta sheet on a lightly floured work surface and trim the edges square. Cut the pasta into 4-inch (10-cm) squares. You should have sixteen to eighteen squares, and they can be used immediately or frozen for up to 1 week.

Butter four to six individual casserole dishes or one large rimmed baking sheet. Bring a large pot of salted water to a boil and fill a large bowl with ice water. Drop the pasta squares in the boiling water, quickly return the water to a boil, and blanch for 10 to 20 seconds. Drain the pasta and immediately transfer to the ice water. Lay the blanched pasta sheets flat on clean kitchen towels.

Raise the oven temperature to 500°F (260°C). Turn on convection if possible. To build the lasagnetta, lay down one pasta sheet in each casserole dish or lay out four to six in a single layer on the baking sheet, leaving about 1 to 2 inches (2.5 to 5 cm) between each pasta sheet. Over each pasta sheet, layer on the ingredients in this order: about 2 tablespoons (30 ml) of béchamel, a slice of roasted squash, about ½ tablespoon (3 g) of Parmesan, and about ¼ cup (28 g) of fontina. Lay on another sheet of pasta and repeat the process. Top each lasagnetta with a third sheet of pasta, a layer of béchamel, a slice of squash, and a sprinkle of Parmesan. Place a pat of butter on top of each lasagnetta and bake until lightly browned and bubbly, 8 to 10 minutes. Serve immediately.

MAKES 4 TO 6 SERVINGS

1 medium-size butternut squash, about 2½ pounds (1.1 kg) total

2 tablespoons (30 ml) olive oil

Salt and freshly ground black pepper

4 ounces (113 g) Egg Pasta Dough (page 282), rolled into 1 sheet, about ¹⁄₁₆ inch (1.5 mm) thick

5⅓ tablespoons (75 g) unsalted butter, sliced into pats, plus more for greasing the dishes or sheet

2 cups (475 ml) Truffle Béchamel (page 281)

2½ ounces (71 g) Parmesan cheese, grated (¾ cup)

12 ounces (340 g) fontina cheese, shredded (about 3 cups)

TOMATO TORTELLINI with BURRATA and BASIL

I'm a big fan of making fresh vegetable and fruit purees as pasta fillings. You just need a little patience. Most vegetables and fruits are pretty watery, and it takes time to drain off the water and concentrate the flavor. Here, I puree fresh tomatoes and suspend the puree over a bowl overnight to drain out the tomato water, resulting in a nice, thick tomato puree. I prefer that thickening method to adding cheese or eggs because it leaves the singular flavor of the tomatoes intact. Save this dish for the height of summer and use the freshest, plumpest tomatoes you can find. The pasta should just explode with fresh, unadulterated tomato flavor—like biting into a raw tomato. A little burrata and basil are all it needs—like a fancy twist on Caprese salad.

MAKES 4 TO 6 SERVINGS

3 large ripe tomatoes (about 5 pounds/2.25 kg)

1½ teaspoons (7 ml) sherry vinegar, plus more as needed

About ¾ cup (175 ml) olive oil, divided

Salt and freshly ground black pepper

Granulated sugar, as needed

4 ounces (113 g) Egg Pasta Dough (page 282), rolled into 1 sheet, about ¹⁄₃₂ inch (0.8 mm) thick

5 ounces (142 g) burrata cheese

2 packed tablespoons (7 g) small fresh basil leaves for garnish

Bring a large pot of water to a boil and fill a large bowl with ice water. Score an X on the bottom of the tomatoes and drop them into the boiling water until the skins split and curl, about 1 minute, working in batches to prevent overcrowding. Immediately transfer the tomatoes to the ice water to shock and loosen the skins. When almost cool, peel and discard the tomato skins. Remove and discard the cores, halve the tomatoes, and remove the seeds. Coarsely chop the tomatoes and then puree in a blender until super-smooth, 2 to 3 minutes.

Make a large, five-layer sack of cheesecloth, using plenty of extra cheesecloth for hanging. Place the sack in a deep bowl or tall stock pot and carefully ladle in the tomato puree in batches. Bring up the corners and gently squeeze out the tomato water after each addition, transferring the drained tomato puree to a bowl as you go. Return all of the thickened tomato puree to the cheesecloth, bring up the corners, and suspend the sack over the bowl, tying the top to a propped-up wooden spoon handle so that the sack hangs well above the bottom of the bowl. You can also set the cheesecloth bundle in a large-mesh sieve and set that over the bowl. Let hang overnight to drain the remaining tomato water, at least 8 hours.

Transfer the thickened puree to a blender, along with the vinegar and about ½ cup (120 ml) of the olive oil. Puree until smooth and emulsified, 1 to 2 minutes. The puree should be smooth and not runny; adjust the amount of oil as necessary. Taste and season with salt, pepper, and additional vinegar, if necessary. If your tomatoes are underripe, add a pinch of sugar, too. Transfer the mixture to a resealable plastic bag and refrigerate for at least 1 hour or up to 1 day.

Lay the pasta sheet on a lightly floured work surface and cut into 2-inch (5-cm) squares. As you work, spray the pasta with water and cover with a towel to keep it from drying out. Cut a corner off the bag of filling and squeeze a ½-inch (1.25-cm)-diameter ball of filling on each square. Fold the pasta corner to corner over the filling to make a triangle. Dampen your fingertips and bring the two opposite corners together up over the filling and then pinch and hold to seal. You should have about fifty tortellini. Use immediately or freeze for up to 1 week.

Bring a large pot of salted water to a boil. Add the tortellini, and cook until tender yet firm, 1 to 2 minutes. Drain, reserving 1 cup of the pasta water. Transfer the pasta to a deep sauté pan, along with the reserved pasta water and the remaining ¼ cup (60 ml) of oil. Simmer over medium-high heat, stirring now and then, until the liquid reduces in volume and becomes light and creamy, 2 to 3 minutes.

Using your fingers, pick the burrata into small, fingertip-size pieces and divide them among plates. Spoon the tortellini over and around the cheese and garnish with the basil leaves and a few grindings of black pepper.

MEAT GRIGLIATA with MIXED BEAN SALAD

Most Italian homes have a fireplace used for both heating the house and cooking food. You don't see a lot of gas or propane grills. They usually build a wood fire in the fireplace, put a grill grate over it, and grill meat there. When we first walked into Agriturismo Armea on our Desenzano culinary tour, I saw a giant fireplace and knew we'd be using it for *grigliata*, a mixed grill dish. I suppose you could cook the meats here on a gas grill with some wood chips, but a wood fire will give you much better flavor. I like to use a mix of red and white oak wood. Sometimes, I add a little mesquite.

For the meat grigliata: Combine the rosemary, garlic, oil, salt, and pepper in a wide, shallow dish. Rub the mixture over the ribs and steak, and then leave the meat in the dish, cover, and marinate in the refrigerator for 2 hours.

Heat a grill to medium heat. Scrape and oil the grill grate, then grill the ribs directly over the heat until tender and crispy, 25 to 30 minutes, turning often. Grill the steak until medium-rare (135°F/57°C internal temperature), about 8 minutes per side. Slice the sausage in half lengthwise but leave it attached at the back end, and then grill until cooked through, 5 to 6 minutes per side. Transfer all of the meat to a platter as it is done and let it rest for 8 to 10 minutes. Slice the flank steak across the grain and arrange the slices on a platter with the ribs and sausage. Drizzle with some olive oil and sprinkle with rock salt and cracked black pepper.

For the mixed bean salad: Drain the borlotti beans and combine with the onion, celery, carrot, and ¼ cup (62 g) of the pancetta in a medium saucepan. Add enough water to cover the ingredients by 1 inch (2.5 cm). Bring to a boil over high heat and then lower the heat to medium-low and simmer gently until the beans are tender, about 1 hour. Season generously with salt and pepper and let the beans cool down in the liquid.

Bring a large pot of salted water to a boil and fill a large bowl with ice water. Add the green beans and wax beans and cook until tender, 2 to 3 minutes. Immediately submerge the beans in ice water to stop the cooking.

Cook the remaining ½ cup (60 g) pancetta in a sauté pan over medium heat until very lightly browned, 2 to 3 minutes. Add the red onion and garlic, and cook until the onion is lightly browned, 3 to 5 minutes more. Use a slotted spoon to remove the borlotti beans and solids from their cooking liquid to the sauté pan (discard the sachet). Add the green and wax beans, season with salt, pepper, parsley, oil, and vinegar. Serve with the meat grigliata.

MAKES 6 SERVINGS

Meat Grigliata:

Leaves from 10 sprigs fresh rosemary

4 garlic cloves, pressed

1 cup (235 ml) olive oil, plus some for drizzling

Salt and freshly ground black pepper

12 country-style spare ribs, cut into individual ribs

1 pound (450 g) flank steak

6 Cotechini (page 244) or other fresh Italian sausage

Rock salt

Mixed Bean Salad:

6 ounces (170 g) dried borlotti (cranberry beans) (about ¾ cup), soaked in water to cover overnight

½ medium-size yellow onion, finely chopped (½ cup/80 g)

1 medium-size rib celery, finely chopped (½ cup/51 g)

1 medium-size carrot, finely chopped (½ cup/61 g)

1 sachet of 1 sprig parsley, 1 sprig rosemary, 2 sprigs thyme, 1 bay leaf and 5 black peppercorns (see page 277)

¾ cup (190 g) finely chopped pancetta, divided

6 ounces (170 g) green beans

6 ounces (170 g) wax beans

½ small red onion, sliced (¼ cup/40 g)

1 garlic clove, minced

Salt and freshly ground black pepper

¼ cup (15 g) minced fresh flat-leaf parsley

⅓ cup (90 ml) extra-virgin olive oil

2 tablespoons (30 ml) red wine vinegar

FRESH PRUNE and ALMOND TART

MAKES 10 TO 12 SERVINGS

Tart Dough:

4 ounces (1 stick/113 g) unsalted butter, at room temperature

¾ cup (90 g) confectioners' sugar

2 large eggs

Grated zest of ½ lemon

1¾ cups (220 g) *tipo* 00 flour (see page 277) or all-purpose flour

Almond Filling and Plums:

1 cup plus 2 tablespoons (106 g) almond flour

3 tablespoons (23 g) *tipo* 00 flour (see page 277) or all-purpose flour

½ cup plus 1 tablespoon (113 g) granulated sugar

4 ounces (1 stick/113 g) unsalted butter, melted

2 large eggs

8 plums

In Italy, plums are called *prugne* (prunes). Don't ask me why. But they're delicious. My favorites are the *susine* (damson plums) that grow on Pina's property in Cene. On our culinary tours, guests pick plums from Pina's trees, and we use the fruit to make tarts. A filling of almond frangipane makes this one special because you press the plums into the filling, which then swells up around the fruit. The filling browns in the oven and cradles each piece of fruit like a warm blanket. Look for ripe, firm plums so they don't completely turn to mush in the oven.

For the tart dough: Cream the butter and sugar in a stand mixer on medium speed until light and fluffy, 1 to 2 minutes. With the mixer running, add the eggs one by one until each is incorporated. Switch to low speed, add the lemon zest and flour, and mix until the dough comes together. Scrape the dough onto a sheet of plastic wrap, shape into a ball, wrap in the plastic, and refrigerate for at least 2 hours or up to 1 day.

Preheat the oven to 350°F (175°C) and coat an 11-inch (28-cm) tart pan with cooking spray. Roll the dough between two large sheets of plastic to a 12-inch (30-cm) diameter. Remove the top sheet and carefully invert the dough onto the tart pan, fitting it in gently. Trim the edges, prick the bottom with a fork, and line the dough with foil. Top with pie weights or dried beans and bake until firm, 15 to 18 minutes. Carefully remove the foil and weights and continue baking until light golden brown, 10 to 15 minutes more. Let cool on a rack.

For the almond filling and plums: Whisk together the flours and sugar in a medium bowl. Stir in the melted butter and then the eggs. Let the mixture rest for 30 minutes, and then spread it over the bottom of the cooled tart shell.

Lower the oven temperature to 325°F (160°C). Cut the plums in half lengthwise and remove the pits. Press the plums, cut-side down, into the almond filling in a circular pattern, and bake until the plums are tender and the filling is set and lightly browned, 35 to 45 minutes. Let cool on a rack and serve warm or at room temperature.

BRAISED BLUEBERRIES with SBRISOLUNA

In the Bergamascan dialect, *sbrisoluna* is a crumbly cookie traditionally broken into pieces and served with coffee. I like to make it about one inch thick in a sheet pan, and then crumble it over buttermilk gelato in a bowl of braised blueberries. With the warm berries, the scoop of ice cream, and the crushed cookies, it's sort of like a deconstructed blueberry crisp.

For the blueberries: Combine the blueberries, sugar, lemon juice, and lemon zest in a medium nonreactive saucepan. Let marinate at room temperature for 2 hours.

Add ¾ cup (175 ml) of the St. Germain, and cook over medium-high heat to 213°F (101°C) on a candy thermometer, 5 to 10 minutes. Use a slotted spoon to transfer the blueberries to a bowl, and then cook the liquid remaining in the pan to 217°F (103°C), 5 to 8 minutes. Remove from the heat, return the blueberries to the liquid, and stir in the remaining ¼ cup (60 ml) of St. Germain. Use immediately or cover and refrigerate for up to 2 days. Reheat gently just before serving.

For the almond sbrisoluna: Preheat the oven to 350°F (175°C), and line a 13 x 9-inch (33 x 23-cm) pan with foil, leaving enough extra foil to use as handles. Spread the almonds on the foil in a single layer and bake until lightly toasted, 5 to 7 minutes, shaking the pan once or twice. Let cool slightly and then chop coarsely and set aside.

Cream the butter, sugar, and vanilla in a stand mixer on medium-high speed. Mix in the egg yolks on low speed, adding one at a time. Mix in the cornmeal and flour on low speed and then mix in the chopped almonds. The dough will be crumbly. Gently press the crumbly dough into the prepared pan so it is about 1 inch (2.5 cm) thick, and then bake until set and lightly browned, 12 to 15 minutes. Let cool in the pan on a rack and then remove the entire sbrisoluna, using the foil sling.

To serve: Spoon the warm blueberries into bowls, top with a scoop of gelato, and crumble on some sbrisoluna. You will likely have some leftover sbrisoluna; it will keep covered for several days. Enjoy it with a cup of coffee.

MAKES 6 TO 8 SERVINGS

Blueberries:

3 pounds (1.3 kg) blueberries

2 cups plus 2 tablespoons (425 g) granulated sugar

6 tablespoons (90 ml) freshly squeezed lemon juice

Grated zest of 3 lemons

1 cup (235 ml) St. Germain liqueur, divided

Almond Sbrisoluna:

1½ cups (215 g) skinless (blanched) almonds

8 ounces (2 sticks/227 g) unsalted butter, at room temperature, plus some for buttering the pan

1 cup (200 g) granulated sugar

½ vanilla bean, split and scraped

2 large egg yolks

1 cup (160 g) coarse cornmeal

2 cups (250 g) *tipo* 00 flour (see page 277) or all-purpose flour

To Serve:

4 cups (1 L) Buttermilk Gelato (page 287)

GRAPPA TORTA

MAKES 10 TO 12 SERVINGS

Unsalted butter, for greasing the pan

6 large eggs

½ packed cup (110 g) light brown sugar

14 ounces (about 3 cups) bittersweet chocolate, preferably 58% cacao

⅓ cup (90 ml) grappa

1 cup (235 ml) heavy cream

One fall, I wanted to make a super-moist chocolate cake with a light texture but rich flavor. Tall order, I know, but I found an old Italian recipe for a mousse-like chocolate cake made with rum. I swapped in grappa for the rum and started experimenting with both dry and fruity grappas. Dry (*secco*) grappas are made with bold grapes, such as pinto nero, while the fruity (*morbida*) grappas are made with lighter grapes, such as moscato and sauvignon blanc. The fruity grappas taste better with chocolate. After a few tries, I ended up with a silky, soft chocolate cake with a light perfume of grappa. It happens to be gluten-free and goes great with cappuccino gelato and a spoonful of softly whipped cream.

Preheat the oven to 350°F (175°C). Butter a 9-inch (23-cm) round springform pan, cut a piece of parchment to fit the bottom of the pan, and then butter the parchment. Wrap the bottom outside perimeter of the pan tightly in a double layer of foil to help prevent leaks.

In the bowl of a mixer, whip the eggs and brown sugar on high speed until the mixture balloons to triple its original volume, 4 to 5 minutes.

Melt the chocolate in a heatproof bowl in the oven or over a double boiler, and then add to the egg mixture on low speed. Fold in the grappa and cream. Pour the batter into the prepared pan and place the pan in a larger pan, such as a roasting pan. Pour in enough hot water to come at least halfway up the sides of the cake pan. Bake for 30 minutes. Cover the pan with foil and bake until the torta is puffed and a toothpick comes out with just a few moist crumbs clinging to it, another 30 minutes.

BASICS AND ESSENTIAL RECIPES

After ten years of cooking in Bergamo and Philadelphia, I've seen some fascinating culinary cross-pollination between the two cities. Chefs travel in both directions to cook in other kitchens, and they end up bringing back with them a taste of each city. This sort of "staging" in restaurants is one of the most important things that chefs do all over the world. It's how we learn from one another and expand our skills. I suppose cookbooks are the home cook's equivalent. Instead of going from restaurant to restaurant, home cooks often move from book to book, cooking different dishes, hearing different perspectives, and improving their kitchen chops.

The recipes in this book should give you a clear picture of my perspective and what it would be like to cook with me at my restaurant. And this chapter includes some of the most essential recipes. These basic preparations are used throughout the rest of the book, but ultimately, they should transcend the book. You can employ these basics in all of your cooking. Veal Stock (page 279) forms the foundation of countless sauces, and you'll find yourself putting a spoonful of Chocolate Sauce (page 285) on dozens of ice creams and other desserts.

Throughout the book, I also use some basic ingredients, techniques, and equipment that bear further explanation. Here's a glossary of culinary fundamentals that clarifies what I'm talking about when a recipe calls for "smashed" garlic or asks you to "sweat" the vegetables. If you came into my kitchen and didn't know these terms, you would definitely understand them when you left.

INGREDIENTS

BLENDED OIL. By itself, extra-virgin olive oil can overpower a delicate vinaigrette or sauce. It also has too low a smoke point for panfrying. For these preparations, I like to cut extra-virgin olive oil with grapeseed oil, which has a milder flavor and higher smoke point. If a recipe calls for blended oil, simply mix together equal parts extra-virgin olive oil and grapeseed oil. Alternatively, you could use canola oil instead of grapeseed oil.

EGGS. Find the best that you can. Eggs from chickens that hunt and peck on pasture usually have a richer flavor and deeper color than eggs from birds that eat standardized feed in crowded indoor facilities. I almost always use large eggs, and sometimes I call for raw or lightly cooked eggs in the recipes in this book. Because of the slight risk of salmonella, be advised that raw eggs should not be served to the very young, the ill or elderly, or to pregnant women.

GARLIC. I'm not a big fan of chomping down on pieces of raw or cooked garlic in my food. But I do like the flavor, so I do what most Italians do: smash whole cloves of garlic, add them to oil or butter for sautéing, and then remove the garlic once it's released its flavor into the dish.

MIREPOIX. Similar to Spain's *sofrito*, mirepoix is a mixture of diced onions, carrots, and celery, often added to soups, stocks, and braised dishes for flavor. The vegetables are also called aromatics.

SACHET. A mixture of herbs and spices, such as parsley, rosemary, thyme, bay leaf, and black peppercorns, tied into a seasoning packet. Also known as bouquet garni, a sachet allows you to season soups, stocks, and braising liquids, and then throw away the seasoning packet to leave behind only the flavors and aromas. Bundle the seasonings together in the center of a double layer of cheesecloth, then tie it tightly with kitchen string. If you don't have cheesecloth, you can tie the seasonings in a clean coffee filter.

SALT. I use Diamond Crystal kosher salt for most cooking and fine sea salt for baking. If you use a different brand, weights and volumes will vary. For reference, Diamond Crystal kosher salt weighs about ⅛ ounce (3 g) per teaspoon; fine sea salt weighs about ¼ ounce (6 g) per teaspoon. For sausages and other cured meats, I add curing salt. There are two types: curing salt #1 and #2. Curing salt #1 (a.k.a. pink salt, Tinted Curing Mix [TCM], Insta Cure #1, and DQ Curing Salt #1), is tinted pink so it's easy to recognize. It contains 6.25 percent sodium nitrite and 93.75 percent salt. Curing salt #2 (a.k.a. Insta Cure #2 and DQ Curing Salt #2) is white, like regular salt. It also contains 6.25 percent sodium nitrite, but it has 4 percent sodium nitrate and 89.75 percent salt. These curing salts are used to help prevent bacterial growth in cured meats. For reference, they weigh about ¼ ounce (6 g) per teaspoon.

SAN MARZANO TOMATOES. These canned plum tomatoes have a deeper flavor than other varieties. Look for San Marzano tomatoes imported from Italy because there are cheap knockoffs on the market using the same name. I usually core and crush the tomatoes by hand. For each tomato, pull it out of the can, hold it in one hand, and use the fingertips of your other hand to pinch the stem end and pull out the core. Discard the core and crush the remaining tomato right into

the dish you are making. Sometimes I drink the canning liquid (tomato puree) or save it for other preparations.

TIPO 00 FLOUR. In Italy, they number different types of flour according to how finely they are milled. *Tipo* (type) 1 is coarse, 0 is fine, and 00 is very fine. The texture of *tipo* 00 flour resembles that of all-purpose flour, which makes a good substitute. The flour weighs about 4.4 ounces (125 g) per cup.

VINAIGRETTE. If you don't know how to make one yet, here's the basic method for making 1 cup (235 ml) of vinaigrette. It's a three-to-one ratio of oil to vinegar. You start with the vinegar. Pour ¼ cup (60 ml) of vinegar into a bowl or blender, start whisking or blending the vinegar, and then slowly drizzle in ¾ cup (175 ml) blended oil (see page 276). You have to add the oil gradually so you don't overwhelm the vinegar with oil all at once, which could keep the mixture from emulsifying or blending evenly. Whisk or blend in the oil in a slow, steady stream until the mixture looks opaque and a little thicker (emulsified), and then season it to taste with salt and freshly ground black pepper. For red wine vinaigrette, use red wine vinegar. For Banyuls vinaigrette, use Banyuls vinegar. For citrus vinaigrette, squeeze the juice of one orange and ½ lemon into a bowl to equal ¼ cup (60 ml), and then whisk or blend in the oil. Experiment with other vinegars and citrus juices to make different kinds of vinaigrette. You can also add finely chopped herbs, shallots, or other aromatics.

TECHNIQUES

ROASTING PEPPERS. I roast peppers right over a hot wood fire. You could also do it on a gas grill, under a broiler, or right on the gas flame on your stovetop. To make about 4 cups (590 g) of roasted peppers, rinse four large bell peppers and pat them dry. Put them over or under a flame or other high heat source until completely blackened on all sides, 4 to 5 minutes per side, turning the peppers several times. Transfer the blackened peppers to a bowl, cover, and let steam for 10 minutes. Peel off and discard the skins, and then pull out and discard the cores and seeds.

SWEATING. Think of this as a kinder, gentler form of sautéing. The goal is to soften the vegetables in a pan without browning them. When sweating vegetables, you want no color because browning introduces new flavors. Those flavors are great for sautéing, but not for sweating, which is usually done over slightly lower heat.

EQUIPMENT

SCALE. Most professional chefs measure ingredients by weight, not volume. Weights are more accurate because volumes change, especially for ingredients that are easily compacted, such as flour. But most home cooks measure by volume, so that's how the recipes in this book are written. You still might need to weigh an ingredient in the odd recipe here or there, and I highly recommend it for accuracy. Just buy a cheap digital scale that can weigh in grams, and keep it on your kitchen counter.

TONGS. I use tongs for everything from tossing pasta in a pan to pulling steaks from the grill. Find a good pair of spring-loaded ones. Edlund's are particularly sturdy and cheap.

Veal Stock

•

Fish Stock

•

Shellfish Stock

•

3-2-1 Brine

•

Polenta

•

Béchamel Sauce

•

Egg Pasta Dough

•

Semolina Pasta Dough

•

Nut Pesto

•

Crème Anglaise

•

Pastry Cream

•

Chocolate Sauce

•

Gelato and Sorbet

•

Candied Citrus Peel

VEAL STOCK

At Osteria, we make very traditional meat stocks by roasting the bones to develop flavor and then heating the bones slowly in water with mirepoix and herbs. We don't add any wine, tomatoes, or other flavorings until we use the stock to make sauces or soups. This method gives you a clear stock that highlights the pure flavor of the bones. For chicken stock, use chicken bones. Or use any other animal bones you like to make pork stock, lamb stock, rabbit stock, and other meat stocks.

MAKES ABOUT 1 QUART (1 L)

5 pounds (2.25 kg) veal bones

2 tablespoons (30 ml) olive oil

1 medium-size yellow onion, chopped (1½ cups/240 g)

2 large carrots, chopped (1½ cups/185 g)

3 medium-size ribs celery, chopped (1½ cups/152 g)

1 sachet of 2 sprigs rosemary, 5 parsley stems, 10 peppercorns, 1 garlic clove, and 1 fresh bay leaf (see page 277)

Preheat the oven to 400°F (205°C). Lay the bones in a single layer in a roasting pan and roast until dark browned, 1½ to 2 hours. Transfer the browned bones to a stockpot and place the roasting pan over medium heat. Add about a cup (235 ml) of cold water to deglaze the pan, scraping all the browned bits from the pan bottom. Scrape into the stockpot and add 3 more cups (750 ml) of cold water.

Bring the liquid to just under a simmer but do not boil. If it boils, your stock will be cloudy. A few bubbles should occasionally and lazily come to the surface. Cook for 1 hour, frequently skimming scum from the surface.

Meanwhile, heat the oil in a large sauté pan over medium heat. Add the onion, carrots, and celery and sauté until deeply browned, 8 to 10 minutes. After the stock has cooked for 1 hour, add the sautéed vegetables. Cook gently for another 6 hours, frequently skimming the surface. Add the sachet, and cook for another 2 hours, skimming the surface. The total cooking time should be about 8 hours.

Remove and discard the bones and big vegetable pieces with tongs. Line a medium-mesh sieve with cheesecloth and strain the stock through the cheesecloth into a quart-size (liter-size) container. Label, date, and refrigerate for up to 1 week or freeze for up to 1 month.

FISH STOCK

Use any white fish bones here, such as those from cod, halibut, or branzino. Be sure to remove the gills from the heads.

MAKES ABOUT 2 QUARTS (2 L)

2 tablespoons (30 ml) olive oil

1 medium-size yellow onion, chopped (1¼ cups/200 g)

4 medium-size ribs celery, chopped (1¼ cups/125 g)

5 pounds (2.25 kg) white fish bones

2 lemons

1 sachet of 1 bay leaf, 10 parsley stems, 10 peppercorns, and 1 garlic clove (see page 277)

Heat the oil in a stockpot over medium heat. Add the onion and celery and sweat until soft but not browned, 4 to 5 minutes. Add the fish bones and sauté for 2 to 3 minutes. Cut the lemons in half and squeeze in the juice. Add the rinds, too. Pour in 2 quarts (2 L) of cold water, drop in the sachet, and bring the liquid to just under a simmer but do not boil. A few bubbles should occasionally and lazily come to the surface. Cook for 45 minutes, skimming any scum that comes to the surface.

Remove and discard the bones and big vegetable pieces with tongs. Line a medium-mesh sieve with cheesecloth. Let the stock cool until warm and then strain it through the cheesecloth into quart-size (liter-size) containers. Label, date, and refrigerate for up to 1 week or freeze for up to 1 month.

SHELLFISH STOCK

This recipe is part stock, part sauce. You gently heat bits of shellfish, such as lobster heads and shrimp shells; puree the shells right along with everything else; and then strain the whole mixture. This method extracts so much flavor—and some protein—from the shellfish that you can simply mix the stock with pasta and seafood, as in Spaghetti al Nero di Seppia with Shrimp (page 104).

MAKES ABOUT 3 QUARTS (3 L)

¼ cup (60 ml) grapeseed oil

2 pounds (1 kg) mixed lobster heads, shrimp shells, and other shellfish bits

1½ cups (375 ml) white wine

1 large yellow onion, chopped (2 cups/320 g)

1 large carrot, chopped (¾ cup/92 g)

2 medium-size ribs celery, chopped (¾ cup/75 g)

3 cups (720 g) canned peeled tomatoes, preferably San Marzano, cored and crushed by hand

1 sachet of 1 sprig rosemary, 2 sprigs thyme, 1 bay leaf, and 10 black peppercorns (see page 277)

Heat the oil in a Dutch oven or large, deep sauté pan over medium-high heat. Add the shells and sauté until pink, 4 to 5 minutes. Add the wine and simmer until most of the liquid evaporates, 8 to 10 minutes. Add the onion, carrot and celery and sweat the vegetables until soft but not brown, 4 to 6 minutes. Add the tomatoes and sachet, and cook until the tomatoes start to break down a little, 4 to 5 minutes. Add water to cover and adjust the heat so that the liquid simmers gently. Simmer for 45 minutes, then remove from the heat and discard the sachet.

Blend the mixture, shells and all, in batches in a blender. Strain each blended batch through a fine-mesh strainer, pressing on the solids to extract the liquids. Let cool. When cool, pack in quart-size (liter-size) containers and refrigerate for up to 1 week or freeze for up to 3 months.

3-2-1 BRINE

Three gallons (12 liters) of water, two pounds (1 k) of salt, and one pound (50 g) of sugar. This brine recipe is easy to remember, and it's the only one you'll ever need. Use it to brine chicken, fish, pork, or almost anything that needs a little extra moisture. I included volume measurements for salt and sugar so you don't have to weigh those out, but weights are more accurate, so if you have a kitchen scale, use it. This recipe makes enough to brine about twenty pounds (9 kg) of meat. Halve or quarter the recipe as needed. You'll need a half-recipe to brine ten pounds (4.5 kg) of meat, or a quarter-recipe to brine five pounds (2.25 kg) of meat. As a rule of thumb, I usually brine meat for about one day per pound (450 g) of bone-in meat—or a little longer if the meat is very thick, like a whole ham.

MAKES ABOUT 3 GALLONS (12 L)

2 pounds/1 kg (about 3 cups) kosher salt

1 pound/450 g (2½ cups) granulated sugar

3 garlic cloves, smashed

10 rosemary sprigs

1 bay leaf, crumbled

15 black peppercorns

Dissolve the kosher salt and sugar in 3 gallons (12 L) of water. Pour 2 cups (475 ml) of the brine into a food processor and add the garlic, rosemary, bay leaf, and black peppercorns. Puree until all the ingredients are finely chopped, and then pour the mixture back into the brine. Submerge the meat in the brine and refrigerate.

POLENTA

Every day I put a big copper pot of polenta over my wood fire at Osteria in Philadelphia, just as Claudia's mother and grandmother did over their home fire in Italy decades ago. It's the best way to make it. Coarsely milled whole-kernel corn makes the best polenta. You can also mix in other grains. *Polenta taragna* includes some buckwheat flour.

MAKES ABOUT 5½ CUPS (1.375 L)

Salt
¾ cup (120 g) coarse yellow cornmeal (polenta)

Bring 6 cups (1.5 L) of water to boil in a large pot and add salt to taste (it should taste like a mild broth; I use about 1½ teaspoons [9 g] salt per quart of water). Gradually whisk in the polenta in a slow, steady stream. Lower the heat just enough to keep the polenta bubbling and then cook, without stirring, until the polenta becomes a very thick porridge, like cooked oatmeal, and burns a little on the bottom and sides of the pan, which adds a nice smoky aroma. The total cooking time will be 45 minutes to 1 hour for medium-coarse polenta or 1½ to 2 hours for very coarse polenta. Avoid stirring to make sure the bottom burns a little.

VARIATIONS

FOR PORCINI POLENTA: Grind ¼ packed cup (a generous ¼ ounce/about 10 g) of dried porcini mushrooms to a powder in a spice grinder or clean coffee mill. You should have about 2 tablespoons (10 g) of powder. When the polenta is thick yet pourable, stir in the porcini powder. Taste and season with additional salt as necessary.

FOR BUCKWHEAT POLENTA: Whisk 1 cup (160 g) of polenta and ½ cup (62 g) of buckwheat flour into 5 cups (1.25 L) of boiling water. Cook over medium heat until the polenta is the texture of stiff pudding but still pourable, 45 minutes to 1 hour. Season to taste with salt and pepper.

BÉCHAMEL SAUCE

Also called *besciamella*, this sauce finds its way into quite a few Italian dishes, such as lasagna, cannelloni, flan, and sformato. I even use flavored béchamel as pizza sauce. It's basically a blank canvas of creaminess that you can flavor however you like.

MAKES ABOUT 2 QUARTS (2 L)

6 tablespoons (85 g) unsalted butter
1 small yellow onion, minced (½ cup/80 g)
⅔ cup (83 g) *tipo* 00 flour (see page 277) or all-purpose flour
2 quarts (2 L) whole milk
⅛ teaspoon (0.3 g) grated nutmeg
Salt and freshly ground black pepper

Melt the butter in a medium saucepan over medium heat. Add the onion and sweat until soft but not browned, 5 to 6 minutes. Whisk in the flour to make a roux (it will look like lumpy batter). Whisk and cook until the flour smells a little nutty but doesn't turn brown, 2 to 3 minutes. Slowly whisk in the milk until it is fully incorporated and the mixture is free of lumps. Season with the nutmeg, plus salt and pepper to taste, and then simmer gently over medium to medium-low heat until thickened, 35 to 45 minutes, stirring occasionally to prevent sticking on the bottom. For a super-smooth sauce, strain through a medium-mesh strainer and cool. The cooled béchamel can be covered with plastic pressed onto the surface (to prevent a skin from forming), and refrigerated for up to 2 days. Reheat gently in a saucepan before using.

VARIATIONS

FOR PORCINI BÉCHAMEL: Omit the nutmeg. Soak 2 ounces (57 g/about 2 cups) of dried porcini in 3 cups (750 ml) of hot water until the porcini are tender, about 15 minutes. Replace 2 cups (475 ml) of the milk with 2 cups (475 ml) of porcini-soaking liquid. Chop the soaked porcini and stir into the sauce, along with the salt and pepper. Skip the straining step to retain the chopped porcini in the sauce.

FOR TRUFFLE BÉCHAMEL: Add 1 tablespoon (15 ml) white truffle paste, along with the nutmeg.

EGG PASTA DOUGH

In both Italy and America, I've come across dozens and dozens of pasta dough recipes. I found the best one while working at Frosio in Alme, Italy. The egg yolks and durum flour give the dough enough stability for it to be stretched super-thin, which is what makes ravioli so tender. This recipe makes enough for four fully rolled sheets of pasta, each 4 to 5 feet (1.25 to 1.5 m) long. That's enough to make about ninety-five 2-inch (5-cm) square or 150 1-inch (2.5-cm) square ravioli.

MAKES ABOUT 1 POUND (450 G)

1¼ cups (155g) *tipo* 00 flour (see page 277) or all-purpose flour, plus more for dusting

½ cup plus 1 tablespoon (70 g) durum flour

9 large egg yolks

1 tablespoon (15 ml) extra-virgin olive oil

Combine both flours in the bowl of a stand mixer with the paddle attachment on medium speed. Add the egg yolks, oil, and 3 tablespoons (45 ml) of water, mixing just until the dough comes together, 2 to 3 minutes. Add up to 1 tablespoon (15 ml) more water, if necessary, for the dough to come together.

Turn the dough out onto a lightly floured work surface and knead until silky and smooth, about 5 minutes, kneading in a little flour, if necessary, to prevent sticking. The dough is ready when it gently pulls back into place when stretched with your hands. Shape the dough into a disk, wrap in plastic wrap, and refrigerate for at least 30 minutes or up to 3 days.

Cut the dough into four equal pieces and let them sit at room temperature for 5 to 10 minutes before rolling out. Shape each piece into an oblong disk that's wide enough to fit the width of your pasta roller. Lightly flour a long work surface and set the pasta roller to its widest setting. Lightly flour one disk of dough, pass it through the roller, and then lightly dust the rolled dough with flour, brushing off the excess with your hands.

Set the roller to the next narrowest setting and again pass the dough through, dusting again with flour and brushing off the excess. Pass the dough once or twice through each progressively narrower setting. For thicker pasta, such as corzetti, you generally want to roll to about ⅛ inch (3 mm) thick or setting #2 or 3 on the KitchenAid attachment. For strand pasta, such as fettuccine, or for cannelloni, you want to roll to about 1/16 inch

(1.5 mm) thick (setting #4 or 5 on the KitchenAid attachment). For ravioli, you want to roll the pasta a little thinner, to about 1/32 inch (0.8 mm) thick (setting #6 or 7); ravioli sheets should be thin enough that you can read a newspaper through the dough.

As you roll and each sheet gets longer, drape the sheet over the backs of your hands to easily feed it through the roller. You should end up with a sheet 4 to 5 feet (1.25 to 1.5 m) long. Lay the pasta sheet on a lightly floured work surface and use a cutting wheel, knife, or the cutter attachment on the pasta machine to create the right pasta shape for the dish you are making.

VARIATIONS

FOR BUCKWHEAT PASTA DOUGH: Replace half of the *tipo* 00 or all-purpose flour with buckwheat flour.

FOR CHESTNUT PASTA DOUGH: Use ¾ cup (94 g) of *tipo* 00 flour (see page 277) or all-purpose flour, ⅓ cup (42 g) of durum flour, and ½ cup (62 g) of chestnut flour.

FOR TAGLIOLINI: Roll the pasta to #5 on the KitchenAid attachment, and then roll it again on #5. The dough should be about as thick as fettuccine. Lay the pasta sheets on a floured surface, lightly dust with flour, and then cut the sheets into 10-inch (25-cm) lengths. Fold each length in half lengthwise over itself, then fold in half lengthwise again. Julienne each folded piece crosswise into thin strips about ⅛ inch (3 mm) wide, and then dust with flour and place on a parchment-lined baking sheet. Use immediately or freeze for up to 1 day.

SEMOLINA PASTA DOUGH

You can easily make dried pasta that blows away the cheap, boxed stuff. The dough is just semolina and water. The trick is to get the dough to the consistency of damp sand. Depending on the humidity in the room, you may need to add more or less water to get to that consistency. You also need a pasta extruder or attachment for your pasta machine. Once extruded into spaghetti, macaroni, or whatever shape you like, just dry the pasta uncovered in your refrigerator, which has the perfect temperature and humidity. After about two days in the fridge, the texture of your dried pasta will be just right.

MAKES ABOUT 1 POUND (450 G)

2¾ cups (460 g) semolina

Put the semolina in a bowl and slowly stir in enough water (about 1 cup/235 ml) for the mixture to resemble damp sand. Knead it a little with your fingers until it clumps together, feels like sandy bubble gum, and sticks together when you pinch it. Too dry is better than too wet, and even though it may appear as if the dough hasn't come together, it will compress when it is extruded through the pasta machine.

Fit your pasta extruder or stand mixer attachment with the plate needed for your desired pasta shape. Set the extruder to medium speed and feed the dough into the extruder in marble-size clumps, using a pushing tool to push the clumps through the extruder. The first few clumps will come out uneven; just throw them away. Continue gradually dropping marble-size clumps into the extruder and pushing them through, being careful not to overload it. As the pasta is extruded, cut it into lengths appropriate for the recipe you are making (examples follow).

Dry the pasta by placing it on wire racks that will fit in your refrigerator (or coil long pasta, such as spaghetti and bucatini, into nests) and refrigerate it uncovered for at least 8 hours or up to 5 days. The pasta will get drier and harder as it sits. For most recipes, the texture is perfect after 2 days in the refrigerator. Two-day-old pasta will cook in about 4 minutes in salted boiling water.

VARIATIONS

FOR SQUID INK PASTA: Mix 2 tablespoons (30 ml) of squid ink into the water before adding to the semolina.

FOR SPAGHETTI: Fit the extruder with the spaghetti plate, set the extruder to high speed, and feed in the dough, cutting the spaghetti to 9-inch (23-cm) lengths.

FOR CANDELE: Fit the extruder with the large macaroni plate, set the extruder to high speed, and feed in the dough, cutting the candele to 6-inch (15-cm) lengths. Dry straight instead of forming into nests.

NUT PESTO

Everyone knows basil pesto made with herbs, pine nuts, and cheese. I like to skip the cheese and put the focus on nuts. Walnuts, almonds, pistachios, pine nuts. . . they all work well here. I keep the recipe ultra-basic as a starting point. If you like, toast the nuts or add some herbs for more flavor. Check out the variation that includes milk and butter as well.

MAKES ABOUT 1½ CUPS (375 ML)

1 cup (135 g) shelled nuts
1 cup (235 ml) blended oil (page 276)

Put the nuts in a blender or small food processor and process until chopped but not too fine; you don't want to make nut butter. With the machine running, gradually add the oil in a slow, steady stream and process until blended and emulsified. Season with salt and pepper and use immediately or cover and store at room temperature for up to 8 hours, refrigerate for up to 2 days, or freeze for up to 2 weeks.

VARIATION

FOR WALNUT PESTO: Toast 6 tablespoons (45 g) of walnuts in a dry pan over medium heat until fragrant, 5 to 6 minutes, shaking the pan now and then. Put the toasted walnuts, 4 teaspoons (19 g) of room-temperature butter, and 1 cup (235 ml) of whole milk in a blender or small food processor. Process on slow speed and gradually increase the speed, adding more milk a little at a time, until the mixture looks smooth (up to ½ cup/120 ml additional milk). Blend until very smooth, about 2 minutes. When smooth, gradually add 2 tablespoons (30 ml) of olive oil in a slow, steady stream. Season with salt and pepper and use immediately or cover and refrigerate for up to 4 days before using. Makes about 2 cups (475 ml).

CRÈME ANGLAISE

You don't need to be a pastry chef to make this dessert sauce. You just need a little patience so you don't scramble the eggs. Once cooled, serve the sauce with almost any dessert. I like to spoon a pool of crème anglaise beneath a slice of pie, cake, or *torta*.

MAKES ABOUT 2½ CUPS (625 ML)

6 large egg yolks
½ cup (100 g) granulated sugar
1 cup (235 ml) whole milk
1 cup (235 ml) heavy cream
1 vanilla bean, split and scraped

Put the egg yolks and sugar in a heatproof bowl that fits tightly over a saucepan or in the top of a double boiler. Whisk until light and pale yellow, 1 to 2 minutes. Heat the milk, cream, and vanilla in a heavy saucepan over medium heat until it begins to simmer, 3 to 4 minutes, and then remove from the heat. Whisk about 1 cup (235 ml) of the hot cream mixture into the yolk mixture until incorporated, then combine the rest. Set the bowl or double boiler top over gently simmering water. Cook and stir constantly but gently until the sauce thickens slightly and registers a temperature of 165°F (74°C), 5 to 8 minutes. Remove from the heat and stir until the sauce thickens to the consistency of heavy cream, about 2 minutes. Strain through a fine-mesh sieve into a bowl and let stand for 10 minutes, stirring occasionally. Let cool completely, and then cover and refrigerate until cold, at least 1 hour or up to 3 days.

PASTRY CREAM

Pastry cream is creamier than crème Anglaise because it's thickened with starch. It's what you see inside a typical chocolate éclair or cream-filled doughnut. The key here is cooking the cream long enough to cook out the starchy taste.

MAKES ABOUT 2 CUPS (475 ML)

¾ cup (150 g) granulated sugar

¼ cup (32 g) cornstarch

9 large egg yolks

1⅔ cups (400 ml) whole milk

6 tablespoons (90 ml) heavy cream

½ vanilla bean, split and scraped

Combine the sugar, cornstarch, and egg yolks in the bowl of a stand mixer fitted with the whisk attachment. Whisk on medium speed until smooth, about 2 minutes.

Bring the milk, cream, and vanilla to a boil in a medium saucepan over medium heat. Remove from the heat and mix about ½ cup (120 ml) of the hot milk mixture into the egg mixture. Scrape all of the egg mixture into the pot of hot milk, and cook over medium-high heat until bubbling, thick, and creamy, stirring constantly, 2 to 3 minutes. Transfer the mixture to the mixer bowl and whip on low speed until cool, 3 to 4 minutes.

CHOCOLATE SAUCE

This is the most badass chocolate sauce ever. It's simple, keeps for a week or two in the fridge, and goes with almost any dessert. You can even make a milk shake with it. For extra-bitter chocolate sauce, use a higher percentage cacao chocolate, such as 65% Manjari from Valrhona.

MAKES ABOUT 5 CUPS (1.25 L)

1½ cups (300 g) granulated sugar

⅓ cup (90 ml) glucose syrup or light corn syrup

1⅓ cups (115 g) unsweetened Dutch-process cocoa powder

1 pound (450 g) bittersweet chocolate (about 58% cacao), melted

Bring the sugar, glucose syrup, and 2 cups (475 ml) of water to a simmer in a medium saucepan over medium-high heat. Put the cocoa powder in a large heatproof bowl and whisk in about ½ cup (120 ml) of the hot sugar syrup to make a smooth paste. Whisk in the remaining sugar syrup until smooth. For a supersilky texture, strain through a fine-mesh sieve. The sauce can be covered and refrigerated for up to 2 weeks before using. Reheat gently over low heat.

GELATO AND SORBET

The recipes that follow are the real-deal gelato and sorbetto. Don't worry about the oddball ingredients here and there; they can all be ordered over the Internet (see Sources on page 289). There are two gelato bases, and different bases are used to make different flavors of gelato. The flavors themselves are given as variations under the base recipes. Note that some of the gelato flavors make about 6 cups (1.5 L). If that's too much volume for your ice-cream machine, make a smaller batch, or churn half of the base at a time. And make sure you check the machine as the gelato churns; overchurning can make the gelato grainy. Stop churning when the gelato is nice and creamy.

YELLOW GELATO BASE

MAKES ABOUT 4 CUPS (1 L)

2 cups (475 ml) whole milk

2 cups (475 ml) heavy cream

15 large egg yolks

1 cup plus 2 tablespoons (225 g) granulated sugar

Bring the milk and cream to a simmer in a saucepan over medium heat, and then remove from the heat. Meanwhile, whip the egg yolks and sugar in the bowl of a stand mixer fitted with the whip attachment on medium-high speed until light, fluffy, and pale yellow, about 3 minutes. Reduce the speed to medium-low and mix about 1 cup (235 ml) of the hot cream mixture into the yolk mixture. Stir the yolk mixture back into the remaining cream mixture in the pan. Return the pan to low heat and cook, stirring frequently, until it registers 160°F (71°C), 5 to 8 minutes. Fill a bowl with ice water, and then strain the mixture through a fine-mesh sieve into a heatproof bowl. Rest the bowl in the ice water to cool it down. It will keep covered in the refrigerator for 1 week.

VARIATIONS

FOR PISTACHIO GELATO: Use an immersion blender, stand blender, or food processor to blend together 2¾ cups (675 ml) of white gelato base (page 287), ⅔ cup (150 ml) of yellow gelato base, ⅓ cup (90 ml) of PreGel pistachio paste (see the Sources on page 290), and 2½ tablespoons (37 ml) sugar syrup (page 288). Blend until smooth, and for a super-silky gelato, strain through a medium-mesh sieve. Transfer to an ice-cream machine and freeze according to the manufacturer's directions. Makes about 6 cups (1.5 L).

FOR CHINOTTO GELATO: Pour 3 quarts (3 L) of chinotto into a large saucepan and boil over medium-high heat until reduced to a thick, molasses-like syrup, 45 to 50 minutes. You should have about 1½ cups (375 ml) of chinotto reduction. Use an immersion blender, stand blender, or food processor to blend together the chinotto reduction, 3 cups (750 ml) of white base (page 287), and ¾ cup (175 ml) of yellow base. Blend until smooth, 1 to 2 minutes, and then freeze in an ice-cream machine according to the manufacturer's directions. Makes about 6 cups (1.5 L).

FOR CANTUCCI GELATO: Use an immersion blender, stand blender, or food processor to blend together 3 cups (750 ml) of white base (page 287) and 1 cup (235 ml) of yellow base. Blend until smooth, and then freeze in an ice-cream machine according to the manufacturer's directions. When the mixture is halfway frozen, fold in 2½ cups (300 g) coarsely crushed Cantucci (page 229) and continue freezing according to the manufacturer's directions. Makes about 6 cups (1.5 L).

WHITE GELATO BASE

MAKES ABOUT 5 CUPS (1.25 L)

4 cups (1 L) whole milk

1 cup (235 ml) heavy cream

¾ cup (150 g) granulated sugar

⅔ cup (85 g) PreGel dry milk powder (see Sources, page 290)

¼ cup (28 ml) dextrose or 3 tablespoons (22 g) superfine sugar

Pinch of salt

2 tablespoons plus 2 teaspoons (52 g) glucose syrup or light corn syrup

Whisk together the milk, cream, sugar, milk powder, dextrose, salt, and glucose syrup in a large saucepan over medium-low heat. Whisk frequently until the mixture registers 140°F (60°C) on a candy thermometer. Lower the heat to its lowest setting so that the mixture maintains a temperature of 140°F (60°C) for 30 minutes (periodically check the temperature, especially during the last 10 minutes of cooking, and adjust the heat as necessary to maintain that temperature). Fill a bowl with ice water and increase the heat under the saucepan to medium. When the temperature of the white base reaches 180°F (82°C), remove the saucepan from the heat, plunge the bottom of the pan into the ice water, and stir until the white base cools. It will keep covered in the refrigerator for 1 week.

VARIATIONS

FOR FIORDILATTE GELATO: Make the white base as directed and freeze in an ice-cream machine according to the manufacturer's directions. Makes about 5 cups (1.25 L).

FOR MASCARPONE GELATO: Use an immersion blender, stand blender, or food processor to blend together 2½ cups (625 ml) of white gelato base, 2 cups (460 g/about 1 pound) of mascarpone, and ½ cup (120 ml) of sugar syrup (page 288). Blend until smooth, and for a super-silky gelato, strain through a medium-mesh sieve. Transfer to an ice-cream machine and freeze according to the manufacturer's directions. Makes about 5 cups (1.25 L).

FOR POPPY SEED GELATO: Bring 9 tablespoons (140 ml) of water, 1 tablespoon (9 g) of poppy seeds, and ⅓ cup (67 g) of granulated sugar to a boil in a small saucepan. Whisk in ½ teaspoon (1 g) of agar powder (a natural thickener carried in health food stores or the Asian section of large supermarkets). Return the liquid to a boil and boil for 30 seconds. Remove from the heat and let cool to room temperature. Whisk in 4 cups (1 L) of white gelato base until blended, and then freeze in an ice-cream machine according to the manufacturer's directions. Makes about 6 cups (1.5 L).

FOR POLENTA GELATO: Bring 4 cups (1 L) of whole milk and ½ teaspoon (3 g) of salt to a simmer in a large saucepan over high heat. Slowly whisk in ½ cup (80 g) of coarse yellow cornmeal (polenta), and then lower the heat to medium-low and cook until the polenta is soft and the milk has been absorbed, 25 to 30 minutes, whisking frequently to prevent the polenta from burning on the bottom. Measure out 2¼ cups (560 ml) of the cooked polenta and refrigerate any extra for another use. Use an immersion blender, stand blender, or food processor to blend together the 2¼ cups (560 ml) of cooked polenta, 2½ cups (625 ml) of white base, and ½ cup (120 ml) of sugar syrup (page 288). Blend until very smooth, 3 to 4 minutes, and then freeze in an ice-cream machine according to the manufacturer's directions. Makes 4 to 5 cups (1 to 1.25 L).

FOR BUTTERMILK GELATO: Use an immersion blender, stand blender, or food processor to blend 2¼ cups (560 ml) of buttermilk, 1⅔ cups (400 ml) of white gelato base, and ¾ cup (175 ml) of sugar syrup (page 288). Blend until smooth, and for a super-silky gelato, strain the mixture through a medium-mesh sieve. Freeze in an ice-cream machine according to the manufacturer's directions. Makes about 4 cups (1 L).

SUGAR SYRUP

MAKES ABOUT 4 CUPS (1 L)

3 cups (600 g) granulated sugar

½ cup (120 ml) glucose syrup or light corn syrup

2 tablespoons (14.25 g) powdered dextrose, or 1½ tablespoons (11.75 g) superfine sugar

Fill a bowl with ice water. Heat the sugar, glucose syrup, dextrose, and 1½ cups (375 ml) of water in a medium saucepan over low heat until the sugars dissolve, 3 to 5 minutes, stirring occasionally. Plunge the pan bottom into the ice water to cool down the syrup. It can be covered and refrigerated for about 2 weeks before using.

VARIATIONS

FOR GOAT CHEESE SORBET: Combine 10 ounces (284 g/about 1⅓ cups) of soft goat cheese, 1¼ cups (310 ml) of sugar syrup, 1 cup (235 ml) of water, and 2 tablespoons (30 ml) of glucose syrup or light corn syrup in a blender. Puree until very smooth, 2 to 3 minutes. Freeze in an ice-cream machine according to the manufacturer's directions. Makes about 4 cups (1 L).

FOR RASPBERRY SORBET: Combine 3¼ cups (14 ounces/400 g) of fresh raspberries, 2 cups (475 ml) of sugar syrup, and ¾ cup plus 2 tablespoons of water (205 ml) in a blender. Puree until very smooth, 2 to 3 minutes, and then strain through a fine-mesh strainer. Freeze in an ice-cream machine according to the manufacturer's directions. Makes about 4 cups (1 L).

FOR PEACH SORBET: Combine 2⅔ cups (14 ounces/400 g) of peeled, pitted and sliced peaches, 2 cups of sugar syrup (475 ml), and ¾ cup plus 2 tablespoons (205 ml) of water in a blender. Puree until very smooth, 2 to 3 minutes, and then strain through a fine-mesh strainer. Freeze in an ice-cream machine according to the manufacturer's directions. Makes about 4 cups (1 L).

CANDIED CITRUS PEEL

Drop a few of these sweet peels on ice cream, cake, or anywhere you want the perfume of citrus. Just be sure to remove all the bitter white pith and to julienne the peels super-fine. The recipe here is for candied orange peel or candied lemon peel, but you could use other citrus. You'll need enough for about one cup (235 ml) of citrus peels.

MAKES ABOUT 1 CUP (235 ML)

5 oranges, or 10 lemons

5 cups (1 kg) granulated sugar

2 cups plus 2 tablespoons (530 ml) water, plus some for
blanching

⅔ cup (150 ml) glucose syrup or light corn syrup

Use a vegetable peeler to remove the zest from the oranges or lemons in strips, leaving behind any white pith. Thinly julienne the peels and then place them in a medium saucepan with cold water to cover. Bring to a boil over high heat. As soon as the water comes to a rolling boil, drain the peels and cover again with cold water. Repeat the process to blanch the peels three times.

Combine the blanched peels, sugar, water, and glucose syrup in a medium saucepan over medium-high heat and cook until the liquid registers 225°F (110°C) on a candy thermometer, 15 to 20 minutes. Let cool and then store the peels in the syrup at room temperature for up to 1 month. Use the citrus-scented syrup for cocktails or to pour over ice cream.

SOURCES FOR THE COOK AND TRAVELER

Most of the ingredients and equipment I call for in my recipes are widely available. But here are some sources for oddball things, such as wild hare and *corzetti* stamps—along with a few of my favorite purveyors. I also listed contact information for most of the markets, shops, restaurants, wineries, bars, hotels, and inns mentioned throughout the book so you can visit these places yourself.

EQUIPMENT

Artisanal Pasta Tools
Sonoma, California
www.artisanalpastatools.com
707-939-6474
Corzetti stamps.

The Baking Pan
www.thebakingpan.com
Brioche molds, tart pans, and other baking supplies.

Barbecue Wood
P.O. Box 8163
Yakima, WA 98908
509-965-0123
www.barbecuewood.com
Oak, hickory, and other woods for grilling, roasting, and smoking.

Fante's
1006 South Ninth Street
Philadelphia PA 19147
215-922-5557
www.fantes.com
Pasta machines and other pasta-making supplies.

Franco Casoni
Via Bighetti 73
16043 Chiavari
Province of Genoa, Italy
+39 0185 301448
www.francocasoni.it
Corzetti stamps custom-made in Italy.

King Arthur Flour
135 US Route 5 South
Norwich, VT 05055
802-649-3361
www.kingarthurflour.com
Metric scales, baking pans, other baking supplies.

KitchenAid
Customer Satisfaction Center
P.O. Box 218
St. Joseph, MI 49085
800-541-6390
www.kitchenaid.com
Stand mixers, extruded pasta presses, pasta rollers, pasta cutters, meat grinders, sausage stuffers, and other attachments.

Previn
2044 Rittenhouse Square
Philadelphia, PA 19103
215-985-1996
www.previninc.com
Ring molds, terrine molds, and other baking supplies.

WEBstaurant Store
717-392-7472
www.webstaurantstore.com
Stand mixers, baking sheets, baking molds, and other kitchen equipment.

MEAT AND FISH

Country Time Farm
3017 Mountain Road
Hamburg, PA 19526
610-562-2090
www.countrytimefarm.com
Pork.

Creekstone Farms
604 Goff Industrial Park Road
Arkansas City, KS 67005
620-741-3100
www.creekstonefarms.com
Dry-aged rib-eye steak.

D'Artagnan
280 Wilson Avenue
Newark, NJ 07105
973-344-0565
www.dartagnan.com
Duck, rabbit, lamb, suckling pig, guinea hen, pheasant, wild hare, and other meats.

Di Bruno Brothers
930 South Ninth Street
Philadelphia, PA 19147
215-922-2876
www.dibrunobrothers.com
Pancetta, prosciutto, and other cured meats.

Jamison Farm
171 Jamison Lane
Latrobe, PA 15650
800-237-5262
www.jamisonfarm.com
Lamb.

Potironne
120 Thornwood Road
Georgetown, TX 78628
512-635-3742
www.potironne.com
Canned snails.

Samuels & Son Seafood Company
3407 South Lawrence Street
Philadelphia, PA 19148
800-580-5810
www.samuelsandsonseafood.com
Halibut, swordfish, squid, cuttlefish, and other seafood.

The Sausage Maker, Inc.
1500 Clinton Street, Building 123
Buffalo, NY 14206
888-490-8525
www.sausagemaker.com
Curing salt and sausage-making supplies.

La Tienda
3601 La Grange Parkway
Toano, VA 23168
800-710-4304
www.tienda.com
Baccalà (salt cod) and squid ink.

Wells Meats
982 North Delaware Avenue
Philadelphia, PA 19123
215-627-3903
www.wellsmeats.com
Duck, rabbit, oxtails, lamb, suckling pig, and other meats.

CHEESE AND DAIRY

Di Bruno Brothers
930 South Ninth Street
Philadelphia, PA 19147
Phone: 215-922-2876
www.dibrunobrothers.com
*Parmigiano-Reggiano, Gorgonzola dolce, mozzarella
di bufala, ricotta salata, and other Italian cheeses.*

Euro Gourmet
10312 Southard Drive
Beltsville, MD 20705
301-937-2888
www.eurogourmet.biz
Burrata, Bra, and other Italian cheeses.

VEGETABLES AND FRUIT

Alma Gourmet Ltd.
39-12 Crescent Street
Long Island City, NY 11101
718-433-1616
www.almagourmet.com
White truffles.

Blue Moon Acres
P.O. Box 201
Buckingham, PA 18912
215-794-3093
www.bluemoonacres.net
Lettuces, microgreens, and herbs.

Buon Italia
75 Ninth Avenue
New York, NY 10011
212-633-9090
www.buonitalia.com
White truffles and truffle paste.

D'Artagnan
280 Wilson Avenue
Newark, NJ 07105
973-344-0565
www.dartagnan.com
White truffles.

L'Épicerie
866-350-7575
www.lepicerie.com
Candied citrus peel.

George Richter Farm
4512 70th Avenue East
Fife, WA 98424
253-922-5649
Fresh berries.

Gourmet Foodstore
3212 NW 64th Street
Boca Raton, FL 33496
877-220-4181
www.gourmetfoodstore.com
White truffles and truffle paste.

Green Meadow Farm
130 South Mount Vernon Road
Gap, PA 17527
717-442-5222
www.glennbrendle.com
Vegetables and fruits.

Linvilla Orchards
137 West Knowlton Road
Media, PA 19063
610-876-7116
www.linvilla.com
Apples, squash, and vegetables.

Maximus International Foods
15 Bicknell Road
Weymouth, MA 02191
617-331-7959
Wild and cultivated mushrooms.

Il Mercato Italiano
P.O. Box 9751
Green Bay, WI 54308
877-202-8881
www.ilmercatoitaliano.net
La Valle San Marzano tomatoes.

DRY GOODS

Allen Creek Farm
P.O. Box 841
Ridgefield, WA 98642
360-887-3669
www.chestnutsonline.com
Chestnut flour.

Amazon.com
866-216-1072
www.amazon.com
*Forno Bonomi ladyfingers, glucose syrup,
and Casa Forcelli Mostarda.*

Buon Italia
75 Ninth Avenue
New York, NY 10011
212-633-9090
www.buonitalia.com
Tipo 00 flour, semolina, and other dry goods.

King Arthur Flour
135 US Route 5 South
Norwich, VT 05055
802-649-3361
www.kingarthurflour.com
*All-purpose flour, durum flour, semolina,
almond flour, SAF instant yeast, food-grade cocoa
butter, and other baking ingredients.*

Il Mercato Italiano
P.O. Box 9751
Green Bay, WI 54308
877-202-8881
www.ilmercatoitaliano.net
Amaretti cookies.

The Meadow
888-388-4633
523 Hudson St
New York, NY 10014
3731 N Mississippi Ave.
Portland, OR 97227
www.atthemeadow.com
Gourmet salts and salt blocks.

PreGel USA
8700 Red Oak Boulevard, Suite A
Charlotte, NC 28217
704-333-6804
www.pregel-usa.com
*Pistachio paste, dry milk powder, and
gelato supplies.*

Whole Foods Market
www.wholefoodsmarket.com
Chestnut flour and other culinary products.

Alla Spina
1410 Mount Vernon Street
Philadelphia, PA 19130
215-600-0017
www.allaspinaphilly.com

Alpine Grove
19 South Depot Road
Hollis, NH 03049
603-882-9051
www.alpinegrove.com

Amis Trattoria
412 South 13th Street
Philadelphia, PA 19147
215-732-2647
www.amisphilly.com

Bedford Village Inn
2 Olde Bedford Way
Bedford, NH 03110
603-472-2001
www.bedfordvillageinn.com

Da Caino
Via della Chiesa, 4
Montemerano, 58050 Manciano
Province of Grosseto, Italy
+39 0564 602817
www.dacaino.it

Da Cesare
Via Umberto, 9
Albaretto della Torre
Province of Cuneo, Italy
+39 0173 520147

Da Guido
Via Fossano, 19 a Pollenzo
12042 Bra
Province of Cuneo, Italy
+39 0172 458422
www.guidoristorante.it

Fiaschetteria Nuvoli
Piazza dell'Olio, 15
50123 Florence
Province of Florence, Italy
+39 055 2396616

Frosio Ristorante
Piazza Lemine, 1
24011 Almé
Province of Bergamo, Italy
+39 035 541633
www.frosioristoranti.it

The Greenhouse Tavern
2038 East 4th Street
Cleveland, OH 44115
216-443-0511
www.thegreenhousetavern.com

Locanda Don Serafino Ristorante
Via Avv. G. Ottaviano
97100 Ragusa Ibla
Province of Ragusa
+39 0932 248778
www.locandadonserafino.it

O'Dea's Pub
Via Borgo Palazzo 211
24125 Bergamo
Province of Bergamo, Italy
+39 035 298511
www.odeaspub.it

Olfà
Via Colleoni, 3
Osio Sotto
24046 Bergamo
Province of Bergamo, Italy
+39 035 881047

Osteria
640 North Broad Street
Philadelphia, PA 19130
215-763-0920
www.osteriaphilly.com

Osteria Boccondivino
Via Mendicita Istruita, 14
12042 Bra
Province of Cuneo, Italy
+39 0172 425674
www.boccondivinoslow.it

Osteria dei Catari
Via Solferino
12065 Monforte d'Alba
Province of Cuneo, Italy
+39 0173 787256
www.osteriadeicatari.com

Osteria dell' Arco
Piazza Savona 5
12051 Alba
Province of Cuneo, Italy
+39 0173 363974
www.osteriadellarco.it

Osteria della Brughiera
Via Brughiera, 49
24018 Villa d'Almé
Province of Bergamo, Italy
+39 035 638008
www.labrughiera.com

Ristorante Antica Torre
Via Torino, 64
Barbaresco
Province of Cuneo, Italy
+39 0173 635170

Ristorante dei Pescatori
Via Doria, 6
19032 Lerici
Province of La Spezia, Italy
+39 0187 965534

Ristorante Flipot
Corso Antonio Gramsci, 17
10066 Torre Pellice
Province of Turin, Italy
+39 0121 91236

Ristorante Il Latini
Via dei Palchetti 6
50123 Florence
Province of Florence, Italy
+39 055 210916
www.illatini.com

Il Ristorante Loro and LoRo&Co
Bistrò/Pizzeria
24069 Via Bruse, 2
Trescore Balneario
Bergamo, Italy
+39 035 945073
www.loroandco.com

Sadler Ristorante
Via Cardinale Ascanio Sforza, 77
20141 Milan
Province of Milan, Italy
+39 02 58104451
www.sadler.it

Tucans Pub
Via Gaetano Donizetti, 25
24129 Bergamo
Province of Bergamo, Italy
+39 035 575538
www.tucans.it

Vetri Ristorante
1312 Spruce Street
Philadelphia, PA 19107
215-732-3478
www.vetriristorante.com

SHOPS AND MARKETS IN ITALY

5 Terre Gelateria e Crêperia
Via Antonio Discovolo, 248
19010 Manarola
La Spezia, Italy

Cazzamali Macelleria
Via Gaspare Vezzoli, 2
26014 Romanengo
Province of Cremona, Italy
+39 0373 72101

Eataly
Via Nizza 230, Lingotto
Turin 10126
Province of Turin, Italy
+39 011 19506801
www.eatalytorino.it

Gelateria Peccati de Gola
Via Mazzini 174, Albino
Lombardia 24021, Italy
+39 035 752299

Mangili Macelleria
Via Roma, 17
Paladina
Bergamo Italy
+39 035 542116

Pesceria Orobica
Via Bianzana, 19
24124 Bergamo
Province of Bergamo, Italy
+39 035 4172611
www.orobicapesca.it

Salone del Gusto
Via Nizza, 280
10100 Turin
Province of Turin, Italy
+39 0172 419611
www.salonedelgusto.it

WINERIES IN ITALY

Bellavista
Via Bellavista, 5
Adro
Province of Brescia, Italy
www.bellavistawine.it

Ca' del Bosco
Via Albano Zanella, 13
Erbusco
Province of Brescia, Italy
+39 030 7766111
www.cadelbosco.com

Ceretto
Località S. Cassiano 34
12051 Alba
Province of Cuneo, Italy
+39 0173 282582
www.ceretto.com

Clerico
Località Manzoni, 22/A
12065 Monforte d'Alba
Province of Cuneo, Italy
+39 0173 78171
www.domenicoclerico.com

Marchesi di Grésy
Strada della Stazione, 21
12050 Barbaresco
Province of Cuneo, Italy
+39 0173 635221
www.marchesidigresy.com

Rocche dei Manzoni
Località Manzoni Soprani , 3
12065 Monforte D'Alba
Province of Cuneo, Italy
+39 0173 78421
www.barolobig.com

Scavino
Via Alba-Barolo, 59
12060 Castiglione Falleto
Province of Cuneo, Italy
+39 0173 62850
www.paoloscavino.com

HOTELS AND INNS IN ITALY AND THE UNITED STATES

Agriturismo Armea
Località Armea
25015 San Martino della Battaglia
Desenzano
Province of Brescia, Italy
+39 030 9910481
www.agriturismoarmea.it

B&B Novecento
Via Ricasoli, 10
50122 Florence
Province of Florence, Italy
+39 05 5214138
www.bbnovecentofirenze.it

Ca' du Rabajà
Localita Rabajà 28
12051 Barbaresco
Province of Cuneo, Italy
+39 0173 635016
www.cadurabaja.com

Donna Franca
Trappitello
Province of Messina, Italy
+39 3473713686
www.discover-sicily.com

Hotel Florida
Via S. Biaggini, 35
19032 Lerici
La Spezia, Italy
+39 0187 967332
www.hotelflorida.it

Locanda Armonia
Località Redona
Trescore Balneario
Province of Bergamo, Italy
+39 035 4258026
www.locanda-armonia.it

Locanda del Biancospino
Via Monte Beio, 26
24026 Leffe
Province of Bergamo, Italy
+39 035 7172161
www.locandadelbiancospino.com

Parson's Post House
62 Shore Road
Ogunquit, ME 03907
207-646-7533
www.parsonsposthouse.com

ACKNOWLEDGMENTS

I slept through English class, so writing this book has been challenging to say the least. It could not have happened without the love, support, and creativity of so many people.

Claudia: Meeting you was the greatest moment in my life. You filled my heart and opened yours to me. I would not be the husband, chef, and father I am today without having you by my side. And this book could not have happened without you. *Sei tutto per me amore e Ti amo con tutto il mio cuore!* (You are everything to me, my love, and I love you with all of my heart!)

Mom and Dad: Thank you for standing by me on every decision I made—even when you thought they were stupid decisions. I know there were times when you couldn't imagine why I was doing what I was doing, but you both were always there for me. I love you both very much.

Marc Vetri: When we first met, I was living larger than life and knew nothing about the simplicities of it. Meeting you showed me that life was as simple as a plate of spaghetti with tomatoes and basil. You changed my life not only professionally but also personally. I couldn't have asked for a better mentor, partner, and best friend.

Jeff Benjamin: When Marc hired me and you weren't so sure about it, there was no way I was going to make you regret taking that chance. Ten years later, I want to say thank you. Without you, I would not have taken my first trip to Italy and fallen in love with the country, about which I knew little. Your knowledge of wine and business is endless, and the classes you held with me were priceless. I continue to learn from you every day as a partner and friend.

Brad Spence: Cooking with you in the kitchen at Vetri was a lot of fun. We shared the same passion and style of cuisine, and it was amazing to bounce ideas off each other and create great tasting menus together. I knew from early on that you were going to fit into this family. Thanks for always inspiring me.

Miles Angelo: Without you, Miles, I would have never met my Claudia, Marc, or Jeff. Thank you for bringing these people into my life and giving me the tools I needed to grow as a young chef.

Clare Pelino: Thanks for finding a home for this book. Your hard work and persistence really paid off, and I look forward to our new friendship and projects in the future.

Osteria Crew: What can I say? You guys are the best!!! I am so lucky to have all of you and can't thank you enough for your hard work, not only for the book, but for every day that you put your heart and soul into Osteria.

Brad Daniels: Since Osteria opened, I have never felt as comfortable with someone's running the kitchen in my absence as I have with you. Your enthusiasm, skill, and dedication never cease to amaze me. Thank you for all the work you did for this book. I couldn't have done it without you.

Vetri family: This is becoming one giant family and it keeps filling up with some of the most caring, talented, and hardworking individuals I know. Together, we have created a family that I am proud to be a part of. Thank you all.

Kelly Campbell: How you were able to capture the rustic essence of my food and the places we visited in Italy is beyond me. You're a rock star, and it was a lot of fun to work with you on this project. Can't wait till the next one.

David Joachim: We finally did it! After revising the proposal four times and wading through endless manuscript revisions, we have put together a very special book. From the beginning, you not only saw my vision but were able to capture my voice. And I don't think I ever saw anyone able to eat as much food as you did in Italy. That was pretty impressive. Thank you for your hard work and for becoming a dear friend.

Running Press: Thank you to my editor Kristen Green Wiewora, book designer Josh McDonnell, and the rest of the team at Running Press for helping to make this a real, live book.

Giuseppina Carrara: *Pina, non ho parole per dirti quanto la tua famiglia ha cambiato la mia vita. Tu sei una persona molto speciale, in tanti modi. Mi hai accettato nella tua casa come fossi un figlio fin dal primo momento. Mi auguro tu senti quanto sei importante per me. Ti voglio tanto bene e grazie per tutte le ricette di famiglia—è il nostro segreto!* (Pina, I don't have the words to describe how your family changed my life. You are a very special person in many ways. You accepted me into your house as if I were your own son. I hope you feel the same. I love you, Pina, and. . . thank you for all the family recipes—it's our little secret!)

Andrea Forcella: *Ciao, Zio! Tutte le volte che ho un dilemma con la pasticceria, tu ci sei. Hai sempre la risposta giusta o la ricetta perfetta per togliermi dai pasticci. In questi anni siamo diventati grandi amici e mi sento molto fortunato di averti nella mia vita. Grazie, Andrea, per la tua amicizia e per condividere la tua "dolce arte" con me.* (Hey, Uncle! Every time I have a problem or question in the pastry kitchen, you are always there. You have the right answer and perfect recipes. Over the years, we have become great friends, and I am very fortunate to have you in my life. Thank you, Andrea, for your friendship and for sharing your culinary knowledge with me.)

Antonio and Francesco: *Ricordo quando ho iniziato da voi a "LoRo" e avevate solo otto tavoli. Sono passati solo pochi anni e adesso avete un ristorante bellissimo e siete stati premiati con la stella Michelin. Complimenti!!! Vi ringrazio per l'opportunità che mi avete dato dieci anni fa senza nemmeno conoscermi. Adesso siete per me come due fratelli e vi considero parte della mia famiglia.* (I remember when I started at LoRo and you only had eight tables. Only a few years have passed and now you have a Michelin Star. Congratulations!!! I want to thank you for the opportunity you gave me ten years ago without even knowing me. Now you both have become like brothers and part of my family.)

Paolo Frosio: *Il lungo periodo che ho passato nella tua casa e nel tuo ristorante è stato una delle migliori esperienze della mia vita. Non solo ho imparato un sacco di cose nella tua cucina ma ho anche incontrato la mia Claudia lì. Frosio rimarrà sempre un posto speciale per noi. Paolo, sei uno chef che ammiro molto e ti ringrazio per tutto quello che hai fatto per me.* (It's been a long time since we worked together, but that time in your kitchen was one of the best experiences of my life. Not only did I learn a lot from you, but I also met Claudia there. For us, Frosio will always remain a special place. Paolo, you are a chef that I admire and I would like to thank you for everything you have done for me.)

Matteo Breda: *Carissimo. . . come si fa a ringraziare cupido? Senza di te non avrei mai conosciuto Claudia. . . La tua passione e creativitá mi hanno sempre affascinato e ci hanno unito al punto di sentirci come due vecchi amici. Questo libro è il frutto dalla mia esperienza in Italia e in parte lo devo a te Cupido-MacGyver!* (My dearest friend. . . how do I say thank-you to a Cupid? Without you, I never would have met my Claudia . . . Your passion and creativity have always fascinated me, and it has united us like two old friends. This book is about all of my experiences in Italy, and I owe it to you, Cupid-MacGyver!)

DAVID JOACHIM THANKS:

Jeff Michaud, for opening a window to your world and letting me climb in, live there, and tell your story.

Brad Daniels, for being supremely organized.

Kelly Campbell, for laughing at all the "hide the salami" jokes with Mr. Bull Dick.

Anthony Christian diMarco, for accepting the job of Key Grip, and for sleeping in Italy.

Carrie Havranek, for smiling during hellish days of recipe-testing and broken ovens.

All the tasters who ate and swooned and critiqued during recipe testing, including Selene Yeager, Dave Pryor, Keith Plunkett, Christine Fennessy, Matt Morrison, Jaime Livingood, Tom Aczel, Andrew Brubaker, Bill Melcher, Doug Ashby, and the Peoples family.

August Joachim and Maddox Joachim, for trying everything, including roasted pig eyes.

And to life's best ride partner, Christine Bucher, for pushing me, picking up my slack, and helping another cookbook to see the light of day.

INDEX

Note: Page references in *italics* indicate recipe photographs.

N

O